Praise for the *New York Times* bestseller *Raising Cain*

"Brilliant . . . Required reading for anyone raising—or educating—a boy."

—*The Washington Post*

"*Raising Cain* gives a long-needed insight into that mysterious, magical land, the psyches of boys. Every parent, teacher—or anyone who wants boys to flourish—should read this book."

—DANIEL GOLEMAN
Author of *Emotional Intelligence*

"*Raising Cain* helps us understand the inner lives of boys much as Mary Pipher's *Reviving Ophelia* shed light on the struggle of the adolescent girl."

—*The Tampa Tribune-Times*

"If you love a boy, were a boy, or care about boys and the men they become, read this book. Perfectly balancing cutting-edge science with engaging anecdotes and arrestingly useful insights, Kindlon and Thompson have written *the* book on boys. It is superb."

—EDWARD M. HALLOWELL
Author of *Driven to Distraction* and *Worry*

"Enormously compelling . . . This thoughtful book is recommended for parents, teachers, or anyone with a vested interest in raising happy, healthy, emotionally whole young men."

—*Publishers Weekly* (starred review)

Speaking of
Boys

ANSWERS TO THE MOST-ASKED
QUESTIONS ABOUT RAISING SONS

Michael Thompson, Ph.D.

with *Teresa Barker*

A Living Planet Book

BALLANTINE BOOKS

NEW YORK

To Theresa McNally
—MGT

To the memory of my mother, Maxine Barker
—THB

Contents

Contents   ix

Contents

Acknowledgments

I would like to acknowledge all I have learned from the faculty, administrators, parents, and students at The Belmont Hill School, and to thank the head of the school, Richard Melvoin, for his support of my work.

My writing partner, Teresa, and I are also grateful to the countless other parents, educators, colleagues, friends, and boys across the country whose shared stories and questions provided the basis for this book. Many who opened their lives to us in the writing of *Raising Cain: Protecting the Emotional Life of Boys* returned with updates and new puzzlements or concerns.

We extend thanks to Liz Perle, who heard me speak at the Town School for Boys in San Francisco and suggested I continue to talk with parents through a question-and-answer book, and to our agent, Gail Ross, for carrying the project

forward. We also appreciate the efforts of Ballantine editor
Joanne Wyckoff and her editorial and production staff, and
the special assistance of Eileen Chetti, Sherry Laten, Leslie
Kagan, and Melissa Jordan-Drummond.

I would like to thank my wife, Theresa, and my children,
Joanna and Will, for their love and support, and their patience with my writing *Speaking of Boys* on our Florida vacation. Teresa thanks her husband, Steve, and her children,
Aaron, Rachel, and Rebecca, for their love, support, and patience on the home front.

Speaking of boys, we offer particular thanks to the sons in
our lives (Will and Aaron) for providing such a vital piece of
our continuing education.

Introduction

In *Raising Cain: Protecting the Emotional Life of Boys*, my coauthor, Dan Kindlon, and I set out to break the traditional silence about boys' emotional lives and advance a more enlightened approach for raising boys to be emotionally whole, moral, and resilient young men. The tragic shootings at Columbine High School focused public attention squarely on these issues, and for more than a year since the publication of *Raising Cain*, we have been on the road continuously, speaking to parent and teacher groups, education leaders, public policy makers, and the media across the nation about the nature and potential of boys.

The silence has certainly been broken. The level and fervor of public dialogue has been gratifying. What has impressed us the most, however, has been the freeing effect this public conversation has had on parents' willingness to seek advice about issues they face with their sons at home. Wherever we go now, and in letters from readers of *Raising Cain*, parents are more eager than ever to share their "boy stories," open up their lives, and air their concerns and questions. The hesitation that used to couch so many questions about boys is gone. What we hear now are more candid questions that reflect the great diversity of boys and boy experience—all kinds of questions about all kinds of boys. This is good.

The value in asking questions out loud is that more people can learn from them. Sometimes the answers offer new ideas or insights. Sometimes they confirm that which a parent already believed, but may have wondered about. And sometimes just hearing that other parents have the same questions can give a feeling of connection to the greater community of caring adults. As child psychologists, we, too, have learned from the questions. The more I hear, the more clearly I can see what perplexes parents and educators about boys and what we can do to help them.

I was asked to write *Speaking of Boys*, not as a textbook on boy psychology, but as an extension of the kind of relaxed discussion of boy life that typically unfolds at my public speaking engagements and in private therapy with boys and their families. While I've answered thousands of questions in these settings, it never occurred to me to write them all down and save them, first because I was too busy listening and talking to do any writing, but also because I have the organizational skills of an average eighth-grade boy. As it turned out, there was no need for old notes.

I invited Teresa Barker, a veteran journalist who collaborated as our writing partner for *Raising Cain*, to join me on this new adventure, collecting fresh stories and questions from parents, teachers, mental health professionals, and other caring adults across the country and from all walks of life. Teresa is the mother of a son, age fourteen, and two daughters. Though not a psychologist, she has a natural gift for putting parents at ease. Many parents who have never attended a parenting talk shared their concerns and questions in personal interviews with her. Many parents who don't have access to private therapy were pleased to bring their concerns to me this way. And many people who would never ask their questions in public found a comfort level in tossing their questions into the pot anonymously and for the common good.

To keep the book a manageable length, we selected questions that best represented the concerns I hear again and again from parents and others engaged in working with boys. To share the rich diversity of life with boys, while protecting everyone's privacy, we changed names and some details in the stories. Every one of these questions reflects a true-life minidrama or sometimes the comic relief also a trademark in the life of boys. We chose not to "clean up" the scenarios to simplify the lives and the issues they raised. In everyday life, parents and teachers—and therapists—are asked to problem-solve with insufficient information. The process of discovery includes looking for more than one explanation and remaining open to more than one kind of response. This is the way we need to talk and think to get closer to the truth.

There was no way to rank the questions. Who's to say that a question about what makes one happy boy tick is any more important than a question about what makes another boy a walking time bomb? When questions come from a caring place, they are all equal. So we grouped the questions in categories by topic. They cover the full range of boy life, from the most serious concerns to the most humorous, and they cover all ages of boys. *Speaking of Boys* addresses physical and emotional development, friendship, sports, money, grades, peer pressure, electronics and video games, cruelty, anger and aggression, body image, family relationships, death and illness, divorce, depression, attention disorders, dating, drugs, and college/career/talent development.

As it happens, the single most-asked question about boys comes last in the book.

When I think of all the comments and questions I've heard, one of the most memorable is a comment—a complaint, actually—from a listener when I was a guest on the *Talk of the Nation* program on National Public Radio. *Raising Cain* had just been published, and the public discussion of the emotional life of boys was just beginning to heat up in the media. During the listener call-in portion of the show, a man called to say how disappointed he was in my remarks about the complexities of boy life. "Boy psychology is so simple," he said, and went on to describe his own life: He'd come back from duty in the Vietnam War and it took him four or five years to get over that. He'd had a number of relationships with women that hadn't worked out, but there were no big mysteries at work there. With every example of the "simplicity" of male life, he was describing a life that clearly had been shaped by emotional pain and troubled relationships. And yet his response was to deny that anything was complex about the emotional lives of boys and men.

Boys are not simple. We must not take them at face value. If you are reading this book, you know that already and you are looking for some help in understanding the riddles of boys' lives. My hope is that *Speaking of Boys* will give you the experience of exploring boys' difficulties in the company of a child psychologist (and former boy) who is now the parent of a nine-year-old boy and a fifteen-year-old girl. My wish is that you find it an easy and enjoyable way to understand the baffling, painful, inspiring, and often funny lives of boys.

Speaking of **Boys**

Speaking of
the Nature of Boys

New Mother of Baby Boy Looks to the Future

Q: This may sound like a stupid question, but I am an expectant mother, and we know it will be a boy. I've never had any experience around little boys. I never had any brothers and my sisters never had boys. My only experience is in seeing other people's little boys, and to be honest, they look like a handful. I'm just wondering if you have some simple (so I can keep it in mind over the years!) advice for raising a son to stay out of trouble and be a good man?

MGT: First of all, congratulations! You are in for an adventure, a learning experience, and a lot of fun. All you need is a loving heart and an open mind. As for boys being a handful, all children are a handful! I have a friend who says, "All human beings are more or less impossible." I think that is true (it certainly describes me). That's why we all need families who love us. As I have traveled around the country talking to parents about boys, I have had many mothers come up to me to say, "Take it from me, boys are easy. It is girls who are tough!" I have had just as many mothers testify that boys are so hard to read, so competitive, so mysterious, and so cruel.

Why do some mothers find boys difficult and others find them to be a delight? Certainly, being raised with brothers or having nephews is a helpful experience, but I don't think that is the crucial element. I have known some wonderful mothers of boys who were not raised in families with brothers. To me the two things that I would wonder about in the mother of a boy are: (1) whether she likes men, and (2) whether she will be able to adapt to her baby's rhythms and temperament.

In some ways, you have to want the end product of boyhood in order to raise a son with a sense of full acceptance. He is going to turn into a man. As our son, Will, has grown up, from time to time my wife has said, "It doesn't seem possible that he is going to grow up to be large and hairy." But he is, and I can see she is practicing in her mind, transforming this sweet, beautiful child into a large, bearded man and still recognizing him. Practice thinking about the man your son will become. Who have been the admirable men in your life? Did you love your father? Did your grandfather dote on you? Do you have a good relationship with your husband? Think about what you have liked in men and how you would like to see your son grow up to be like that. If you have a picture in your mind of the way you'd like him to be, it will help you to guide him.

Please don't think about boys as a problem; don't brace yourself for their energy or their competitiveness. Think about what your loving grandfather must have been like as a boy. Does your grandmother or mother have any stories about him? Ask your husband about his boyhood. What was he like? What did he do? Ask your husband enough questions so you get beyond the polished family stories about his bringing the frog to the table or throwing a football through the window. Families tend to hold on to gender-stereotyped stories that do not really illuminate the nature of the child. Ask your husband how it *really* was for him when he was a boy. What scared him, what was he passionate about?

May I suggest that you read books about boyhood? How about *Angela's Ashes*? You'll read it with new eyes, now that you have a son. It will teach you something about boy grief, boy endurance, and boy humor. Reread *Tom Sawyer*. Read some autobiographies of admirable men. It will be helpful to discover that Mahatma Gandhi got into fights at school or the Dalai Lama and his brother were so boisterous and competitive that his brother was sent away from the monastery.

Of course, you are going to be reading books to your son at night. The books that he loves will be an education for you. He will identify with the angry Max in *Where the Wild Things Are*, and he will admire the elephant, Horton, who steadfastly hatches the egg while balanced on that little tree, and you will both marvel at the imagination of that boy fishing in McElligot's pool. You will see your son in all of these characters, and you will be introduced to things you had never spent much time thinking about, such as what occupies a boy's mind when he is fishing. Reading to children is as much an education for parents as it is for children.

As for my second point, adapting to a child's temperament, that is the crucial thing for parenting any child, boy or girl. You are going to have to get on your son's wavelength without his being able to tell you what channel he is broadcasting from. You will get that from the experience of knowing him as a baby, holding him, responding to his cries, calming him during a plane ride, and holding him back as he is about to run into the street. He will make you stretch your personality and your limits, and you will become more adaptable than you ever thought possible. That's parenting.

For a mother to raise a boy means she gets as close as one can get to crossing the lines of gender. She will see the world through her son's eyes, and the world won't look the same. Mothers get to be adored by their sons, and that is really fun. She'll get to celebrate everything she has loved in men and help her son to become a good man. She will struggle with everything she has found regrettable in men, and at moments she will despair and say, "They're hopeless." It will be an amazing trip, just as it is for fathers who have daughters. Your son will open your eyes, broaden your knowledge, and help your sense of humor. I guarantee it.

For a father to raise a boy means he gets to replay the best of his own father's fathering of him. To teach your son how to fish, if that's what your father did with you, will be intensely gratifying. Fathering children, especially boys, means that we get to take care of ourselves as well as them. It will also give a father a chance to improve on his own father's harsh or punitive fathering of him. The experience will be good for his son and healing for him. Finally, if a man has struggled inarticulately in the past to explain himself and his life in boy terms to his puzzled wife, his son will provide a walking, talking illustration. Their son will do something very "boy" and the dad can say, "See! That's what I meant!"

Bombs Away! Blocks and Barbies

Q: We have a daughter in first grade and twin three-year-old boys. We have all kinds of toys in the playroom and we encourage everyone to play with everything—trucks, dolls, and building blocks. We've noticed that when our daughter plays with the Barbie dolls she gives them little places to live and has them cook and do things like real people might do. When the boys play with Barbie, they use her as a torpedo down the slide into the sandbox. We see the same kind of behavior in other boys—they turn everything into an action figure or a weapon. Why do boys do that?

MGT: You have asked the central unanswerable question of psychology, what is called the "Nature or Nurture" question. It is also a question I am asked by parents all the time. They are so surprised by how "boy" their boy is and how "girl" their girl is. They want to know where the child's gender choices came from.

In 1952 Erik Erikson started his landmark study of child psychology, *Childhood and Society*, with exactly the observations of children's play that you describe, namely, the different ways in which boys and girls use blocks. The girls built circular, contained cities, and the boys built towers and rockets. Many scientists have studied the nature of children's play since then. Is what we see in boys and girls the result of biology or training? Is what we see in children the result of their biological wiring, their hormones, some inborn plan, or is it the result of the expectations of their parents and the thousands of messages they get from the culture about what it means to be a boy or a girl?

We know that children show signs of gender identity very early, though not quite as early as the old Mel Brooks skit about the two-hour-old baby suggested. In the skit, a miracle baby with the ability to speak (Mel Brooks) is born at the UCLA Medical Center and is hurriedly interviewed by a reporter (Carl Reiner). The baby believes he is a girl until he looks down and sees that he is swaddled in a blue blanket. "Oh, I'm a boy," he shouts. "I'm going to go to baseball games, get drunk, and throw up!"

The humor here is just a slight exaggeration of the truth: our culture creates gender scripts for both boys and girls, and just as soon as a boy realizes what gender he is, he is inevitably going to feel inclined to play out some version of the script. Many parents play an eager supporting role by buying into the traditional "boy theme" colors and designs in clothes, cribs, clocks, wallpaper, blankets, and such. Others want to resist this kind of overt directing, yet will pick up their newborn son and describe him as "strong" and "rugged," while parents of newborn girls hold them and describe them as "beautiful" and "sweet." Even before babies are born, they are stereotyped. Mothers who know they are carrying a boy often describe the baby's kicks in the uterus as "very strong." Mothers of girls don't tend to describe their girl's kicks in terms of strength. In truth, the kicks of boys in utero are no stronger than the kicks of girls. So the messages that boys receive about what they should be—very strong, for instance— begin before they are even born. Boys see thousands of messages that tell them that boys like guns, torpedoes, and action. Girls get thousands of messages that tell them that girls grow up to be women who manage homes, offices, families, and relationships. Think of how many visual reinforcing messages boys receive from their parents. If he picks up a truck, everyone smiles: he's a boy! If he were to pick up a doll, it might make everyone nervous. When you think about how much reinforcement a boy receives for acting "like a boy" and how much discouragement he encounters when he acts "like a girl," it is not surprising that boys come to like "boy" things.

Most parents don't experience themselves as influencing their boys to be boys or their girls to be girls. Their child's boyness or girlness seems so strong, so inevitable, that most parents experience their gender behavior as a biological imperative. I cannot tell you how many times mothers have said to me, "I never understood about boys until I had one. They really are *boys!*" By that they mean that biology—nature—must have something to do with these early, distinctive differences in behavior. We do know that young boys typically exhibit a higher activity level, physicality, and impulsivity than do girls. We know that boys engage in more play fighting than girls. However, it is clear that testosterone alone is not responsible for boy aggression, nor are boys condemned by their biology to be violent. There are many cultural factors that influence boy behavior along with their biology.

We do not yet have the answers about gender behavior. Unfortunately, the complexity of human beings and the limits of psychology do not allow scientists to say definitively what makes a boy want to play with boy toys. Most psychologists believe that children's choices reflect some combination of nature—genes, hormones, body, brain chemistry—and experience, including seeing what men do, seeing what their older brothers play with, and especially receiving the toys their parents give them.

One professor of psychology wrote an essay in his retirement claiming that he had decided the question of genetics vs. environment. Genetics wins, he said, at 52 percent! Life experience is responsible for 48 percent. Of course, that is a joke. No one knows exactly what percentage of boy behavior is nature and what is nurture. The safest bet is that it is a complex interaction between the two that will provide doctoral dissertation material for neurologists, psychologists, and geneticists for years to come. For parents, it means continued years of amusement as we watch our children play, and an occasional rescue mission when Barbie the bomb is needed back at the dollhouse.

Dad's Retreat from Obstinate Four-Year-Old

Q: Sean is four years old and very, very active and sometimes also is very obstinate when it comes to cooperating about getting dressed to go places or getting into the car. The need to be constantly "on duty" is wearing out my husband and me, and then when Sean is difficult to deal with, my husband has no patience left. Recently he smacked Sean on the bottom— some people would call it a spank—which upset me. My husband's father was very harsh this way when my husband was a boy, and we had agreed that we wouldn't use this kind of physical discipline with Sean. Since that incident, when it's my husband's turn to get Sean dressed to go out, at the first sign of trouble he throws his hands up, leaves the room, and says he can't deal with it. That leaves me to do more and more, and I am exhausted by Sean and resentful of my husband's attitude. I've suggested we go to a parenting seminar, but my husband won't go. How can I get my husband to stop walking away at the first sign of trouble but control his temper so he doesn't hit Sean?

MGT: One of the difficulties men face when they become fathers—no matter what kind of discipline they experienced in their families—is that they have not had enough practice dealing with the activity level and willfulness of small children. Most women have had some experience as baby-sitters; most women took a more active role in raising their younger brothers and sisters when they were young. Women tend to have a larger repertoire of strategies for dealing with the stubborn defiance of small children. Men are often surprised by how helpless they can be made to feel, and they are humiliated by how angry they become at a four-year-old.

People often believe that men are without compassion or do not want to deal with problems, when, in fact, a man is struggling to manage his own internal level of distress. Research has shown that boys respond just as strongly as girls to a crying baby—their heart rate and skin response are often more aroused than that of girls—but they do not have the experience in calming babies and so they remain in a more overwhelmed state longer than girls do. They don't have self-confidence that they can handle the situation.

The best part of what your husband is doing (and I hear that you do appreciate this) is that he is separating himself from your son so that he doesn't spank him. If he spanks, he is going to feel ashamed of himself and a failure in front of you. You should let him know that you respect and appreciate that he is trying not to hurt his son. You should let him know that you, too, feel like hitting your son sometimes. You should let him know that you feel stressed out by your son. It will help him to know that even though you do a more effective job with your son, you struggle, too. Your husband may have turned you into a bit of a saint in his mind and that's a problem. (Despite our respect for saints, no one wants to be married to one because the unsaintly one constantly feels inadequate by comparison.) You are resenting his abandonment of you; he may be resenting your competence in comparison to him. This is how children can stress their parents' marriage. It would help the two of you if you could both acknowledge how lonely, how scary, and how difficult parenting can be and let one another know that you both need help. You need relief; he needs strategies.

How do you help him develop the skills he needs to help you? He has rejected the idea of a parenting class. That's understandable. He does not want to be humiliated in front of strangers either, and he cannot imagine that a class could make him feel better. Why don't you take the class alone and leave your husband home to put your son to bed? I'm only half joking. If your husband handles bedtime all right with your son, this might give them some needed time to enjoy each other without the stress of deadline departures. Do you have friends with a seven-year-old version of your son? Why don't you get together for dinner and ask them how they managed? It will be a great relief to your husband to hear that someone else's marriage was put under stress by a small child. They may also have some practical suggestions for you. Even if they don't, it will make you and your husband feel closer to see that others survived.

It sounds to me as if you have some good strategies already in place when you work with your son, but that your feeling of not being supported is contributing to your sense of exhaustion. Enlist your husband as a partner and help educate him by reviewing with him how you handled issues with your son during the day. This not only welcomes him as a consultant but also helps him understand all the steps in responding responsibly to your son. If you find you need specific suggestions, begin by briefing him about what went wrong with your son in the morning. Very often, going back over the events together can illuminate where the glitches were and what might be done about them. If you cannot come up with some creative solutions together, reading some practical books that deal specifically with how to avoid power struggles with stubborn children or children with high activity levels might help. Ask other parents for tips on dealing with obstinate behavior and getting a child dressed in the morning. Take some notes and share them with your husband. Ask him which ones he thinks would be effective. Then split the work of getting your son dressed, and each take the parts that you think you can do most effectively. Develop a tag-team or hand-off system, so that you can give your son to your husband when you feel resentful and he can give his son back to you when he feels overwhelmed. I would bet that when your son experiences the two of you as working together, he will much more easily give up his oppositional behavior.

In the early evening, when you both still have some energy, debrief each other about the morning battle. Share your impressions. Try to laugh about it when you can. Isn't it amazing and ridiculous that children can make us feel so powerless?

Preening at Thirteen

Q: Our son is thirteen and has always been an attractive enough boy but never did seem to care a lot about his appearance. Suddenly, he is living in the shower and has become very meticulous about his hair before he goes out to school or even to the grocery store. What is the thing with all the showers and why this sudden urge to preen?

MGT: A boy's wish to shower, put on deodorant, stare in the mirror, and run a comb through his hair is an unmistakable sign that he has discovered a new sense of pleasure and pride in his body. For most boys, it suggests that they've come to realize that girls care about the way boys look, and it is iron-clad evidence that a boy is interested in girls and their looks, their hair, and the way they smell.

A frequent complaint of mothers of boys under the age of eleven is that they are messy, don't like to take baths, wear torn clothes, put on clothes that don't match, and are willing to wear the same pair of underpants for days on end. (This is not true of all boys, of course; nothing is true of all boys, but it may be true of a majority.) You'd think, given these complaints, that mothers would rejoice when their sons begin showering two and three times a day, wearing deodorant, and combing their hair. More often, mothers and fathers get a bit annoyed about it.

First of all, parents get upset because the behavior is so obviously self-absorbed. Indeed, the act of running a comb repeatedly through your hair in front of other people is almost the definition of self-centeredness. (Remember Kookie on *77 Sunset Strip?*) For those of us adults who have gradually given up thinking we are the center of the universe, it is disconcerting to see our children suddenly think that they are the center of the universe. Can't we pass down our hard-won discovery of humility to them? We try. As one exasperated mother said to her thirteen-year-old son, "One billion Chinese people do not go to bed at night with your name on their lips!"—an example of adult sarcasm that was undoubtedly lost on her son. We can try, but we can't crack our children's egocentrism in the years from thirteen to fifteen. Their self-absorption and egocentrism are impregnable. What does break it down? Life does it. The teasing of other kids does it. A girl may do that by dismissing your son, by telling him he isn't as handsome or as cool as he thinks. And then you'll want to scream at her, "Don't you hurt my son. He's a wonderful boy."

The second thing that bothers parents about a son's sudden self-absorption is that it slows things down. He stays in the shower too long, he'd rather comb his hair than pull his schoolbooks together in the morning, etc. That's annoying to an adult who is trying to get everyone in the family moving toward the car and school and tasks and lessons. And it makes you want to shout, "All the combing isn't making very much difference. You're still a kid, you're still a wonderfully hand-some and funny-looking thirteen-year-old. Nothing but time— a couple of years of growth—is going to change that, so let's get in the car and go to school!"

Third and most profoundly, our children's interest in their appearance tells us that they are becoming sexual beings, and that involves a sense of loss for parents. His combing his hair means he is thinking of himself as someone who might be at-tractive to a girl. And a boy's sexual interest in girls means that his loving bond with his mother, though it may be strong throughout his life, is not going to be as exciting as what he is going to feel about another girl in the next few years. That can hurt a mother's feelings. She may feel she has become the old love, now discarded. It can hurt a father's feelings, too, when his son would rather talk with a girl on the phone than go to a boat show with his father, the way they did when he was ten. When he was ten, being with his dad was real ex-citing, and his love for his mom was huge. It is hard for par-ents to give up the feeling of being the central love in their child's life. That's the parental side of the old Oedipus com-plex. You see, it is not just boys who love their moms; moms love their boys, too. They love them a lot, but they know that all that hair combing isn't for them; it is for someone else.

Just thinking of a son as having a sexual life, which includes masturbation, fantasy, and eventually sexual intercourse, is more than most of us want to think about when we're wait-ing impatiently for our turn in the family bathroom. But that's what's behind this preening, and that's why it drives parents nuts.

Chin Hairs and a Boy's Pride

Q: BJ is sixteen, and in the past few months several hairs have begun to grow from his chin—like a beard, only just about five hairs. I've encouraged him to shave them off because they look odd, but he just leaves them there. His dad just shrugs and laughs at it. BJ's so sensitive about how he looks in other ways, I'd think he'd want to shave this little spot. But he doesn't. Am I missing something? Is there something "sacred" about these few hairs?

MGT: Of course there is something sacred about his five hairs. That's 500 percent more hair on his face than he had two years ago. He's a man now, with a man's body. And the hair on his chin is evidence of it. He's also advertising, symbolically; he's letting people know that he has hair on other places on his body as well. His father understands that and that's why he just shrugs and laughs. He doesn't want to have to explain to you how important pubic hair can be to a boy. Boys on athletic teams shower with other boys. It matters to them to look masculine because they are going to be naked in "public." I know a twelve-year-old boy who was just starting puberty and came out of the bathroom at home and announced to his mother that he had "eleven pubic hairs." He'd counted them. He was very proud. She hardly knew what to say. What's the right response in that situation? How about "That's wonderful, son! Keep it up!" or "I'm so proud of you!" Probably a wise smile and accepting nod is the best way to go.

Fascination with these physical changes is not just a boy thing. Don't girls between the ages of eleven and fifteen pay attention to their breast size? Don't they study their changing figure in the mirror? Don't they think a lot about bras and buying them? I know they do. I'm the parent of a teenage daughter. Girl friends that age spend an enormous amount of time discussing clothes, changing clothes, trading clothes, and then coming downstairs to say, "How does this look?" They rotate on their feet like professional models, showing you the front and the back and the front again, just in case you missed seeing how different their bodies are than they were three or four years ago. And it is not just the clothes. Sometimes the clothes are odd or ugly to a father's eyes, just like the five hairs on a son's chin, but the girls need the acknowledgment that they have changed, that they are growing.

Relax and enjoy your son. Don't worry about the hairs looking odd. They're less odd than a nose ring or an eyebrow ring. (With sixteen-year-old children it is always important to be grateful for what they are not doing.) The moment a girl at school in whom he is interested says, "Why do you have those? I think you'd look better without them," they will disappear in the flash of a razor.

"In Your Face" Boy Arrogance

Q: What makes boys so arrogant? I am the mother of four children—boys and girls all in their teens now—and although I know these children and their friends are "good kids," I also have noticed that boys, no matter what age they are, have an arrogance about them that I just don't see in most girls. The young ones say and do immature things they know offend other people, and the older ones do things that can actually be dangerous or intimidating to other people. They stroll across the street in front of traffic, shout at each other using R-rated language or worse—even when they're friends— or refuse to do things when they're asked, in much more defiant ways than girls. Why do they impose on other people this way?

MGT: Some people play piano. Some people sing. Some people act. In the boy realm, arrogance is a performance art. It communicates a feeling, and part of its allure is the reaction it receives from the audience—it makes people stop and take notice.

There are five explanations for boy "arrogance." I will list the reasons and then I will explain each one. First, some of these displays of arrogance may have biological roots in primate dominance displays. Second, it is part of their adolescent separation from adults. Third, it is immaturity dressed up to look intimidating. Fourth, it is the end result of powerful social modeling which boys receive. Fifth, in some sense arrogance works. It succeeds in confusing and sometimes frightening adult women and girls, especially because it breaks so many of their social rules.

When you see little boys or teenage boys strut their stuff, it is almost impossible not to think that there are biological roots to such behavior. It may be that such boy behavior is linked to primate sexual displays or intimidation behaviors. It is not unusual to see a football player make a tackle and then get up and beat his own chest like a gorilla. When I drive past Cambridge Rindge and Latin School on my way to my office, boys often cross the street in front of my car and slow it down in a deliberate, challenging way. Their body posture has aspects of biological display to it. I am crossing their "territory" and they let me know it.

That said, it is always hard to know what is biological in humans because boys see so many models of arrogant behavior that they learn to imitate. Have you ever watched the World Wrestling Federation, which so many boys watch? All the wrestlers come into the ring swaggering and acting arrogant. What about Muhammad Ali's prefight performances, sticking his face in the camera and shouting, "I am the greatest!" Just look at the sports and media models that are offered to boys. How could boys not learn to act in the same arrogant fashion? We imitate what we see famous people do.

Adolescent boys not only need to show off their new, muscular bodies, but they also want to flaunt their autonomy and their expanded sense of self. "Watch out, world, here we come!" is often the teenage message, from both boys and girls. Girls are generally more keenly aware of their relational bond to others and are more likely to act in a nonthreatening way. Boys are much less inhibited about their competitiveness, and so they thrust themselves forward in loud and obnoxious ways.

Though boys are competitive and full of bravado, they are also likely to be developmentally immature, especially in comparison to girls of the same age. In my experience, boys often cover up social anxiety and ignorance with arrogant displays. If a boy is afraid of the unit that they are beginning in third grade, he is likely to say, "I hate this class!" Or, "I hate Ms. Jones, she's a terrible teacher." If a tenth-grade class is about to have a serious discussion with the psychologist, some boy will make an offensive comment about what a pointless waste of time it is going to be. If you work with adolescent boys, it is important to understand that they appear arrogant when they are afraid.

Finally, boys find that acting arrogant is a source of power. Adults on a subway move away from a bunch of macho boys. Teachers become rigid and punitive when challenged by an arrogant boy; too many back down subtly when challenged in front of the class. Mothers can become frightened and overwhelmed; fathers sometimes feel challenged and retaliate physically. In whatever way, adults change their behavior when a boy acts in an arrogant way, and that tells the boy he is powerful.

A star athlete was once sent to me for therapy by his

coach, after an angry outburst at a referee. He started out the session with me by literally shouting in my face, "This is the wrong way to go about helping me!" "Oh," I said, as calmly as I could, "why do you say that?" He continued to lead with his anger until I had involved his frightened parents and some crucial members of the faculty in seeing behind his anger at the loneliness that afflicted him. Many high-achieving boys, particularly athletes, are so respected by the adult community that everyone assumes that everything is all right inside them. Sometimes it's not, but they don't know how to say so except by being angry. At some point in the next few months he accepted that the adults in his life were worried about him and were not going to go away, and he began to soften and ultimately to open up.

A wise psychoanalyst once explained a patient's behavior to me by saying, "Anger is a young man's game." I try to remember that it is a game. I believe that the only way to deal with boy arrogance is to disarm it. Don't rise to the bait, don't lecture and moralize, don't become frightened, and don't patronize. These are boys, here: young, dependent, and sometimes immature boys. Don't be too impressed or upset.

Is Annoying Nine-Year-Old Asking to Be Hit?

Q: The other day I was in the den watching TV and my nine-year-old son was running around and yelling and jumping on the furniture. I asked him several times to stop and he didn't stop, so I shouted at him, but he kept it up. Finally I hit him and he stopped. It seems to be the only thing that works. Sometimes a boy is just plain asking to be hit, isn't he?

MGT: No boy that age ever asks to be hit. I don't believe that a boy of any age wants to be struck by a parent, unless it is a teenager who wants to discover whether he is actually as strong as his father (I will discuss that at the end of my answer). A boy might, through his actions, ask to be contained, restrained, held, or settled down. His running into the street can demonstrate that he is reckless and needs to be closely monitored. A boy might show you, by throwing snowballs wildly or losing control with his brother, that he cannot manage his own excitement at that moment. But the instant you hit a boy, you will see immediately that that was not what he was looking for. He will be frightened, hurt, and confused, and he will look at you with hatred. Your hitting him might make him stop jumping on the couch, but if you hit your son, the two of you are headed down a sad road.

If you hit your son, especially if you have hit him regularly, you have put yourself in a position where you are likely going to hit him again, because he won't really believe that your words mean anything until you back them up with something physical. By hitting, you create a physical standard for "I really mean what I'm saying." Once you have established the precedent of hitting, then your words *don't* really mean what you say. You only really mean it if you are willing to hit. All children, and boys in particular, push the envelope with their parents to discover the true limits of parental authority. Once you start to hit children, your words are devalued, and you will have created a "communication style" based on hitting.

Furthermore, hitting boys undermines the development of conscience and moral maturity. Consider this paradox: we punish boys much more harshly than we do girls, and yet they grow up to commit far more crimes than girls. By any measure, boys are our moral failures. Why? You can either blame their biology, which takes adults off the hook, or you can look more closely at what adults are doing wrong.

Research shows us that when children are physically punished, or harshly criticized, they only have a memory of how angry the adult was or how hard they were struck. They don't remember the content of the lesson. They learn to fear and to become resentful, rather than learning morals. I cannot tell you how many boys I have seen in therapy who say about their fathers, "He's always yelling at me." They never say— and no longer care—what the lesson is supposed to be about. All they retain is the image of a red-faced, angry father. And they mentally write him off.

In therapy, boys can always recall incidents of being hit. I wish you could be there with me in my office, because you can see in their faces that they experience their fathers as *losing* their moral authority when they resort to physical punishment. They often say, "He's an asshole . . . he's a jerk . . . he doesn't know anything, he just hits me." If a boy has been struck often, he often looks defeated and angry himself; at the same time, he has a tough choice to make about whether or not to discuss the punishment with me. If he has been bruised, or struck regularly, or really beaten—if I have any reason to believe that a child has suffered psychological or physical harm—I must report the parent to the state's child protective services. In all fifty states, teachers and mental health professionals are mandated reporters of child abuse. Why? Because the overwhelming conclusion of research on hitting children is that it is harmful to them. The state has stepped in to protect children from their own families because the long-term effects are so injurious.

You need to know that one of the long-term effects of being hit is that it lays the foundation for a boy to become a domestic batterer. A colleague of mine who runs groups for men who abuse their wives says that you never get an adult batterer who was not himself hit as a child. Boys learn to do what their fathers show them to do. If you model physical punishment as a way to solve problems, he will think that it is masculine and will take that identification into adulthood with him. The research tells us that the most aggressive boys in kindergarten are boys who are hit or yelled at at home.

What if your boisterous boy turns into a teenager who threatens you, hits you, or challenges you to fight? This happens extremely rarely. Because children love and forgive their parents, they will often not fight back when they are being physically punished, even when they are of an age where they could inflict some damage. However, when a son gets to be a certain size, he may strike back. I have had sons at age fourteen or fifteen describe punching their fathers. They always say, "That's the last time he'll hit me. That put a stop to it."

And it does. Sons who have been hit may take revenge.

Sometimes sons will want to wrestle their dads in a peaceful moment, just to test their strength against their fathers. Perhaps this is biological behavior, like a young buck challenging an older one. The young like to put us on notice that they are strong now and a force to be reckoned with.

But we have come a long way from the nine-year-old boy running around your den. Let me offer some suggestions: When your son starts leaping around the room, speak to him quickly in a firm voice. Try not to let him get up a head of steam. If speaking firmly doesn't work, stand up in an authoritative—not a threatening—way. Your movement will convey that you are serious. Do something to get his attention. Turn off the TV, or turn the light switch off and on, or count down from ten. Say in a firm but quiet voice, "If this continues, you are going to lose TV privileges for the rest of the weekend." If he is already in such an excited state that he cannot stop, go and stand in a spot that is in the way of his jumping. Don't grab him, or turn it into a "hunt and chase" game. That may increase his excitement and fear. If you feel yourself starting to lose your temper and wanting to hit him, you should leave the room until *you* have calmed down again. There is nothing he can hurt in the den that is so valuable that you cannot take the time to regain your cool. If you cannot get control of yourself, just don't go back into the room.

Simply depriving him of an audience for his antics will slow him down. Your relationship with your son is more important than the couch, the TV, or Aunt Sarah's vase on the table. Material things can be replaced. It is much harder to heal your relationship with your son after you have hit him.

You didn't mention whether this is an ongoing problem or whether it happens only at certain times—for instance, before meals when your son might be hungry and running on empty. If you identify a pattern to his activity in relation to hunger, or to stimulation by TV, or to a certain time of day, then you will be able to anticipate those frantic times and intervene with a snack or some parental attention. If there is no pattern, and such activity is chronic, you have to consider that your child may have a form of what used to be called "hyperactivity" and is now known as Attention Deficit Hyperactivity Disorder (ADHD).

One final thing I'd like you to think about. Is it possible that your son is trying to get your attention? Is it possible that he's trying to pry you away from the TV to go outside with him and play ball or go swimming? It could easily be that your son simply wants contact with you. He may be asking for loving contact with you.

Body Piercing: What's the Message?

Q: Our son has always been a bit of a maverick, but he recently went out with some friends and when he returned we saw that he had had his ear pierced in two places. We accepted that, but now he says he wants a nose ring, also. He's seventeen and we can accept that his body is his own, but we're a little concerned about the effect of all this on his job prospects as he looks for summer work, and on the way he's defining himself in the world. Also, is there some deeper meaning to all this piercing stuff that we don't know about or that we should be concerned about? Boys didn't used to pierce their ears at all, and then a few years ago I thought it was a sign of being gay. But now I don't know what to make of it.

MGT: Don't you remember long hair in the sixties? Don't you remember how upset parents were about their boys wearing their hair past their shoulders and dressing like hippies? One generation always finds a way to upset and outrage the older generation. John Jay Chapman wrote that "every generation is a secret society and has incommunicable enthusiasms, taste, and interests, which are a mystery both to its predecessors and to posterity." Although I believe there are a lot of things to worry about with respect to boys and their high levels of anger, risk taking, and violence, body piercing is not one of my big concerns. From a boy's point of view, it is a very useful way of upsetting your parents and making them worry that you won't turn out to be a productive member of society.

Of all the people I know who went to Woodstock or smoked dope in college in decades past, most now have families, pay their mortgages, and worry about whether their children will look respectable enough in an interview to get a decent job. Your son either has to be smart enough to apply for jobs where they don't object to body piercing (the cashiers at my grocery store have earrings) or, having been turned down for four jobs, he might remove the nose ring. There is a theory of child rearing that is called "natural consequences." Not getting offered a job you very much want because the boss stared unhappily at your nose ring is a "natural consequence." (I should mention that the year I graduated from college I applied for a job as a bartender at a fancy restaurant. I'd had a nice interview, and then the boss looked at me and said, "I'm ready to give you the job. How attached are you to those whiskers?" The beard came off the next day.)

As any anthropologist would tell you, body decoration and body piercing are as old as human society. I think that for adolescents, body piercing fulfills the same need it did in primitive cultures: to establish identity, to help young people mark their growing up, their independence, and their power. We live in a society that is terribly impoverished with respect to meaningful rites of passage for the young, and especially for boys. So they take the human impulse to scar and decorate the human body into their own hands. They create their own rituals because the adult world has done such an inadequate job of providing boys with a way to say, "I have arrived!"

A minority of teenagers who engage in body piercing are also depressed, alienated, and angry. Certainly, some of the most extreme forms of body piercing—below-the-waist pierc-

ings, for example—are associated with mental illness. However, many violent and depressed teenagers don't have earrings or nose rings, so it is not a reliable diagnostic indicator.

Mark McConville, a psychologist in Cleveland, wrote that
for adolescents, clothes are the "psyche worn on the outside."
I agree. For that reason it is important to read a child's dress
or piercing as a psychological statement. The more extreme
the fashion, then presumably the more extreme the statement, unless everyone in his or her group is doing it and they
are otherwise functioning normally. That is, there is less
likely to be a serious emotional issue behind the fact that
your college freshman gets his tongue pierced when many of
his friends are doing the same thing. If he is meeting his responsibilities in college and is emotionally available to some
adults in his life, it is most likely a group phenomenon, not a
serious psychological statement by an individual about his or
her depression, for example.

As for body piercing being a sign that a young man is homosexual, a lot of times it connotes exactly the opposite. "I
am so confident of my heterosexuality," these decorations
proclaim, "I don't care what you think." Many young women
find them bold and very sexy. Your son knows the message he
is sending and the audience for which it is intended.

Speaking of
Mothers and Sons

Can Moms Stay Cool?

Q: When my son was younger we used to get along fine—we could go places together and make small talk and enjoy some laughs together. He's thirteen now, and in the past year he's become much more "one of the guys" with his friends, which I can understand, but it hurts my feelings that he's not at all interested in spending any time with me in even the most ordinary ways—like running errands together. My husband doesn't notice any difference in him and says I'm being overly sensitive. I know it's not my imagination. What's going on, and is there any way for me to be "cool" again in the eyes of my son?

MGT: No, there isn't much chance of your ever being "cool" again in the eyes of your son, at least not in the way you once were. It may happen that when he's sixteen or seventeen, he'll have a friend over to the house, and perhaps the three of you will get in a conversation about some important topic. Perhaps you will say something unexpected or something particularly insightful about the nature of girls, and as your son and his friend are leaving the house, the friend might say to your son, "Your mom's pretty cool." Your son will be momentarily surprised and he'll say, "Yeah, she's not bad." Later that evening he might—with an emphasis on the word "might"—tell you, "Matt thought what you said was pretty cool." You will be stunned because by that time you will have become long accustomed to not being cool. You will vaguely remember that at one time in his life you were cool in his eyes, but it will be a distant memory.

You see, your son is growing up and beginning to transform his relationship with his parents. His peer group is beginning to feel more important to him than at any time in his past. His sense of identity is also changing. He is no longer willing to be the child who simply loves his mom in a take-it-for-granted way. He is tall, and growing taller now. Perhaps he is able to look right into your eyes or soon will be able to do so. We know that when young adolescents grow to be close in height to their parents they begin to redefine the relationship. "Why is this person giving me orders? Why is she in charge of everything? I'm as tall as she is. I can decide what I want to do." Once a teenager decides that he (or she—this isn't just a boy issue) is the size of an adult, he also comes to believe that he is entitled to adult privileges.

The simplest of all adult privileges is the ability to say "no" to someone and have them not be able to coax, cajole, or force you into doing something. That's what two-year-olds do, just to get the feel of self-assertion; that's what early adolescents do to declare the early stages of their adulthood. That is why saying "no" to running errands with his mother becomes an act of independence. Not wanting to go becomes a way of saying to himself: "I am my own man!" It also becomes a way of declaring his loyalty to his friends because he believes that they also refuse to run errands with their mothers. A lot of conversation in the group has been about how they dislike their parents, how "dumb" things are at home, what a "dork" their younger brother or sister is. They verbally compete with one another to show how independent they are from their families.

As I wrote earlier, this is not just a boy issue. Girls become independent from their parents just as boys do. Sometimes, they are more polite about it than boys are, because the boys' group may require a particular negative attitude, but I assure you that girls feel the same things. I know a girl who was considering going to boarding school and was on her visit to the campus. At lunch in the cafeteria one of the students asked her why she wanted to go to boarding school. She replied, "To get away from my parents." Immediately, another girl said, "That's why I came to boarding school, too!" "Me, too," another girl laughed. "Isn't that amazing," declared another. "We all hate our parents!" And suddenly there was a feeling of solidarity and friendship. They were all bold, independent young women who did not need their parents. Yeah . . . right.

Here is the hard part for parents. Your adolescent son is going to need you for many more years. He needs you to love him, to attend to him, to be present for him. He also needs— and I mean *needs* in the strongest sense—you to do this for him while he acts as if he doesn't need you. He needs you to do this while he defines what is cool and what is not. This is the infuriating and wounding aspect of adolescent children. They take what they require, all the while disavowing their providers. However, it is important that you do not get too hurt by him, that you do not get too mad at him, that you do not dislike his growing up. It is important that you do not grieve for your lost "coolness" and status in his eyes. It is important not to communicate that you preferred him when he was small. Quite rightly, he will resent that. He wants you to begin to take him as he is: a big guy, a cool guy who doesn't like to do errands anymore. As long as he is civil and responsible—and I do believe you can require teenagers to behave in a civil way—you have to accept that he is not going to idealize you the way he did when he was a child.

One of the most famous of Mark Twain's observations is relevant here: "When I was a boy of fourteen, my father was so ignorant I could hardly stand to have the old man around. But when I got to be twenty-one, I was astonished at how much the old man had learned in seven years."

Help! Micromanaging Mom Struggling to Let Go

Q: I quit a successful career to stay home and raise our only son. I love him and admire him. He's a good kid, now twelve. After years of being in charge of his life and teaching him what to do and how, I am having trouble backing off, letting go, knowing when to push and when to step back. This is a daily struggle for me. I hate myself when I see myself micromanaging his life, but I get impatient with him when he balks at taking the initiative or doing his best. How can I let go and not be disappointed when he makes mistakes or makes choices that are different from those I would make, or simply doesn't apply himself the way I think he should?

MGT: First of all, I want to say that I admire the choice that you made. Not every family is economically able to manage a mom without an outside income, nor is it the right choice, psychologically speaking, for every woman, but I am sure that your son has benefited from the love and attention you have given him. Second, I respect that you have already diagnosed the situation and are very close to seeing the solution, both for yourself and your son. You have just asked me to give you a small push in the right direction and I'm going to oblige.

I spend a lot of time in schools, and I am going to tell you bluntly that middle school teachers routinely struggle with how to communicate and work effectively with moms who micromanage. Typically, the mother is anxious and overinvolved, believing it's necessary, while the teacher's experience of the boy is that he is quite able to manage himself if he's given the freedom and responsibility to do so. If a mother's "full-time job" is to manage her son's school career, a motivated mother becomes a micromanaging mother. It doesn't have to be this way.

I am assuming that you are not dealing with a son who has special needs, an ADHD boy, for example, or a child with learning disabilities that might affect his memory or executive functioning. There are some children who need their parents—and it is usually the mothers—to stay involved for longer than an average boy would need his mother. Children with special needs by definition need more adult care for a longer period of time. Then it becomes difficult, but absolutely essential, for the parent to step back and allow that child to leave the nest as well. A colleague of mine has just arranged to have her son, an autistic "boy" of twenty-five, move into an assisted living situation for autistic adults. It was, developmentally speaking, time for him and for her, but it could not have come any sooner. He needed the parenting for a long time.

Your son needs you to have some other focus than him right now. He cannot feel his own initiative if your initiative is all too present. He cannot make mistakes because you take his mistakes and project them catastrophically out into the future. He cannot do his best because he cannot feel what his best is; he can only react to what you think his best should be.

He needs to come into possession of his own life, and he cannot do that until you begin the process of resigning as manager of his life. It is not an immediate resignation, of course; it is a gradual retirement. He will still need you to come to his plays, his science fairs, and his football games. He would be very upset if you suddenly took an all-consuming job and were never home. The change would be too abrupt. I know a mother who started medical school when her children were twelve and ten, and they reacted as if they had been abandoned. In some sense they had been, and neither boys nor girls want to be dropped when they become competent adolescents.

Adolescent boys need someone to be in the house when they get home, at least some days of the week. They need someone to ask them if they have done their homework, or to be available for questions when the assignment is too difficult. They want a mother to listen to their stories of injustice and woe at the end of a hard day (don't we all need that?).

When I went into high school and on to college, my mother—who had been a stay-at-home mother all of my childhood—began tutoring children in reading at a public school in New York. The school where she worked was on the edge of Harlem and contained many disadvantaged African-American children. I did not need her so much anymore, but these kids sure did. I know my mother felt very committed to the children there; she would talk about them with great pride and pleasure. And I felt relieved. My mom was occupied, she was feeling useful, and she wasn't burdening me with her worry. I could grow up and feel more responsible for myself. Perhaps most important, I did not have to feel guilty about abandoning her.

Has it occurred to you that while your son may fight with you over your involvement and may often feel annoyed by your perfectionism, he is also worried about you? His growth and development are robbing you of a job. He is "firing" you and I am sure there are times—moments when he is experiencing his love and gratitude—when he thinks, "What's going to happen to my mom?" I have had many boys in therapy describe these concerns about their mothers, though customarily they only tell me after they have told many stories about their mother's irritating, micromanaging behavior.

Your son needs to be able to grow up the rest of the way without being the central source of meaning and employment in your life. There are exciting projects out there in the world of work; there are other children who need your attention. Is there a graduate degree you have always thought about earning? He will be inspired by your doing your homework in the evenings; he will respect the courage you display in taking on something new in the world. Your personal growth—and attention to homework—will serve as a model for him.

Loving Well vs. Loving Equally

Q: I have two sons. One is five and one is eight. This is hard for me to admit, but I have never felt as close to my younger son as I do to my older one. The older one seems more like me—we often have similar reactions to things, I anticipate his needs, and understand his moods, much more easily than I do with the younger one. My younger boy is much more a mystery to me—he is more unpredictable and mischievous, more active, and less thoughtful. My husband is out of town for his work much of the time, so he isn't much help in this regard. I'm worried that I'm shortchanging my younger son or that he'll think I don't love him, when it's really more that I feel like I don't understand him. What can I do to change this situation or keep it from having a negative effect on my son?

MGT: Not loving children equally—or equally easily—is a source of guilt to most parents. Parents sometimes tie themselves in knots to deny what is perfectly obvious to their children: that they have a favorite child. But what exactly do we mean by a "favorite" child? Does that mean that one child is loved and the other is not? Does it really mean that one is loved "better" or "best"? No, that's not what actually happens. I think it usually means that a particular child is easier for one parent to love than another child. One child is a more natural temperamental fit with a parent than is another. You say that your older son is "like you," and your younger son is a "mystery." I might argue that your younger son is the one that you love more because it is more of a struggle to understand that child than it is to feel in the groove with your older son.

Do you remember the old comedy routine made famous

by the Smothers Brothers? The one in which the brothers, Tom and Dick, would be talking and suddenly Tom would say to Dick, reproachfully, "Mom loved you best." And this would either be denied or it would be acknowledged with quiet satisfaction (and not enough guilt) by Dick, with a shrug that suggested, "Of course I was loved best. I deserved it." When they talked about which of them was the favorite, it made you laugh and made you wince, because it was close to the truth—in every family. The joke hits a universal nerve for anyone who has had brothers and sisters, because children monitor their parents carefully to make sure they are not favoring one child. Despite all the careful supervision and the best efforts of parents, every child is certain that his or her older brother (or younger brother or sister) is spoiled, is believed when they shouldn't be believed, and in sum ". . . gets away with murder."

Because children are so quick to point to sibling injustice, it makes parents nervous that their inner feelings and motivations are showing when they feel different things toward their various children. That's your worry. As a psychologist, I have to wonder whether you experienced some of these tensions when you were growing up. Are you guilty about being the favored one? Or are you angry at a brother or sister who seemed to be favored? Or perhaps you are an only child, and the inevitable tensions between siblings are foreign to you. Whatever your family history, it is clear that you want to be as perfect a mother as you can be, and you don't want to be "caught" loving one child more than another. Yet the fact that you harbor the worry that the younger one won't feel as loved suggests that you love him a lot.

Your wish to be perceived as an absolutely fair mother who loves both boys equally easily is understandable, and totally futile. They both know that the one who is "like you" enjoys a certain advantage, at least for now. That's okay. Don't worry. They will both survive it. It will not traumatize them, as long as there is enough love in the house. As English pediatrician turned psychoanalyst Donald W. Winnicott always said to mothers, you do not have to be perfect; you only have to be "good enough." Who knows? Your younger son might appreciate that you have to reach out to understand him in his mysteriousness, or he might enjoy the fact that he has a bit more psychological freedom than his transparent older brother.

One last thing I should warn you about. Parents typically fight with the child who is most "like them" in adolescence. There is something extraordinarily frustrating for a parent about understanding everything about a child and still not being able to control him. And teenagers sometimes have to fight against the parent with whom they have had the most intuitive bond, in order to develop a sense of separateness. Such a fate is not foreordained, but it is not out of the question, either.

Mother Love Goes the Distance

Q: I'm the mother of an older boy. I have a son who is twenty-three and lives a couple of hours away. I realize we're not going to be as close in the same way we were all his growing-up years, but what are some ways I can keep a loving connection to my son without using home maintenance questions as an excuse for calling him?

MGT: Well, speaking of maintaining homes, you could buy a ski condo or a beachfront vacation cottage. There is nothing that keeps a young adult in touch like a second home in a recreation area! I'm joking, of course, about the house anyway, but not about the recreation or leisure time pursuits. If you can continue any mutually enjoyable activity with a son, especially something you did as a family when he was younger, that will allow you to be together in a relaxed and unguarded way.

It helps to understand the psychology of many children in their twenties, especially boys. They want to be grown-up, they want to be independent, they want to be seen as adults, and yet many of them are still lost and confused. After a career of doing therapy with people from the age of three to sixty-six, I'm inclined to say that I think the two or three years after college are among the most miserable in the life cycle. As a therapist, I have run into it with twentysomethings who have come into therapy depressed and without a vocation, really needing an adult hand, wishing for some trickle-down wisdom, yet awkward about turning to their parents for it, especially if communication has been thin or brittle.

Here are the ways that a mother can stay in touch with her son in his twenties:

1. E-mail. He's probably on e-mail every day at his job or every night at home. E-mail has opened up some wonderful channels of communication between sons and parents who are separated geographically. There is no reason that it couldn't be used by sons and mothers who are close geographically. He'll think you're cool, he can respond in the middle of the night, and if he has difficulty talking on the phone or in person, e-mail is perfect. Send him an e-mail greeting card that flashes or jumps or sings. Send him a joke. Invite him to send you jokes over e-mail. A shared laugh lasts.

2. Ask for help. If there is something that you cannot do, something you think your son could do handily, ask him. Ask him especially if it is in his area of expertise. Ask him well in advance, ask him without being pathetic or making him feel guilty, don't nag about it, and accept it graciously if he says "no." I know a widow who had to buy a new car. She didn't have a very close relationship with her thirty-year-old son, but she knew he was very knowledgeable about automobiles. She asked him to help her scout out cars. He was there in a flash! And their relationship improved after they had been to five auto dealers together. He would have gone to eleven dealerships if she had had the stamina for it.

3. Travel or vacation together. If your son has to drive back from Baltimore to Chicago by himself, offer to go with him and share the driving. I'm not kidding. There is more intimate conversation in automobiles in the United States than there is almost anyplace else in this country. People talk in cars.

If you can afford it, invite him and any siblings on a vacation with you. Decide on a destination together. Perhaps you can help finance a vacation that your son couldn't do on his own. My aunt created a July 4th tradition of having her son throw a party for all of his friends at her house. He did all the work, but she provided the big backyard and access to a pool and helped pay for the paper plates and other fun stuff. She got to meet and enjoy his adult friends as a result.

4. Make friends with the girl—or girls—he loves. Respect his relationship, befriend his lady friend. Invite them over, talk with her when he is busy doing something else. Ask her about her family and her aunts. She'll leave with him and say, "Your mom is pretty nice," and he'll say, "Yeah, right, I knew that." Don't intrude, don't give advice, don't ask them about birth control or when they're getting married, don't criticize her if she's a vegetarian, etc. Just appreciate their young love. My bet is that he will then start to turn to you with relationship questions. If you let on that you don't really like her, he cannot ask you about problems in the relationship, because he's sure you'll say: "Get rid of her." If they talk with anyone, most sons talk to their mothers about problems in relationships.

5. Ask him questions about his work. Don't ask, "Shouldn't you have a better job?" Ask him about the details, the scut work, the technical aspects. Let him teach you something. Boys and young men love to teach their parents something.

6. Tell him you love him without any nostalgia in your voice. Young men are exquisitely sensitive to maternal longing for their boyhoods. Forget their boyhoods. You can talk to them about how cute they were when they have children. In the meantime, love the young man you raised.

Speaking of
Fathers and Sons

Father Misses Special Tuck-in Time with Nine-Year-Old Son

Q: I am a busy father, someone who travels during the week, and even when I'm in town, I often can't get home until seven o'clock. Because of that, tucking my son in at bedtime and reading with him then is one of the best times I have with him. My son doesn't play organized sports, so we're not going to his practices together the way I do sometimes with my daughter, and I really can't get into Pokémon and Legos, so this reading time together has always been "our thing." Now my son is nine and lately has told me he can put himself to bed and doesn't need me to come in and read. Even when I've invited myself in and asked to read, he has said he's too tired and just wants to go to bed. I feel I'm losing my most important connection to him. What should I do?

MGT: I don't often hear this question from fathers, but that's only because fathers don't come to parenting talks or therapy nearly as much as mothers do, and when they do, they aren't as comfortable bringing up issues about closeness or loss of it as a boy grows up. I do know that caring fathers experience this kind of loss all the time and struggle with feelings of rejection, just as caring mothers do. I know because I eventually do hear about it in the rare Fathers-Only parenting talks I'm asked to lead or in therapy with boys and their fathers, and because I have a young son myself and have been the dad booted from the bedside at tuck-in time. It helps to understand why your son is doing what he's doing and why it hurts your feelings that he wants to put himself to bed. From there it becomes easier to see how to keep the connection you treasure so much. Here's what I can tell you:

The process of child development means that you lose your child over and over. Your child is constantly growing, and like a snake he discards his old skins. You fall in love with an infant, and then suddenly the infant is gone, turned into a toddler. You fall in love with your toddler, and all of a sudden he's not a little guy anymore, he's a big boy now. Then you fall in love with taking him to Little League games or coaching him, and one day he tells you he doesn't like baseball anymore. Heartbreak for Dad. That's what has happened with you and your son around this bedtime ritual. He needs to feel strong and independent. Most boys want to feel that way around the age of eight or nine.

The truth is that you have been lucky that he has let you

put him to bed for all these years. Many boys might have wanted the feeling of being grown-up and independent at bedtime at an even earlier age. Count yourself lucky and be graceful about it. You are going to have to let him put himself to bed from time to time now, and it has to be his call. You have to turn the control over to him or risk making him feel like a baby. If you insist on treating him in baby ways, it will turn into a power struggle in which he needs to fight you in order to feel big. That happens to many fathers and sons. The father won't give up control and the son ends up having to "back him off."

Here is one comforting thought. My experience as a therapist tells me that boys enjoy being put to bed right up until late adolescence. Many boys and mothers report to me that they still talk at bedtime. Many mothers still rub their sons' backs at bedtime. Why is it always mothers and not fathers? Fathers don't like losing control and they don't like being rejected. Or they have an ideological belief in independence and want to support it. The problem is that in the process of cultivating a son's independence, fathers often become isolated from them.

You should keep offering to read with your son; you should keep showing up at his doorway when he is in bed "just to say good night." Perhaps you will sit at the edge of his bed and he'll talk to you. That's what many moms do. My advice to you is this: don't try to control this process, celebrate your son's growth, let him know that this is hard for you, allow yourself to feel some grief, but don't withdraw. Stay in the game. If sharing literature isn't going to keep his interest any-more at bedtime, and sitting quietly with him to chat about the day seems awkward, try picking up a book of humor columns or jokes. Maybe *he'd* like to read to *you*. And finally, remember that his changing interests can work in your favor. Look at what's important to him now and see if there's an-other way to make special time for the two of you.

Why Can't Dads Be More Like Grandfathers?

Q: My husband and our ten-year-old son Christopher often lock horns over everyday things—whether he's dressed right for school, whether he's handling his household chores well enough, and other issues that come up again and again. In the past few years I've noticed that Christopher seems tense and uncomfortable with his father but is very relaxed with his grandfather, who lives nearby and whom he sees often. I wish Christopher had that kind of relationship with his dad. Why is it so hard for a father and son to get along?

MGT: Christopher is very lucky to have a grandfather close by who sees him frequently. The grandson-grandfather rela-tionship can be incredibly close and loving. I am happy for them both. Why is it that they can enjoy each other in a way that your son and your husband cannot? There is a very popular bumper sticker in Florida, often seen on cars belong-ing to retired people. It says, "If I had known grandchildren were so wonderful, I would have had them first." There is a certain ease in the grandson-grandfather relationship—often paralleled in the granddaughter-grandmother relationship—that is difficult to achieve in the father-son relationship. The secret lies in the fact that the grandfather does not have frontline responsibilities for the boy. He cannot be sucked into power struggles as easily as the father is. The grandfather is in a different stage of life; he may be wiser than he was when he was a father. Fathers are far more susceptible to struggling with their sons because of their life stage and their inexperience with child development.

Young fathers are often extraordinarily proud of having a son, but they also worry a lot about whether their sons are going to be disciplined and productive. If a first-time father of a boy is in his late twenties or thirties, he may be at the height of his own ambition. Some of his striving is going to rub off on his wishes for his son, and he may be intensely focused on helping his son turn out well. I have watched fathers talk to their boys, and a great percentage of the time they are talking to their sons about improving themselves, thinking ahead, about what it takes to get into college, etc. Fathers often see in a young boy's disorganization signs of future laziness, and it worries the dad. Your husband may look at the way Christopher does chores and think, "Uh-oh, he's not going to be very successful on a job; I'd better teach him how to *really* mow the lawn, or *really* clean up the garage." Your husband may also have forgotten what he was like at ten years of age.

Many men have a story about their lives that goes, "I used to be a screwup, I didn't do what I should have done in school, I wasn't as productive a student as I could have been. I only got a high school degree," they think regretfully. Alternatively they imagine, "I could have gone to a better college, and many of my colleagues at work seem to have gone to better colleges. If I hadn't wasted so much time, if I hadn't drunk so much beer and chased girls so much, I would have gotten further in life sooner." The conclusion that many men come to is that they should bear down on their sons and save their sons those lost years in their own lives. In my experience fathers don't trust development as much as mothers do, even though they are often the very successful products of their own development. But that's not the life history that they remember. They remember that they "finally took hold" and "saw the light" after great amounts of wasted time. Their sons, they hope, will do better sooner.

Unfortunately, however, too few men have had experience with children. They don't know much about what children at certain ages are capable of doing. Moms tend to see other children in action, and they are constantly making comparisons between their own children and other people's children. These are not competitive comparisons, they are reality checks: Am I asking too much or too little of my son? Most fathers don't have the same depth of information about children that moms do. Unfortunately, many men lack the patience that women develop in baby-sitting or taking care of younger siblings; therefore, when they encounter willfulness or dawdling in their sons, they don't have patience for it.

If a father asks for too much from his son or he displays a

lot of impatience, the son may try to rise to the level of his father's expectations, but if he cannot, he will become anxious. The son is thinking, "There is no pleasing my dad. No matter what I do, he seems disappointed." When boys feel that they are not going to be able to be successful in their father's eyes, they often start to resent their fathers. Or they go into a worried kind of stalling behavior. "Uh-oh, when is he going to get upset?"

Now you have a father thinking, "My son cannot even find his boots. How is he going to get into a good college?" And his son is thinking, "Oh no, I can't find my boots and my father's going to get mad at me and it's not fair because he didn't put my boots out for me the way Mom does." The result is a tense father and a tense son.

Enter the grandfather. He made his mistakes with his children; he had fights with his son. Indeed, they hardly spoke to each other for a year when his son was twenty-three. He has a lot of regrets about the way he criticized his son because he sees that it wasn't necessary; perhaps there is a residue of tension between the two of them. His son—your husband—has turned out to be a good and loving man with high standards. The grandfather thinks, "I must have done a few things right. Maybe I wasn't so bad a father after all." Now he has a wonderful grandson whom he adores and who loves him back. He has no need to find the boy's boots most days of the week. He doesn't have to struggle to get him off to school and he doesn't have to speak to him about his report card. And deep down, he knows that he may not live to see this boy grow into adulthood. He wants to fully enjoy the relationship now. The grandfather's orientation is the present. They get to do fun things together. The grandfather is in a mellow stage of life, glad to be alive and glad to have the chance to be a companion to this wonderful boy. And the grandson feels totally accepted by his grandfather.

Is there hope for your husband? Yes. As your son begins to become more capable and independent, your husband will see that development is working. As soon as your son doesn't need someone to supervise his putting on his boots, your husband may be reassured that his fathering has been effective. Alternatively, your son's anxiety may turn into anger and he may express his fury at his father in a way that gets his dad's attention. Your son may say to his father, "Dad, when you criticize me and nag at me, it makes me hate you." Sons can often be the agents of their fathers' change. Fathers have said to me, "I could see that getting mad at him wasn't working any longer. It was pointless."

You did not say whether or not your husband ever asks you for your thoughts about how he is managing his son. If he does, you have an opportunity to speak. Please don't criticize your husband; he probably feels amateurish and ashamed about the power struggles he has with your son. Just say to your husband, "I think Christopher is constantly tense around you because he is frightened that he's a disappointment to you." A father may have high expectations for his son; he may think his son has bad habits that need a father's attention. However, no father wants his son to think that he is chronically disappointed in him.

Wishful Dad Wants to Be in on the Conversation

Q: My son, Spencer, is eleven. He and I get along fine, but whenever he has something on his mind, it seems like he always talks with his mother about it, not me. They have these long bedtime chats, but when I go in there, he's happy enough to see me but he never brings up the kinds of things he shares with my wife, like problems at school. Frankly, I feel left out. I'm not suggesting my wife is somehow to "blame," but why won't my son talk with me?

MGT: I am so glad to hear that you want your son to talk to you and that you are hurt that he doesn't. Your wish to be closer to him is admirable, and you will be successful in getting closer to him if you work at it. I also think I can give you some advice to help you, but first I have to ask you some questions—tough questions—that will enable you to assess whether or not you have been disqualified by your son because you don't know enough about his life.

In my experience, sons don't talk to fathers because they do not think fathers have enough of a frame of reference to understand their concerns. Do you know the name of your son's homeroom teacher? Have you met her or him? Do you know the name of his P.E. teacher? Does he like P.E. or is he self-conscious because he is not as good an athlete as other boys? When was the last time you helped him with his homework? Do you know the name of his science teacher, his music teacher? Do you take him to school or pick him up from school? Can you name his closest friend and five other friends of his? Can you name the most powerful boy in his class? Can you name the girl in his class that he sort of likes and sort of hates? Do you know the name of his principal? Do you know when his science project is due?

I am willing to bet that your wife knows the answers to many, or even all, these questions. If you do, too, I congratulate you. If you don't, then your son may want to protect you from looking stupid. Most sons do not want to have to bring their fathers up to speed on their lives because it makes the son feel sad that their dads don't know, and it makes the son embarrassed for his father. No boy wants to feel that. He'd rather protect you. He'd rather have you be a benevolent, distant dad than confront the fact that you are somewhat clueless about the details of his life.

If you want your son to trust you in more intimate conversation, you have to know the characters and the plotline of his life. If he is going to talk to you about his problems in school, you need to be able to say, "I'm sorry to hear that you hate science. I thought you and Mr. Miller were getting along better than you were in the fall." He can then reply, "Well, we were for a while, but things are bad again." But if you don't know Mr. Miller's name, and you don't know the history of his experience in class, when he starts to talk to you, you're going to say, "Well, don't you think you should do what your science teacher asks of you?" The answer to that is a silent look from your son; inside his head he's saying, "Why are you telling me to pay more attention to my science teacher; you don't even know his name! You don't know how mean he can be! You don't know anything!" But your son loves you and he does not want to go down that road.

What if you did know the answers to all those questions, and your son still doesn't talk to you about matters of the heart? Possibly he believes that strong boys shouldn't show weakness to their fathers. Perhaps he wants you to see him as very capable, and so he shares his frightened, more needy side to his mom, who he assumes will understand his fears. Boys very often believe that their fathers won't understand or be able to tolerate their son's fears because the fathers don't often show their sons their own uncertainty, their vulnerability. When was the last time you told your son about a struggle or a failure in your life? Does he know that things aren't always good on your job? Does he know some of the details? Fathers tend to present themselves to their sons in a very strong way, and the sons mirror back that image. Fathers don't share the concerns of their souls, and the sons imitate them.

I am not recommending that you suddenly become a blubbering whiner. I do suggest that you show him something from your heart. Perhaps you can sit on the edge of his bed one night and say simply: "I worry that we're not very close. My dad and I had trouble talking and I always imagined that it would be different between you and me. Have I done any-thing to shut things down between us?" Three sentences is plenty. Then you have to sit there and accept his answer, whatever it is. Perhaps he will say, "No, Dad, things are great. It's just that Mom knows more about what happened with Mr. Miller." Perhaps he will be stunned; he might not know what to say. Go back the next night and say something about your day, tell him something that you wish for in life that you haven't gotten. Rub his back. Admire the poster on his closet door. Ask him about the CD that he is playing. Listen to his answer.

Father Withdrawing as Son Grows Older

Q: Eight years ago, when Drew was born, my husband was as involved as his work allowed him to be in the routine things like feeding and bathing the baby. As time has gone on, though, now that Drew can do those kinds of things for him-self, I notice that my husband spends much less time with him and doesn't show the same interest in Drew's day-to-day life as he once did. It often feels as though I'm the only one who cares about some school and social issues that I know are troubling Drew. The problem is, I often can't figure out what the problem is, and Drew won't necessarily offer much detail. I believe my husband must know more about the struggles of being a boy—after all, he was one once, himself—but he never wants to talk about these things with me or even with Drew. I've asked him to share more stories from his growing-up years, so Drew can see that things work out, but my husband just shrugs and says it's got nothing to do with life today. I love my husband and I know he loves our son, but I resent always being the one to notice when Drew seems troubled or needy in some way. How can I get my husband to be more of a partner in this part of parenting? I'd ask my other mother friends, but we all have the same problem with our husbands.

MGT: Whenever my *Raising Cain* coauthor, Dan Kindlon, is asked by a woman how to get her husband more involved in child care, he always answers, "Take a long trip and leave your husband with the children." The answer gets a laugh, and because it is funny, I'm afraid that many women don't take his advice seriously. I do. If you want your husband to become reengaged with your son, you have to put him back into a position of responsibility. Being disappointed in him is not going to work; asking him to think about his son in the way you do seems not to have worked. You have to rethink what has happened in your family.

There are two main reasons why fathers fall out of touch with their children. First, they come to regard their wives as the "experts" in child rearing and they withdraw into different areas of expertise where they feel more competent. Second, the emotional complexity of raising children conflicts with their image of themselves as men (or what they learned from their own fathers about being a father).

Many men find themselves falling behind their wives in their knowledge base as their children grow older. This must be true of you and your husband because you said he did child care consistent with what his work allowed. I do not know whether you work full time, but your question implies that you are the more on-the-job parent. You are driving car pool. You hear the stories from school. You know something about your child's friends and enemies and his social anxieties. Most men do not want to look incompetent, and so they do not try to keep up in your area of expertise. A family is an emotional system where people take reciprocal roles and, indeed, are forced into reciprocal roles. Yours is hardly the first marriage that has fallen into a more traditional pattern as the children have gotten older. The problem is that both you and your husband may now regard him as the associate parent. If you are the one in charge, how can he give you advice and counsel? Your situation has become a marital issue, not just a parenting issue, and probably has to be addressed that way, because not only is your husband out of touch with your son, you are out of touch with each other.

Why is your husband not interested in the minutiae of your son's school and emotional life? The simple answer is that his father was not interested in those things and he is unconsciously or consciously repeating his father's fathering of him in his relationship with Drew. Furthermore, he has shown Drew a model of masculinity that is emotionally closed. He does not talk much and neither does Drew. I have a lot of empathy for you. Many men believe that silence is strength and that real men do not discuss emotional matters in the way that women do. As a psychologist, I worry about men who are "emotionally illiterate" and who model that emotional style for their boys. However, it would not be fair of me to say whether that is true of your husband without meeting him. I have to give him the benefit of the doubt and imagine that he is shy or introverted and that stylistically your son, Drew, is just like his dad.

What you need to develop is confidence in your husband's fathering of your son. The way he does it may be different from what you would do. He's not likely to change his personal style a lot. If he misses out on some aspects of his son's life, that is a shame for them both, but your critiquing him will not help. He needs to be requalified as a father in your mind and his mind. I have seen many fathers become better fathers after they were divorced from their children's mother. They finally realized that they had to do the job because "the expert" was gone. (You might rent the old movie *Kramer vs. Kramer* and watch that father's transformation from an unengaged father to one who is energized and expert once the mother has departed.) How do you achieve your goal without getting divorced?

My advice is the same as Dan Kindlon's humorous suggestion. I think that you should take a long trip and leave your husband in charge. Let him struggle with your son's anxieties; let him hear the news from school. Go somewhere with your sister or your mother or a group of women friends. Leave all your husbands with all the children for two weeks. When you get back, your husband will have something to say about your son. I guarantee it.

Father's Depression: How Does It Affect a Son?

Q. My husband suffers from depression and is trying some treatments, but on a day-to-day basis at home, he often comes across as a basically unhappy person. For years our son has made every effort to greet his dad cheerfully after work and try to engage him in occasional small talk. He is nine years old now, and has begun to mention to me that his efforts to "cheer up" his dad are futile. Sometimes I think this makes him sad. Other times I think he resents his father for being so glum. What are the effects of a father's depression on a son, and how can I help my son understand and cope with his father and his own feelings?

MGT: In my clinical practice I have seen many boys deeply affected by a father's depression. In fact, I have seen boys who have become deeply sad in identification with their father's depression, following the roller coaster of their moods with unconscious loyalty. All children love their parents very much and try to support their mental health by pleasing them, cheering them up, or telling them a joke when they are down. One of the great secrets of childhood is how hard children strive to be their parents' therapists when there is trouble in a home. They will at first deny their fathers' trouble and try to rationalize it. "He's a good dad, he's just in a bad mood sometimes." They will try to get their fathers interested in activities, the way your son does. Ultimately, they may themselves become symptomatic in an effort to bring out the best fathering in their deeply preoccupied parent. When you work with boys, you cannot help but admire their efforts to lift the household onto their backs, and you always understand when, having failed in the effort, they become discouraged and angry themselves.

I was once asked to present to a middle school audience on short notice without any prepared topic and, on a whim, I asked the children in what ways they took care of their parents. They all described how they tried to keep their parents from "stressing out," how they tried to intervene in fights between their parents or between their older siblings and their parents, or how they tried—often without success—to get their parents to give up smoking. They were so honest in that very public setting, it is a good thing that news of our discussion in assembly did not get to many parents. It was an eye-opening look into the inner struggles of children in their family settings.

I admire your son's efforts on behalf of his father. He is being his best healing self. Depression is a tough illness, however, and it is likely to beat back the efforts of anyone who tries to help. Depressed people often give off the silent plea, "Help, help, throw me a rope." And when you throw them a rope, they say, "No, not that rope, another rope." And when you throw them another rope they say, "No, no, not that rope, another rope." They don't do it intentionally. It is what happens to people caught in a depressive loop. I assure you, it is enough to try the patience of a trained therapist who is getting paid to be persistent! Imagine how confusing it is for a loving child.

What I worry about for your son is that he will begin to measure his worth by his success in being able to cheer up his father. He has to be relieved of his burden. He has to know that his father has an illness, that his father is trying to get treatment for it (He is trying, isn't he? He has tried therapy and medications, hasn't he? I hope so. Both forms of treatment can really help.), and that it is completely natural for your son to want to cure his father of this disorder. He has to know that you have tried, too, and that you still try and sometimes feel discouraged because you have had only limited success. He needs his therapeutic strivings honored and his sense of failure acknowledged. Most of all, however, he needs to hear that you and his father, especially his father, know how much he wishes that his father weren't depressed.

What I wish for is a conversation between your husband and your son in which your husband tells his son about the nature of depression, how long he has suffered from it, and what he has tried *and is currently trying* in order to heal himself of depression. He has to let your son know that he sees his loving efforts and really appreciates them. If your husband can tell his son these things, he will personally lift a burden off his shoulders. If he cannot, perhaps you can explain these issues to your son. Otherwise, your son may eventually have to distance himself from his father in order to avoid the feelings of failure that his father's depression engenders in him. Having a seriously depressed parent is a burden in the life of a child. You need to lift it off him as much as you can.

Whatever your son's experience of his father, or home life in general, it will become part of the man he grows up to be. He may choose to be a psychologist, a psychiatrist, or a social worker! Many in this line of work had troubled parents and learned how to be good caretakers from an early age. When they became adults, they found a "natural talent" for the work and often a lot more satisfaction because they were able to help other people in ways they could not as children of emotionally needy parents.

Speaking of
Siblings

Cain and Abel: Will They Ever Be Friends?

Q: I have two sons, one twelve and one eight. They used to play a lot together, but in just the past year the older one has become more insulting to the younger one, and the younger one has become more explosive in his anger when his older brother puts him down. Even so, the younger one tries so hard to impress his brother, engage him in conversation, lure him into playing the old way; it's clear that he adores his older brother. I'd like to think that will be a bond that lasts for life, but it breaks my heart to see my older boy turn on his little brother and the little one explode in a rage. How can I help them be better to each other? Is it just a phase? Is there some relationship rut they're getting into that will follow them into adulthood?

MGT: Are Cain and Abel going to be friends when they grow up? I get asked this question a lot by mothers and it is a tough one because I'm pretty sure that I know what is going on developmentally, but I am not a psychic and I cannot predict how things are going to turn out in adulthood. That's what you really want to know. Mothers study their children's relationships and are constantly extrapolating from the present moment into the future: Will they be friends? Will their families be close? Are the fights they are having now going to injure their future relationship? When I am gone will they be a comfort to each other?

To reassure you, I would like to declare authoritatively that "this is a phase. They are going to be friends in adulthood." Unfortunately, the best I can do is tell you that it is likely to be just a phase, that my best guess is that they will turn out to be friends in later years. If you read Anne Tyler's novels, you will see that she believes siblings always end up with each other, happily or ambivalently. *Dinner at the Homesick Restaurant* is a favorite of mine. In the novel, the brothers and sisters keep re-creating their childhood dinnertime dramas in a restaurant owned by one of the sisters. Anne Tyler seems to think that parents die, friendship is uncertain, spouses come and go, but your brothers and sisters are forever. That's what I have seen in life. With a few exceptions, everyone in my acquaintance has developed stronger relationships with their siblings in middle age. It is the few exceptions that trouble me, because they are generally brothers.

What happens between brothers that potentially drives

them apart? There are three things going on between your boys that create conflict in a relationship. The first is the inherent feelings of rivalry that exist between all siblings. The first child always has "feelings" about the presence of the second, and though they may love each other, there is always some residual sense on the part of the first that the younger one ruined a great setup. Second, competition is such a part of boy culture out in the world that inevitably brothers bring it home and try it out on each other. Third, the brother-brother relationship can fall victim to some of the expectable adolescent stresses that hit the older brother, in particular his wish for independence and the kind of cruelty he is beginning to experience in his peer group. His peers may be attacking him for loving his mother, for having tender feelings toward his family. This attack on a twelve-year-old's masculinity, which Dan Kindlon and I called the "culture of cruelty" in *Raising Cain*, may then be displaced onto the younger brother.

Most early adolescent boys feel under an obligation to begin to create some distance between themselves and their families in order to demonstrate that they are growing up. Many boys of this age make a personal Declaration of Independence by becoming rude to their parents, hating school, being unwilling to follow rules, or by treating their siblings in a cruel and shabby way. Parents dislike this change and often get caught up in it. It is hard for parents to understand why their growing child has to become so unpleasant as a part of his (or her) emerging autonomy. Parents want to say, "We know you're getting to be an adult. Do you have to be obnoxious as well?" As unpleasant as it is for the parents, it can be truly bewildering to the younger siblings.

Some teenagers—and I'm putting your twelve-year-old adolescent "wanna-be" in this category—don't take on their parents directly; rather, they proclaim their new status by torturing their brothers and sisters. They disavow their families and their own childhood by having contempt for their younger siblings. They all sound like Angelica, the wicked older cousin in the Rugrats cartoon. The psychological message that your older boy is sending is this, put as cruelly as I can write it: "I am growing up now and going out into the world. I have contempt for you pitiful, stay-at-home babies. I never was young and little like you. Just seeing your love for me reminds me that I once adored this family, and that makes me puke! What was I thinking? Now that I am mature and cool, I will rub your face in your adoration of me, your love for me, and I will make you think that I never loved any of you at all. Long live ME!"

My older brother, Peter, when he was fourteen, would saunter into the house, walk up to me, and run his hand over my face. "You don't have facial hair, do you?" he would say, and I would be mortified. To me, he seemed so powerful, so grown-up, and so enraging. I would fight him at every opportunity. We would wrestle and throw things and declare our hate for each other. My brother Peter and I are now very close. We talk twice a week on the phone, our families vacation together in Florida every Christmas, and he would be the first person I called in an emergency.

I hope the same thing is true for your two boys. If they had a good relationship in their early years—and it sounds as if they did—and they both receive loving support from their parents during their teenage years, there is no reason to worry. That is, if there is no scarcity of love in their lives, if you give them separate-but-equal time with you and your husband, they should be okay. If they are not permitted to brutalize each other, with the older one repeatedly humiliating the younger, then they will both be able to forgive one another. They should begin to refind one another and admire one another in their late teens or twenties. Try to imagine the two of them home from college, one a senior and the other a freshman. They'll have dinner with you and hang around and talk, and just as you're getting ready for bed, the two of them will head out in a car together, bonded by the realization that they are both cool dudes now and their parents are hopelessly "other."

Teasing with Intent: Brother's Barbs Hurt Sister

Q. Robb is fourteen and our daughter, Jennie, is eleven. Robb has always teased Jennie and gotten the best of her that way—she's not as quick with comebacks. Lately, he's begun teasing her about her appearance, calling her fat and stupid. Even if she were fat, it wouldn't be right to tease her about it, but she isn't overweight. She's a normal, rounded, eleven-year-old girl who is, like all of them, very self-conscious about her shape and weight. She also happens to be a very bright girl and makes good grades. I've talked with Robb privately about how hurtful his comments are to her and how especially vulnerable girls are when it comes to comments about their appearance. I've explained girls' problems with eating disorders, and I've asked him to stop this kind of teasing. He stops for a day and then is at it again as if I never said anything. How can I make him understand that what he's doing is wrong? And how can I get him to stop?

MGT: I have to ask you a number of questions before I can know how to advise you. Getting him to stop is in some ways the easiest part of this situation. I have confidence that you are going to be able to do that. Once you know why this is happening, you will be able to design a creative and meaningful negative consequence that stops it or you will create an incentive that will help him change his behavior. The problem here, however, is that we do not understand why he is doing this. Without knowing that, we cannot address anything but the offensive behavior; without understanding, we have no door into his heart. Do you know why he is willing to be so cruel to his sister? If you asked him why, he might just say, "All boys tease their sisters." However, that answer is insufficient here.

Is Jennie just a victim in this conflict, or does she do things that irritate him? Are there things she does actively, like lording her "goodness" over him? Are there things about her that annoy him, which neither of them can help? For example, is she more physically mature—or at least comparably mature—at eleven than he is at fourteen? Is she a much better student than he is? Has she always gotten better report cards than he has? Is she brighter than he is? These are tough questions to ask yourself, but we need to understand whether he feels defensive and feels that his attacks on her are in some way justified.

Boys, unless they have been abused themselves, are rarely just randomly mean and cruel. They usually have a story of hurt—from their point of view—that justifies their teasing. Does your son have such a story? Do you believe his reasons are authentic, or are they a cover story for some deeper feeling of injustice on his part? You asked me, "How can I get him to see that what he is doing is wrong?" The answer is that you cannot if he thinks she deserves it. You need to make sure that he does not have some grievance against her, or you, that he is expressing in this way. If he does hold a grudge, you need to sort out that issue with him.

Does he have a capacity for empathy? I know that you have told him how hurtful the comments are, but does she show a lot of pain when he teases her? Does she cry? When her pain is obvious, does it make him stop? Is he a good judge of her pain or does he have a limited capacity for empathy? It may be that Robb is trying to draw blood, psychologically speaking, and he cannot tell whether he is succeeding. He may be lousy at reading her facial expressions.

Maybe he wants to have an impact on his "perfect sister" and she does not give him the satisfaction of letting him know that it hurts. It may be that when he sees that he has succeeded he stops but that you do not see that he is relenting. It may be that his early insults ring in *your ears* and that you cannot forget them, even when his sister has.

It is important for you to be clear on whether his insults are primarily upsetting to you on an ideological basis. Attacking girls for being "fat" in a country where eating disorders are epidemic should be offensive to adults; however, that is different than your being upset because his remarks are so hurtful to her. If you are going to be effective in your discipline, you have to be clear about why you are trying to make him stop. If you cite a dishonest reason, he will use that as a reason not to stop.

Honesty compels me to discuss a topic that may make you uncomfortable. I have to tell you that based on my experience, many fourteen-year-old boys are now noticing the bodies, breasts, and hips of girls all day in school. If a boy comes home and there is a beautiful, developing girl in his house, he is going to stare at her and be attracted to her. If that girl is his sister, his incest guilt may click in and make him feel weird. That is one reason why he may be calling her fat. He may be saying, "You are my sister and I don't want to be attracted to you in any way, so I declare you to be unattractive." That would be confusing and hurtful to his sister, and it is doubtful that you can talk to him about it at that level.

It may be that he is simply bringing home samples of the

culture of cruelty that he is experiencing among boys at school. Boys at this age are incredibly hard on one another. They laugh at each other's small size, lack of pubertal development, lack of coordination. Ninth grade can be a very tough place, and your son may be importing the cruelty he experiences at school.

Since you are not here and cannot answer these questions, let me turn to the issue of changing your son's behavior. I can tell from your question that you have not really made a huge effort to get him to stop. Pulling him aside later and explaining how hurtful his comments are is not a sufficient consequence. As you point out, it works for a day but doesn't last longer. If you want him to stop, you have to do four things.

First, you have to put your moral weight and personal feelings behind your comments to him: "I cannot tolerate listening to you tease your sister in this way, I really can't, and I am going to find some way to get you to stop."

Second, find a meaningful consequence. Either ask him what a meaningful punishment would be, one that would really work, or experiment with different strategies. If you are driving to a restaurant and he starts to tease her, turn around, drive back home, and drop him off. Go to the restaurant without him. I bet if you do that, he won't ever do it on the way to somewhere he wants to go. If he starts in on her in a restaurant, or at his grandparents' house, ask him to leave the room. Ask him publicly to leave. If he objects to being embarrassed in public, remind him that you warned him that you were going to find a way to stop him from teasing his sister that way, and that's all you're doing. If he teases her in the TV room, suspend his TV privileges for a couple of days. Or do as a friend of mine does and pull the plug on computer time. Her one-line lecture: "In computer games people don't have feelings, but real people have real feelings, and until I see a return of respectful, civil behavior in my own home, the virtual world is unplugged."

Third, ask him if there is some incentive that you could give him to control this behavior. Offer him something he can work toward, perhaps a weekend skiing with a friend. Take it away from him if he breaks his pledge and continues to tease his sister.

Fourth and finally, if none of the previous ideas work and he insists on being the bully in the household (and I suspect it will work and you won't have to get to this), make a stinging comment to him immediately after he tries to hurt his sister. With full adult conviction, say something short and hurtful such as, "That's ugly, Robb. I didn't know you were so cruel." "Gee, Robb, do you talk to the girls in school about their bodies this way? Hasn't anybody taught you about sexual harassment?" If the problem is that his sister isn't very good with comeback remarks, you can step into the vacuum and get off some zingers yourself. It is my least favorite way of handling sibling teasing because it means you are getting right into their conflict and using their methods yourself. In politics, I think it is called getting into the gutter with your opponent.

Sometimes if a boy is hooked on his own power, it is the only thing that lets him know that you mean what you say. Try not to use it.

Competitive Brothers: Will They Ever "Get a Life"?

Q. Our sons are close in age—nine and eleven—and they have always been intensely competitive about everything. Sometimes it is clear that they choose the same activities just to compete with one another, and other times it seems they make their choices precisely to avoid doing something the other likes. How can we encourage each of them to make their choices on the basis of genuine interest rather than a desire to beat or avoid one another? How can they learn to just be themselves instead of comparing themselves constantly with each other?

A. I'm going to ask you to do a small mental exercise. I want you to imagine that you had given birth to identical twin boys. If you had twins, they would be amazingly alike and probably would be constantly competitive as well. They would also be each other's primary reality; they would compare their performances on everything. Because they were twins, everyone would have been delighted by how similar they were. You would have had to answer the question, "Do you ever have trouble telling them apart?" a million times. Their closeness would have been unmistakable and their teachers would have been charmed by it as well as being attentive to any differences in the two. My point is this: we have unconscious assumptions about how close or how far apart brothers and sisters should be. When we have twins, we know they'll be the main act in each other's lives; we know that their "individuality" will always be colored by being a twin. We accept that intuitively. When we have two boys close in age, there is no guidebook to how tied in with each other they "should" be.

The gap of two years is sufficiently small that your two boys read each other as approximately equal. In a way, it is terrific for both of them. They have a companion, a teammate, a yardstick, and an opponent right at hand. No need to be lonely, no need to go down the street to find a friend. However, it is also pretty intense, and that is what your letter is about. The older one cannot ever be sure of his position; he's always thinking, "Gee, I have to stay on top here. I'm supposed to be first." The younger boy gets to think, "Gee, I'm so close, I can overtake him."

What I didn't hear in your question is that these boys are unhappy or that they fight constantly. What I hear is that they are extremely competitive. Well, that happens with boys two years apart (and I should know, my older brother is two years minus one day ahead of me). If you have two children that close in age they may feel—as with twins—that they have to deal with this other person all the time. Is that inherently bad or destructive? Does that mean that they will not grow up to

be individuals in their own right? I do not think that there is a
big risk of that. Indeed, I know people who grew up in families of five, or eight, or even thirteen and they are very much
individuals. However, they spent their childhoods competing
with, reacting to, hating, and loving their siblings.

If you took a stopwatch and clocked the amount of time
your sons spent together cooperating or competing, I bet
that you would find that they spend much more time playing
together—talking, comparing notes, deciding what to do, setting up a game—than they do actually competing. I bet that
they don't like being separated for too long, that they seek
each other out. If you want to test my theory, you and your
spouse could start doing different activities with the two
boys; spend some "away time" with each of them and then
observe how eager (or not) they are to be back together. My
best guess is that you will find that they like being with one
another. They are living an intense life, but it is not inherently destructive for either of them. If they want space from
one another, or if you want to have them do different things
without reference to each other, that time is coming fast. The
gap between a ninth grader and a seventh grader is huge.

Kid Brother as Mascot to Older Sisters

Q: John is four years old, and our older children are girls, ten
and seven years old. John loves his sisters and wants nothing
more than to play with them and their friends. Fortunately,
they welcome him, but they treat him more like a pet than a

play partner. John has buddies his own age at preschool, but he'd rather play with his sisters. Is there any harm in this?

MGT: There is no harm in this situation. In my experience, most younger brothers with older sisters who have loved them and included them in their play are very grateful for the attention and remain grateful into adulthood. It can make for a very close sister-brother relationship. The girls are practicing their mothering skills, and the younger brother is the lucky recipient of a lot of loving. If there is any potential problem here, it is that the younger brother might grow up thinking that all women will fetch and carry for him. Typically, a boy with a lot of older sisters can come to feel like a young prince. That is okay, as long as the sisters are willing to continue to take care of him. Of course, he might turn out to be somewhat incompetent around the house because the girls have done so many things for him. I think it is important that the girls not just practice their household skills on him, but teach him to be competent as well.

It can also happen at some point that a boy's older sisters will drop him, so to speak, because he is not so cute anymore, or he challenges them and they retaliate, and that can lead to conflict. I have seen sisters turn cruel and contemptuous toward a younger brother as they become adolescent, and it can be bewildering for the boy. At a later age, he will need his own friends to fall back on.

But I hear in your question two deeper worries: is your son avoiding friendships with other boys, and is it good for him to participate in girl play? In my opinion, the peer group is overrated as an experience in the early years. If he is in preschool and has some buddies to play with there, he is fine. It is far more important for him to have peaceful and satisfying play at home. Your son has a friendship with his sisters. That makes home a joyful and accepting place for him and that is what a four-year-old needs to feel.

I have heard many fathers—and hardly any mothers— worry about their sons' playing with sisters because the play is so feminine that the fathers become afraid that the boy will be made into a sissy. Girls will often play with their brother's hair, or put barrettes in it. I know an older sister who fixed her brother's hair, put makeup on him, dressed him in girls' clothes, and brought him downstairs. Happily, his parents were totally cool about it. But I know that in other situations such a makeover has made the boy's father extremely uncomfortable, and he has demanded that the mother put a stop to it. The father's worry is unfounded. Sisters cannot turn their younger brothers into homosexuals any more than mothers can. It is a fact of life in our culture that many men are totally unnerved by their sons' doing anything feminine. It is a shame. Such fears are irrational. If anything, a boy raised with sisters is going to be very successful with women in later life because he has an ease with the ways of women and he can talk to them. With his experience, he'll make a better husband and a good father to a daughter.

Adding to the Family: Best Timing for New Sibling

Q: What's the best age for a boy to have a younger sibling added to the family? We adopted our first son at birth three years ago, and want to add to our family. If we have a choice of timing, how can we decide whether our son is ready to accept a new sister or brother? What should we watch out for?

MGT: If you asked this question of my older brother, Peter, he might say there never is and never was a good time to add another sibling to the family. No, I am just kidding about my brother; we made our peace years ago.

I don't know where you were in the sibling order in your family. If you are a firstborn, your empathy with your son is total. If you are a second-born, you may share my sense that the arrival of a second child is something of a shock to an older brother from which he recovers slowly. For the first-born, the arrival of a second child always disrupts the Garden of Eden in which he has been living. He has been the only child; he has had his father and mother's focused attention and adoration. When a second baby arrives, everything is chaotic and divided. He has to wait his turn; he has to watch his parents get all gushy over the new baby. And it cannot help but make the first child feel as if he has been discarded, that he wasn't good enough or lovable enough for the parents. Why else would they have gone and gotten another child?

I had friends who had a two-year-old boy who became something of a monster when his little sister was born. He literally waged a kind of war against her existence. Finally, when the boy was just short of four years old and his parents were exhausted by his unrelenting hostility to her, the father sat down with the boy. He asked, "Steven, do you think that if you act horribly toward Sarah we will eventually give in and send her back to where she came from?" Steven stared at his father and then slowly nodded "yes." The father then declared, "Steven, I am sorry you have felt this way. Nothing you can do will ever make us send Sarah back. She is here to stay and you have to make your peace with that fact." From that time onward, Steven's behavior toward his sister was markedly less hostile than it had been for two years.

Having a younger sibling is a survivable problem for most boys. Most do not try to fill the cultural role that many older sisters are ambitious to fill when a baby arrives, namely to be a kind of assistant mother. Older sisters tend to see themselves as aiding their mothers and therefore feel closer to them. Boys are not preparing mentally to be like their mothers, and though they are fascinated with the new baby and often very loving, they may not see a future in caring for the child. The best hope for a boy is that his younger sibling will grow up to be a playmate for him. And that's what happens in an overwhelming number of families, whether the new baby is a boy or a girl.

The conventional wisdom in psychology is that if children are spaced three years apart, the parents can avoid the worst competitive feelings that arise between siblings. If a child does not have to share his or her parents with another baby for three years, then that child will have gotten most of what he or she needs emotionally and cognitively in the crucial first three years of life. The sibling research suggests that children born six years apart, with no intervening brothers or sisters, are both "only" children, psychologically speaking. Six-year spacing means their worlds hardly overlap at all. They do not have a day-to-day impact on one another. They cannot annoy one another very much, nor can they share very much. So the best wisdom a psychologist has to offer is that you should bring a new brother or sister into your son's life between the ages of three and six if you want to have the siblings have a real relationship.

I did notice that your son was adopted. Adopted children always have the psychological burden of knowing they were given up by their biological parent; that is a problem that they wonder about off and on throughout their lives. I think parents of adopted children (I am the father of two adopted children, my wife was herself adopted, and my younger sister is adopted) feel a special responsibility to not present their children with another problem in life.

Having said above that a new baby always presents the firstborn with a problem, let me also say that a brother or sister can be a great gift in life as well as a problem. They are a source of delight, play, creativity, conflict, blame, and annoyance. It would be very lonely not to have brothers and sisters.

Speaking of
Divorce

Divided Loyalties: A Boy's Reaction
to Divorce and Father's Affairs

Q: I am recently divorced, and my fourteen-year-old son lives with my ex-wife. Our marriage was an unhappy one for a long time, and I had an affair or two, which caused fighting between my wife and me, but I was always a good father. I'm living on my own now, and although I could stay busy with friends on weekends, when my son is scheduled to visit I keep the calendar clear. The problem is that he has become very negative about visiting me, and when he is with me, he has a really foul attitude. I'm beginning to think my ex-wife is turning him against me, but I don't know what to do about it. How can I make this work out better?

MGT: From a child's point of view, there is no good time for parents to get divorced. That said, fourteen is a particularly tough time in which to try to start a new household and a new style of relationship with your son. You have four things going against you, and your ex-wife's opinions about you may be the least of your worries. Here are your problems, in order of difficulty: first, your son's need for control over his life; second, the normal fourteen-year-old's difficulty in managing transitions and emotional ambiguity; third, your son's sense of judgment about your affairs; and finally, your son's loyalty to his mother and her views of you.

Many fourteen-year-olds, both boys and girls, are difficult—or at least unreliable—weekend companions. Their growing sense of autonomy and their wish to spend a maximum amount of time with their peers means that they can often "throw an atmosphere" when they are at home. But at least at home they can retreat to their rooms or settle in front of the computer or get on the phone and talk to their friends. At home, the moments of closeness between parent and child can then be spontaneous and unself-conscious, an accidental meeting in front of the refrigerator, for example. Your new arrangement requires your son to actually "be" with you. When forced to relate to adults they can often act truculent, as if they have been burdened by this social demand. (Let me say that this is not true of all fourteen-year-olds; many are lovely, but I agree with the family therapist, Jay Haley, who says that one of the most difficult challenges for a family is adjusting to the expanding need for autonomy of a young adolescent.)

Your new home violates your son's sense of place. His new room isn't really "his" yet; his friends don't know your place and he may not be comfortable inviting them over, and he did not necessarily want to have to adjust to something new. Teenage children like to think of themselves as cool and able to "go with the flow," but in truth they can be extraordinarily stodgy. Early adolescence is also a very egocentric age, for physical and perhaps for neurological reasons. They are focused on their own physical and pubertal growth; that is the most interesting thing to them. There is evidence that early adolescents do not read facial expressions as accurately as adults do. Until their frontal lobes develop, they are often having a different experience—*different at the level of the brain*—than adults are having.

If a child is not reading feelings particularly accurately, understanding his own complex feelings about a divorce is going to be a real challenge. My guess is that during the bad years of your marriage you were often closed, your life a secret. You may have been a wonderful dad, but I guess that you weren't a model of emotional openness. Your son may have modeled himself on a more tight-lipped and emotionally shut-down father than you remember yourself being. He may be trying to resolve the issue of your affairs without talking to you about them. (How did he find out about them? Did he discover them through his mother, from seeing her shock and anguish? Or did he hear about them directly from you?)

Finally, if your ex-wife is running you down in front of your son, she wouldn't be the first angry spouse to do so. It is regrettable and it doesn't help your son, but the problem is that she is angry; he loves both of you, and his loyalty to his mother makes him open to her persuasion. It takes children of divorce years to realize that they can love and appreciate—and feel critical of—both their parents independently. That is a significant emotional achievement and it does not come easily.

I have some practical suggestions for you. Try inviting your son over with a friend of his, take them to a restaurant they will enjoy, watch TV with the two of them. Sit side by side on the sofa with them. Laugh together at the same things; speak when spoken to. (Always good advice for the parent of a fourteen-year-old. There is nothing that shuts a teenager down like having a parent ask him a question when he comes into the kitchen. There is nothing that induces him to talk faster than your looking at him quietly without saying anything.) You should do things with your friends and include your son as an adult companion. They will treat him well and he may appreciate the respect they give him. He is more likely to answer their questions than to answer your inquiries. Arrange activities that get both of you out. Go to sports events or rock concerts, go bike riding or skiing; don't buy his friendship, but do consult him on what would be fun for him. Do anything that involves driving in a car together (the scene of parent-child intimacy in so many American families).

Finally, and most painfully, ask him whether he has bitter feelings about your affairs. Be brief and straightforward. Say, "I've wondered whether you are angry at me for having affairs behind your mother's back." Stop, try to be as non-defensive as you can be, and wait for his answer. If he says, "Of course not, Dad, that's your business," listen for his tone. Perhaps he said it too quickly, in which case you can reply, "No feelings at all? I would have been pissed off at my father had he cheated on my mother." He has to know that you can receive his feelings if he is angry at you. Don't ask him whether his mother is attacking you verbally, it puts him in a bind. And don't attack her. Two wrongs don't make a right.

This is not going to be easy, but in time children learn to accept a divorce, learn to love their parents as separate people, and come to know them in a more adult way. I have known many fathers who have become better fathers after a divorce, but with a fourteen-year-old, it is going to take some time. Hang in there.

Divorce No Excuse for Sloppy Son

Q: My husband and I are going through a very bitter divorce, and my son and I are already living on our own. I used to keep house pretty diligently, but now I have more than I can handle and we can't afford maid service. My son, who is now thirteen, refuses to clean up after himself. He leaves dirty dishes everywhere, leaves his laundry lying around, and won't help with any housework. I realize he's going through a very hard time, and there are more important things we should be talking about right now than whether he's picking up his dishes from the table. So I've let it go, cleaned up after him, kept his clothes clean and neat, and the whole thing. I'm trying to be sensitive to how painful this must be for him. But he's only gotten worse instead of better, and now he gets angry if I even bring up the need for him to help out. I think I may have made a mistake by starting out our new situation being so sympathetic and acting like his maid. What's reasonable to ask of him, and how do I do that, when he's already used to things the way they are now?

MGT: Learning how to clean up after yourself in life and your parents getting divorced are two entirely different things. You are comparing apples and oranges. Losing the stability of an intact family and having your father move out of the house are painful events for a thirteen-year-old boy. However, even in an orphanage, where no one has parents at all, children have to learn how to tidy up, how to keep track of their things, and be part of a community.

I'm afraid your guilt about this divorce, and your fears that you are damaging your son as a result of this bitter process, have made you forget that *all* thirteen-year-olds need help in remembering the needs of other people. Thirteen is a famously egocentric age, arguably the most self-centered period in a person's life. Thirteen-year-old boys secretly hope that they can have it both ways, that they can be respected as a growing adult and that they can have their mothers rescue them, organize them, and pick up after them like maids. They cannot have it both ways. Boys who try remain entitled princes who never truly grow up and become responsible. They get older, they look grown-up, but they make lousy husbands and fathers; they are often a burden to their wives.

It is clear that you know divorce is painful for your son. You can see that he is saddened by it. The research tells us that a majority of children in divorcing families are emotionally hurt by the split between their parents. Some children of divorce develop adaptive and coping skills that they might not otherwise have developed at that age and seem more mature than their peers because of the troubling events in their lives. They are in the minority. The majority of children of divorce struggle emotionally at least for a time. What you and your husband have to try to do—as soon as you are able—is to establish as peaceful and cooperative a coparenting relationship between you as you possibly can.

In the meantime, you have to help your son become an independent and self-sufficient person. He has to clean up after himself. He has to learn to do his laundry. He could make one meal per week, for the both of you. At the very least he could do the dishes after dinner several nights per week. He will not learn any of this until you stop doing it for him. That's human nature. All of us would like to have a maid to do the chores we hate—at least once in a while. That's why people who can afford to go to hotels when they are on vacation. Other people make the beds and clean the bathroom. It is pretty nice.

What you are forgetting is that completing tasks takes your mind off your troubles. I bet that after you have been through a period of distress about this divorce, you calm yourself by straightening up the place, by shopping, by bringing order into your world. Why should it be any different for your son? Don't you think it might be distracting, diverting, and ultimately satisfying for him to pull his room together?

Pick one thing that you would like him to do, announce that you are going to stop doing it for him, *and stick to your promise.* He'll wait to see if you buckle. I think the best things to pick are tasks where his hunger, his need for clothes, his wish to look good will force him to become more competent. My personal choice would be to let him do his own wash. I've known many bright young men whose mothers had so consistently done their clothes for them that they arrived in their college dorms and stared at washing machines as if they were spaceships from Mars. I think that is a good place to start. Once he has mastered one skill, let him pick up another. (Drop him off at the supermarket with a list and some money and let him do the shopping. He'll feel great about himself.)

Leaving dishes in the sink until he notices them probably won't work. He'll spend ten minutes rummaging through the cabinets to find paper plates and plastic spoons from last summer's picnic before he'll wash a plate and a stainless steel fork. That is, don't leave him tasks that you care about and he doesn't, and if he doesn't do them it will drive you crazy. Choose something that is invisible to you, or something you can make disappear. I counseled a single, divorced father of two boys to stop constantly nagging his boys about picking up their jackets and stuff from the floor and simply to put them in a large cardboard box in the cellar. As they frantically whined, "I can't find my jacket," it gave the father great satisfaction—one might even say sadistic pleasure—to say to them, "Have you looked in the cellar?"

I wouldn't fight too much about the thing you choose; there has been enough fighting in your family. Be matter-of-fact and consistent and find some other room to go to if he starts to throw a tantrum or tries to make you feel guilty. What's he going to say? "Mom, things are so bad with this divorce, I shouldn't have to wash my clothes!" It is absurd on the face of it. Children whose parents die of terrible diseases have to learn, handicapped children have to learn, every person has to learn how to take care of himself. There are enough entitled, incompetent boys out there in the world. Please don't let your son become one of them.

Breaking Up Is Hard to Do—For Son of Divorced, Dating Mom

Q: I have been divorced since my son was three, and have never really dated because I was too busy with work and housework and trying to be there for him when he was young. He's twelve now and we get along really well. He's a good boy and I'm proud of the kind of person he is. I met a man through my work last year and although he lives several hours away we have maintained a nice dating relationship. He likes my son and my son enjoys him a lot. While this man is a good person, I don't feel we're compatible for a long-term commitment. I'm in the process of pulling away and can handle a breakup, but how do I help my son deal with it? I think he is assuming we'll get married eventually and this will be his new dad.

MGT: I am sorry for your son that it hasn't worked out between you and this man. Your son took a risk in extending himself to a stranger, becoming his friend, and perhaps wishing that he would have a new father. It is going to be awkward for him to keep the relationship alive when you end things with this man, partly because of geography, but also because I am sure this man was, in part, courting you by befriending your son. That is an intelligent strategy for someone who wants an enduring relationship with a divorced woman. One sure way to her heart is through her children's hearts. It can be painful, however, in situations like this one.

But relationships don't always work out. There are no guarantees in this life. Now, you need advice on how to talk to your son about this impending breakup. First, take stock. You have a lot of things going for you in this situation. Your son is a good guy, you have an excellent relationship with

him, and he has an open heart (we know that because he
took this man into his heart). My guess is that you should
have confidence that you and he will get through it together.
Second, I think you should begin to notify your son that
things are not working out so well between you and your
man friend, that you are having second thoughts. It will
help him prepare himself. Don't surprise him with a sudden
announcement.

Third and most important, you should ask him how it is
going to affect him if the relationship does end. Now, if he is
a typical boy, he may say, "Fine . . . no problem." He might
appear distressed and clam up. Or he might have a lot to say.
I cannot tell from your question whether he is a "talker."
What you should do is ask him for advice on how you should
handle aspects of the relationship that affect him. Use him as
a consultant on himself.

This is tricky. It is important not to rely too much on adolescent children as confidants in matters of adult relationships. At the same time, however, this breakup will affect him
and—without any doubt—it will revive any deeply buried
feelings he has about the divorce from long ago. He may feel,
"Why can't my mom hold on to a dad for me?" "Why am I
not strong enough to keep a family together?" "Why am I not
an appealing enough boy for a dad to really love me and have
things turn out wonderfully?" I believe that all children of divorce have a small place in them where they blame themselves for the divorce. They're not always wrong; sometimes a

child is the straw that breaks the camel's back in a relationship, if the camel wasn't all that strong to begin with. I'm just
warning you that this may, unconsciously, feel to your son like
the loss of a second father.

You could be surprised. We don't know what is in your
son's unconscious. Your son may have been holding himself
back from this man in ways you did not know. He may have
had reservations. Not every thirteen-year-old wants to share
his mother after so many years. There is part of him that
might be relieved. Perhaps, in the back of his mind, he just
wanted someone to take care of you so he could go off to high
school, fall in love with a girl, and feel that you were going to
be all right. Your strength in ending the relationship might be
comforting to him.

The point of all this theorizing is simply this: you need to
know what he is thinking. If he won't tell you up front, tell
him what you imagine he is thinking and let him correct your
misapprehensions. Sons like to correct the record. Sit still, let
him tell you how it is for him, and my guess is that you'll get
through it pretty well.

Young Boy Nervous around Hostile Divorced Dad

Q: My husband and I were divorced last year after being
married seven years. He couldn't keep a job, did drugs, and
would threaten to hurt me when he'd get angry or frustrated,
which was often. I finally did divorce him after he beat me up

one day, and he now lives a couple of hours away. Our son
Ron is six years old and lives with me. Although his father
never hit him, Ron is uneasy around his father and has very
mixed feelings about seeing him, although most of the time it
works out fine. My concern is that I believe my ex-husband
still smokes marijuana at home, and possibly does other drugs.
He has various girlfriends. He is constantly blaming other
people for his inability to keep a job, and he belittles people
who are achievers. He is very sarcastic about my own choice
to go back to school and get a good job. Basically, he's not a
good example for my son. Often when Ron comes home
from a weekend with his dad, he's sort of brash and a little
"tough guy." Should Ron continue to see his father or should
I try to cut back on his visits?

MGT: Your question is a difficult and painful one. Is a troubled and potentially violent dad better than no dad at all?
The short answer to your question is "no." It is better to have
just one parent, a loving mother, than to have frightening visits with a father who is unstable and dangerous.

Your son's anxiety is the key here. You have to pay serious
attention to his uneasiness and his mixed feelings. Most six-
year-olds don't express mixed feelings about their fathers because they love their fathers. However, your son has reason
to be afraid; he has heard his father threaten you; he knows
that his father beat his mother up. If he actually saw the beat-
ing, he may have been traumatized. Research has shown that

children who are present for such violence are themselves damaged by it. Furthermore, he has to worry that if he unintentionally makes his father angry, his father might turn on him. He must be at least a little bit frightened when he is with his father, and particularly when he sees his father's personality or mood altered by drugs.

The fact that your son returns from visits to his father full of swagger and "tough guy" mannerisms is easily understood in two ways. Like any boy, he wants to be like his father, and wants to please him. Imitation is the most obvious form of love. However, his need to imitate his father's "tough guy" mannerisms suggests to me that he is afraid of his father. When children, especially boys, feel frightened by someone, they often identify with the person who is actually scaring them. Freud described this phenomenon as "identification with the aggressor." It is why bullies often have followers (but not real friends). Oftentimes the followers are afraid of the bully, but want to stay on the right side of this scary person.

You do not say whether you have full custody of your son. You do not say what kind of visitation has been arranged as part of the divorce. Most courts recognize the importance of both parents in the lives of their children. However, I would use your son's level of fear and anxiety as a guide. If you get evidence that your ex-husband is using drugs, particularly at times when your son is there, you should take appropriate steps to protect your son and put these issues before the judge.

I cannot give you a definitive opinion here, because I

remain cautious about entering into a divorce issue without full and objective data. Because the facts of your case are so persuasive, especially your ex-husband's history of violence, I would suggest that if they are to be together, they should be with some other trustworthy adult (such as a grandfather, uncle, trustworthy family friend, or someone appointed by a court). However, I would feel better if your son had an evaluation by a child psychologist or psychiatrist. If he is afraid of his father, if he has been traumatized by his father's violence, he needs to have his trauma recognized and treated. He needs an advocate other than you who can make recommendations about his welfare. You may also need a professional's opinion in a review of visitation rights.

The only hopeful thing I can say here is that I have seen drug-using fathers clean up their acts in order to have visits with their sons. Sadly, I have often seen fathers abandon their children rather than pay support, or change their reckless ways. I hope your son's father can rise to the challenge of creating a more stable and safe environment for his son to visit.

Son Behaves Like Verbally Abusive Ex-Husband

Q. My controlling, verbally abusive ex-husband has finally moved out, but now my fifteen-year-old son seems to be taking over the abusive role his father practiced with me. My son now talks to me in demeaning ways and insists that I put his needs and expectations before my own. How can I keep my son from turning into the husband who has caused me so much pain?

MGT: Your son is in a dilemma. He knows that he *is* the son of the controlling, verbally abusive ex-husband whom you are divorcing. That is the only father he has ever known and loved. When he grows up he is going to—at least in part—look like his father, think in similar ways to his father, and have adult power as well. At fifteen, he does not know whether he is destined to be totally like his father or totally different. The question he is asking unconsciously is: can he pick and choose from different aspects of his father in order to become the adult he—and you—want him to be. Your difficult job is to persuade him that he can love his father and hold on to his relationship with his father without actually becoming his father.

There is a human tendency to identify strongly with a person who is lost to us. We see parents who have lost their children to drunk drivers become advocates for Mothers Against Drunk Driving. We see the father of a boy killed at Columbine High School plunge into the fight for gun control. We have often seen the wives of congressmen who have died take over their seats in Congress. All of these are ways of identifying with the lost person. Children of divorce often deal with the pain, helplessness, and ambiguity of separation by taking control of the situation and disavowing the departed parent, or by imitating the departed parent. Your son has done the latter. He may not have consciously chosen to do so. If you were to ask him why he is trying to act like his father, he might well deny it. But this is what has happened.

Your son may also be blaming you for the failure of the marriage. Children typically hold the more adult and controlled parent (all too often it is the mother) responsible for the breakup. He may be taking out his anger about the separation on you, using the same style of anger that his father used.

All of this has to make you a little crazy, especially at the moment when you are suddenly seeing, in your son's voice and behavior, the replay of a terrible tape of your husband's anger. It would only be human for you to become confused in that second. Why would you not wonder whether your son is destined to be a bastard like his father? Why would you not feel anger at him as if he were his father?

What you need to do—when you are feeling calm and lucid and under control—is say to your son, "There was much about your father that I loved. I know and respect that you love him and that you always will. However, he had a very bad temper, he said abusive things to people, especially to women, especially to members of his family. His out-of-control behavior destroyed my love for him. Nothing that you can do can ever kill my love for you, but I do not want you to become an abusive man. I will do everything in my power to help you to develop control over your temper. Not only do I want you to treat me with respect, but I want you to learn to treat all women with respect so that some woman doesn't have to divorce you in order to feel accepted and safe in her own life. I don't want any woman to ever feel about you the way I have felt about your father."

Once you give him the long version, you can re-evoke it by simply saying, "You need to learn to control your temper." If he has outbursts, there should be consequences. You don't drive him where he wants to go; you ground him for the weekend. This isn't a war, but it is a hard lesson. You need to win this parenting struggle, for your son's sake.

Speaking of
Friendship

Is Fourteen-Year-Old Boy Okay without a Group of Friends?

Q: My son is involved in a lot of after-school activities and seems to be doing okay socially at school, but he doesn't have any really close friends—never invites friends to the house, never gets calls to go to anyone else's house. I would think he'd be lonely without a "best friend" to confide in, but I hear the same thing from many other mothers. Do boys not have close friends, or what?

MGT: This is a common question from a lot of mothers. Almost no fathers ask it. Why is there such a big gender split in this concern about friends? It has to do with the friendship patterns of boys and girls and the kinds of expectations that those patterns have on the concerns of mothers and fathers.

That is to say, many mothers worry when their son's social scene doesn't resemble the social scene that they remember from the same age. However, a mother cannot judge her son's social life by a girl standard.

If you walk onto an elementary school playground during recess, you are likely to see the following scene: a majority of the boys are playing soccer in the field, perhaps with one or two girls participating; some boys and girls are playing on the tires and monkey bars; and many girls are playing four square or they are standing together talking in pairs. You are not likely to see a lot of pairs of boys regularly together on the playground, and when you see two boys together, they are generally not talking personally; they are playing a competitive game or building something together.

Having a single "best friend" is something more valued by girls than by boys. Girls in a group will admire, respect, and even envy two "best friends." Girls also value self-disclosure as the currency of friendship. To have a friend share your secret thoughts is considered vital by many, especially girls in middle school.

For boys, things work differently. Though many boys do have a close friend or friends, group membership is more highly valued than a "best friend." Boys tend to hang out in larger groups than girls. The games they play, such as soccer or touch football, require a large number of boys and so, the research tells us, boys' groups tend to be larger than girls' groups. Where girls might spend a lot of time discussing the degree of closeness between themselves and other girls—for they live in a "relational" world—it would be embarrassing to boys to spend a lot of time discussing who was closer to whom. Indeed, if a boy seemed to value a friend too much, it might open him up to teasing. So, when two boys are close friends, even when they constantly seek each other out, they will often act incredibly casually about it. As they part, they might say, "See ya," but they won't promise to call one another or be in touch by a certain time.

Part of this reluctance is homophobia. Part of this reluctance is the fear of showing too much emotion or dependence, because that would be considered unmasculine. However, it is masculine to simply have a friend to do things with.

What about your boy then? Why doesn't he have close friends? There are four possible explanations. First, at age twelve or thirteen, he may be so invested in looking cool and strong that he cannot bring himself to reveal his need for a friend. When one boy moved into a new neighborhood one summer, and was obviously lonely for company, his mother suggested that he introduce himself to the boy across the street, who looked to be exactly his age. Her son said, "I can't do that, Mom, I'd look like I really needed a friend!" Now, if he was out there and happened to be doing something neat and the other boy asked about what he was doing, or asked if he was new, then that might lead to something. But no way was he going to take a chance on drawing attention to himself and his status as a newcomer.

Second, your boy might lack some social skills and not feel confident about himself outside of the group, so he doesn't try for friendship outside of the group. Boys often don't have the ease in conversation that girls of the same age have, so making phone calls to initiate friendship can be awkward and exposing. He might also know that he is "lower status" on the ladder of popularity in the sixth or seventh grade and might be afraid of rejection. He'd rather be alone than risk calling someone and being turned down (and having that other boy go to school and make fun of him to the group: "Guess who called me over the weekend? What a dork!").

Possibly your son is shy or reserved in some way. I often encounter very social mothers who have more introverted sons. The question I ask is this: "Is he like his father?" And the mother says, "Yes, but I was hoping he wouldn't be." There is no guarantee that a boy won't get his father's social temperament, no matter what his mother's wishes.

Finally, it may be that your son is simply happy at home. It may be that he enjoys playing with his brother or his sister or needs the "downtime" after school on his computer. We're a pretty driven and active people in the United States, and often a bit suspicious of people who need solitude, but the need exists in many people, boys and girls, men and women.

The important thing is to find out whether your son is happy being alone. (Though he probably won't tell you if you simply ask the question: "Are you happy being alone?" He'll have to say "Yes.") Watch him and compare his happiness when he has companionship and when he doesn't. See how excited he gets when he does get the rare call from someone in his school group. If he appears eager for those calls, that tells you he is mentally waiting for others to reach out to him. If he is, then try to get him involved in a community group, or one at your church or synagogue, where kids and adults socialize after the service. Or take him to a family summer camp for a week, where kids and adults all hike together. Your husband might take the initiative and arrange for a father-son activity with another father and son in the neighborhood. There are ways you can support your son socially without treating him as if he is defective socially.

Circle of Friends: Affirmative Action for Gender Balance?

Q: Our eight-year-old son is a happy kid. Our concern is that all of his friends are boys. I think it would be good for him to have some friends who are girls. How can I get him to have more contact with girls?

MGT: As the comedian Steve Martin used to say, "Excuuuuu-uuuuse me!" What's the matter with boys as friends? Would you want someone to pick your friends for you or tell you that you need more gender balance in your choice of friendships? What is the matter with boys as friends? Are they destructive or unkind? Do they treat him badly? Do they swear and act badly in the house? If so, then there is something serious to talk about, but if not, why are you concerned?

Or is this an ideological thing? Do you—as his mother and father—find boy play repetitive or boring? Do you think girls would be more civilizing, more artistic, more edifying? The greatest likelihood is that your son spends all day at school with girls and that he does have a lot of contact with girls as reading group partners, as science partners, in lines, and doing classroom cleanup. These are somewhat formal, but often lovely relationships, but they don't qualify in a boy's mind as friendships. The boy rules are that he cannot have friendships with girls. Get used to the idea that he may be friendly with girls at school without identifying one girl as a friend in the obvious way you wish, and may never invite her to your home—at least not for a few more years.

The plain truth of the matter is that the boy and girl groups split into gender-exclusive groupings around the age of six or seven and the groups stay largely separated for a period of five or six years. When my Will was in first grade at a lovely Montessori School he came home one day and said, "Dad, I can't play with the girls anymore." I asked, "Why not?" And he replied, " 'Cause Mitchell says so." Mitchell was the biggest and most socially powerful boy in the Montessori classroom at Will's school, and his word was law. Boys make the rule that boys shouldn't play with girls. Girls tell each other that there is something wrong with boys. One fourth-grade girl said, "In second grade we discovered that boys have cooties!" Both boys and girls intentionally avoid the other gender when they are in groups of their own for a period of many years.

For a boy to keep a girl as a friend or spend a lot of time with girls would be highly unusual, unless they were friends of his sister's and were just around the house by chance. If a boy were to cultivate a friendship with a girl, he would be found out and teased by the boy group, for breaking the norms of the boy group. The boy group takes all boys and spends a lot of time encouraging boy activities and discouraging non-boy activities. Playing Game Boy is good, playing sports is worthwhile, the World Wrestling Federation is cool, and all of these things are especially good because not so many girls are interested in them. Even though more and more girls are playing sports, boys often experience sports as meaning something different to girls—somehow not as essential to girls as sports are to boys. (They are wrong, but they have conviction.)

Much of this activity is gender identity formation. "We know we're boys because we're different from girls." If the idea is upsetting, please recall that girls do much the same thing. They disdain boy things and reinforce in one another the obvious truth that the things they are interested in are more mature, more interesting, and vastly less stupid than what the boys like.

Now, there are some boys who really like to hang out with girls and do so despite some occasional teasing. There are boys who like the conversational flow and share many of the interests, but they often encounter resistance from the girls' group. "Oh, no, a boy!" they will say, and turn away from him.

All of this starts to break down, of course, in early adolescence when heterosexual interests emerge on both sides of the gender divide. Don't worry about your eight-year-old. He's going to have boy friends for four or five more years.

Then he will begin to have girls-as-friends again, and then he will begin to have girlfriends. And then there will be a whole other set of things to worry about!

Stories, Boasts, and Lies: How to Help a Cheating Boy

Q. My eleven-year-old son is friends with a boy he has known for years, and for years this boy has been a dishonest child. I don't know any other way to put it. He tells careful lies about his life at home, his family's money, and his father's job— things that most kids don't know anything about or care about anyway, but which I happen to know aren't true. I've not said anything to my own son about this, but more recently small groups of boys have been getting together at our house to play cards, and betting small change, and I have seen this boy cheating routinely to win. I'm not worried about the money—it's truly small change—but I don't like to see this cheating boy get away with taking advantage of these other boys, and I wonder if he needs some kind of help to stop doing this. His parents would never take him to a counselor—they just don't believe in that kind of thing—but I wonder if I might help him by talking with him or by alerting my son and his other friends to the cheating that's going on so they can handle it in their own way. What do you think?

MGT: I know this boy, I know him very well and I feel terrible for him. This kind of routine dishonesty, a boy trying to dress up his family life so that it looks normal, is a sign that things are pretty bad for this guy. And the techniques he has chosen to persuade other people—and himself—that his life is good will backfire very soon. Truthfully, I am surprised that they haven't backfired with his peers already. Boys are usually pretty sharp about ferreting out boasting and lies by other boys. I am surprised that eleven-year-olds haven't caught him cheating in the card game.

It is possible that they understand that he has a need to cheat, and they do not know how to confront him with it. More likely, they will call him on it soon and when they do, they will do it harshly. Boys care about fairness, and they don't like "cheaters." That's what I recommend you say to this dishonest boy. Take him aside and tell him that you have seen him cheating and you hope he stops before the other boys find him out, because it will be pretty bad when they do.

D. W. Winnicott, the English pediatrician turned psycho-analyst, wrote beautifully about the "antisocial tendency" in boys. In his generous interpretation, Winnicott felt that a boy who lies or steals is unconsciously looking for good "mother-ing," the effective early parenting to which he was entitled but which he has unfortunately failed to receive. If this dis-honest boy had a parent who was on the job, he would have had someone to steer him toward honesty. An effective par-ent does not allow his or her child to boast and lie. That he does so routinely suggests to me that he has parents who lie themselves, or a dominant parent who does, and he has learned it from them, or he has parents who are totally inef-fectual and do not notice much about this boy. They probably do not listen to much that he says. He is psychologically neglected.

You have noticed him. You have paid attention to him. You are providing him with some thoughtful mothering. It will shame him and upset him when you mention his cheating, but at least he will feel that an adult knows that he exists. After you mention it to him, make sure you are around when he is playing cards with your son and the other boys. Catch this boy's eye; let him know that you are there and watching him. Someone should have done that for him when he was eighteen months or two years old. He needed a loving parent's eye on him, a gentle shaking of the head when he started to do something wrong. This boy did not have anything like that, I bet. My guess is that no one was paying attention to him at all. My intuition tells me that there are severe psychological and substance abuse problems in his family, and he knows at some level that no one can parent him. So he makes up the parents he wishes he had.

Your small intervention is a drop in the bucket compared with what he needs, but every drop of love and attention will be a help to this boy. If enough people make loving interventions in this boy's life over the next few years, he may be able to stay out of jail.

Exploiting "Friends" Are No Friends

Q. Casey is in fifth grade. He has always been very shy, but he is desperate to be liked. A couple of boys in his class have recently become especially chummy, but it's clear that they're doing it to get things from him. They started out asking to borrow things, which they never gave back. And most recently we discovered they're telling him to buy things to give to them. We hate to pop the bubble about this supposed "friendship," but we also hate to see Casey used this way. What can we do? We are hesitant to contact the parents of the other boys because the boys are part of the "popular" crowd and Casey has said if we make trouble for them, everybody will hate him and this will only make his life worse at school.

MGT: One of the hardest things for parents to watch is their child being exploited by other children. Casey is right in the middle of the popularity wars that are waged in fourth through eighth grade. Boys and girls begin to explicitly rank order one another in terms of "popularity," which is the group's consensus that you have some attractive traits—athleticism, height, extroversion, humor, and wealth—that make you "cool." Boys who are shy or unathletic become painfully aware that certain kids enjoy high status while they occupy a lower rung in the dominance hierarchy. This occurs in all groups of children, no matter how loving their parents or how cozy their school. As one fifth-grade boy said to me, "In this class it is like we have a king and queen, the court, and the commoners." I asked him what he was and he said, "A commoner." I asked him if that was okay with him and he said, "It's not bad, I have friends."

Casey's difficulty is that he is looking for friends in the wrong places. He has fallen victim to some boys who are experimenting with their social power as they manipulate him. Their bogus friendship with him is a bubble that is going to pop, sooner or later. Casey will come to understand that he is being used. The question here is whether you want him to come to the truth himself, or whether you should help him arrive at it sooner. Either way, he is going to feel stupid and ashamed—at least momentarily—by the discovery. If it is his discovery, that might give him some satisfaction. If he discovers it in a consultative conversation with you, he might feel respected, comforted, and relieved.

I wouldn't recommend that you say, "Don't you know that they are taking advantage of you?" or "Don't give them stuff, they are really bullies!" If you do that, you are implying, "Casey, how could you be so naïve?" I would ask specific questions about his motivations and the intentions of these boys: "Casey, did you want to buy them those trading cards? I thought you were saving that money to get yourself a Game Boy game." If he says, "Well, yes, I was, but they really wanted me to get them the cards," you can say, "Why did they ask you? Did they know you had money? Do they make other kids buy them stuff?" It would be especially important for you to imply that this kind of treatment happens to many children in schools and that other kids have to figure out what they feel about this kind of behavior.

It may be that you can help Casey discover the truth of the situation and his own feelings, namely that he fears he is being manipulated but is hoping against hope that he can win these guys over. While he is coming to that decision—and it might take him three weeks to psychologically accept the truth—you should try to support a friendship of Casey's that has promise. Perhaps one of those boys is a potential friend, at least in a one-on-one situation. If you are planning a weekend outing, ask Casey if he would like to invite that one boy. If you know the parents of that boy, invite the entire family to do something with your family—an outing or a trip to a carnival. One of those boys is likely to treat Casey very differently when it is just the two of them surrounded by their families.

Shy boys may need that kind of support for their social efforts. One study showed that children who moved to a new town made a better social adjustment if their families engaged with other families of other children. Casey is shy. He may need you to help create a context where he can make a real friend. Once he has a real friend, he won't be as vulnerable to the manipulations of other boys.

Hanging at the Mall

Q. Our son is fifteen and he's always shown pretty good judgment about most things, but lately he's become friends with some boys who make my husband and me uncomfortable. They smoke, they hang out at a mall after school and on weekends, and it seems like they do it at all hours because no matter what time our son is free to socialize, he always says he'll go to the mall and find these boys. One of them goes to school with my son, but the other is from another school. And when they get together at these places, other kids join them and some of them look a little old to be doing this kind of thing. Our son is making decent grades in school and hasn't suddenly begun to act like a vagrant, but we're more than a little worried about this company he's keeping. We're also afraid that if we say anything bad about this crowd, or even question his choice of friends, he might spend even more time with them just to prove himself. What can we do?

MGT: I am very glad that you recognize that attacking your son's choice of friends is not a good strategy. You want to avoid getting into an open conflict with his friends as long as you possibly can. Please be assured that your son already knows what you think of them. Children know their parents inside and out. He has seen your nose wrinkle or your face drop or your shoulders sag a bit when he has told you he is going over to the mall. He is fully aware that you are disappointed in his choices. Your disappointment may give him the feeling that he is growing up because his judgment is now different and therefore independent of yours.

Boys often feel that they have to prove they are now adults, that they are no longer "little boys," by doing something reckless or antisocial. It is for this reason that twelve- to fifteen-year-old boys, together in groups, commit acts of vandalism, write graffiti on walls, or put themselves through some other "test." I had a patient once, a lovely, educated man who was beloved by his parents. At the age of twelve he was out at the edge of the highway at night with a group of friends. They took turns lying in the road, seeing how close they would let eighteen-wheeler trucks get to them before jumping up and getting out of harm's way. Boys do really scary things in these years. The leading cause of death in adolescence is fatal accidents, and boys are twice as likely to die of a fatal accident than girls are.

Now, I have told you all this for two reasons: one is to support your concern about your son; the other is to reassure you that he's involved in pretty tame stuff. Hanging out at the mall is generally quite safe. There are adults around, there are security guards; the boys are even protected from the weather. It is the modern equivalent of standing outside the drugstore on Main Street in a small town. Your son has chosen a very protected way to express his independence. Try not to panic.

The question here is not with whom he hangs out, but whether his behavior changes in worrisome ways. I believe that parents have to stay on the job when their boys become adolescents. Normally, teenagers want more private time, more time away from their parents, more opportunities to be with their friends. That's natural. Parents have to manage their own separation anxiety, support their child's development, and at the same time monitor their activities. Parents have to be alert and clued in. Has he started to smoke? Can you smell it on his hands or his breath? Do you want to choose that as a battleground with your son? (You won't win the battle if either of you smoke.) Has he started to drink? Do you have any evidence that they are leaving the mall and going to unsupervised houses? Has this group of boys done anything destructive that you know of? Was your son involved?

If your son hangs out with kids who don't appeal to you,

but your son's behavior has not changed in any significant way, I do not think you have any cause for worry. Every parent thinks their child's teenage friends look slightly disreputable. Please remember that your son might look suspicious to some other boy's parents. If your son keeps up his grades, if he meets his responsibilities in the home, if he is respectful of his grandparents, and (mostly) kind to his brother and sister, then you have no cause for alarm. If he has started to engage in antisocial behaviors, then there should be clear, consistent consequences for that behavior. Address his behavior, not his choice of friends.

What would I say to a family of a boy whose behavior had begun to change in dramatic and ominous ways? You must address such changes directly. Don't wait. Don't dismiss them as a phase. Tell him of your concerns. "We are worried that you are hanging out with a crowd that uses drugs, and we believe we see signs that you are beginning to take drugs yourself. Can you do anything to reassure us that you are not? Would you be willing to take a drug test?" Shouting, screaming, and accusing are useless. Increase your vigilance, look for opportunities to talk, and seek out adults who know your child in other contexts. Talk to his coaches, teachers, and guidance counselors. If he is starting to careen out of control, you should put limits on him regarding curfew, car use, and unsupervised time. If he cannot accept any limits, and rages against them, you may have to turn to family therapy or petition the courts for help in supervising him. A boy may need limits and boundaries so that he does not spin out of control.

Speaking of
Girls, Love, and Sexuality

How Can I Talk with My Son about Dating?

Q: My son is thirteen and hasn't started dating yet, but as he moves into that stage I want to be able to talk with him about showing respect for girls and acting with integrity as he ventures out into the world of girl-boy relationships. His father is not comfortable with approaching the subject with him at all, so that leaves it up to me. How can I establish some kind of comfort level for the two of us discussing this subject? I have no idea how to even start.

MGT: I think this is a perfect subject for a mother to discuss with her son. I don't think you should leave it up to his father, especially if he is inarticulate or uncomfortable. Your son will respect the fact that you want to know how he views women because you are saying, "Has the way I have raised you given you respect for women that can hold up to the stereotyping and exploitation of women that is everywhere in our culture?"

Does your son already show respect for girls? Does he treat his girl classmates well? Does he speak of them in kind and generous ways? Does he recognize their talents? Or, unhappily, does he say misogynistic or cruel things about girls? These are your opportunities. The attitudes that he brings to bear on specific girls and situations give you all the conversational openers you need.

Let's say that Katie has run against his friend, Matt, for the presidency of the eighth grade; you can ask, "What would be the difference between them in terms of their leadership?" "Would it be hard for you to vote for a girl?" "Why?"

Does he have a sister? When he speaks to her does he attack her personality—as almost all siblings do from time to time—or does he attack her gender?

I don't know exactly what you mean by acting with integrity, but that is usually code for not sexually exploiting girls. So you have to ask him, "Do you believe boys are more interested in sex than girls?" "Do you believe girls can get hurt in sex more than boys?" "If so, how?"

The newspaper and news stories can provide you with a lot of openings. "Do you know what rape is, son?" His answer is likely to be, "Of course, Mom, do you think I'm stupid?" Your follow-up question might go as follows: "Do you know the difference between rape and date rape?" Or, "What's your theory about why men rape women?"

In my experience, boys and girls love to discuss gender. It is one of the easiest subjects to get kids to discuss. Go for it.

Should My Son Be a More Responsive Friend to the Girls He Knows?

Q: Girls are starting to call my fourteen-year-old son at home, and he chats with them at some length. One of these friends invited him to the movies once and another time out to eat with her family. He seems very relaxed about this friendship, but I notice he never initiates any of the calls and he has never reciprocated by inviting her out. I'm not eager for him to start dating, but on the other hand, I wonder if he should be a bit more responsive as a friend, just as he would if this were one of his male friends. His dad says, "Forget it."

MGT: I think there are two problems in this situation. One problem has to do with social confidence, the other is about the blurred line between what a "friend" is and what a "girlfriend" or "boyfriend" is at this age. This is a classic question from mothers, and a classic response from fathers. I have never heard a father say, "I wonder if he should be more responsive as a friend." There is a gender gap here in the assumption that what is involved is friendship. It's quite likely your fourteen-year-old son doesn't experience a girl's invitation to a movie or to her house as being an invitation to friendship. His friendships are with boys, and if he appears to be making friends with a girl, he has to worry about what his (boy) friends will think and what they might make of it.

On average, girls are more socially self-confident than boys at age fourteen and they like to practice their skills. One study of boys and girls found that all of them experienced a drop in self-confidence as they entered junior high school in seventh grade. Happily, their confidence had returned by the ninth grade, but it was regained differentially along gender lines. Boys rebounded in their confidence in math and science and sports; girls recovered their confidence in English, any subjects involving writing, and in their social lives. The average girl of fourteen has much more confidence in her ability to carry on a relationship and a conversation than does a boy of the same age. She is happy to practice her skills because she values them, just as a boy might value kicking a soccer ball against the side of the garage for two or three hours.

The greater social confidence of girls relative to boys of this age is an obvious fact of life in schools. Whenever I visit schools that end in eighth grade, I ask the girls and the boys what they are looking forward to in high school. The most mature girls invariably answer, with an almost dismissive wave of the hand, "We can't wait to get to high school where there will be some real guys." The boys don't protest. Their feelings are hurt, and they know they are being insulted, but their faces say, "Good riddance. We have no hope of keeping up with them."

A boy knows what to say to his guy friends, he knows how

to do activities with the group, and he is happy to talk about sex, tell dirty jokes, and discuss girls' bodies. When his friend says something, he knows he can reply, "Oh, you're full of shit!" and the conversation will go right on. That is territory that he knows. Talking to girls is different.

An evening in person with a girl involves two things, both of which are going to make him uncomfortable: extended, face-to-face conversation and the possibility of sex. You see, during a phone call, a boy can end the call by saying, "I have to do my homework," or "My mom says I have to get off the phone." Or he can let a girl do the bulk of the talking. But mainly, he doesn't have to be looking at her while they're talking. It is easier for a boy to talk to a girl when he doesn't have to look into her face, or appear responsive, intelligent, or understanding—or wonder whether he is saying the right thing. He knows he cannot say to a girl one of twenty things he might say to a guy, something along the lines of, "Oh, you're full of shit," but he doesn't know what to say instead.

Most important, on the phone he doesn't have to make conversation while looking at her breasts (or not looking at her breasts). It is tough to converse with a girl when you are thinking about her breasts. (Adult men often have difficulty with this task until late middle age, which is around age eighty-nine.) It is for all of these reasons that boys and girls often like to "date" in groups, meet at the mall, go to a movie together, wander into stores, or meet at Papa Gino's, where they can debate the merits of Papa Gino's pizza versus Domino's.

If you are a fourteen-year-old boy, when you are actually

alone with a fourteen-year-old girl, what do you do if conversation fails or you become obsessed with the idea of sex? If the conversation fails, you are going to experience the worst kind of excruciating self-consciousness (I can remember it in my own life and it makes me squirm thirty-eight years after the fact) and you are convinced that the girl thinks you are the world's biggest loser. If you are interested in sex, how do you find out if she is also interested in sex? What if she knows how to kiss and you don't? What if she has done something pretty advanced and you are a total novice? How do you get started?

It is much better, from your son's point of view, to not take the lead in these matters. It is much better to let the girl practice her social skills on him, enjoy the flattery of the invitation, hope that her parents will rescue the conversation, etc. And he can do this all without actually thinking through the question: is this a friend or is this someone to have a more intimate relationship with? His friends may ask him or tease him. He can just say, "I don't know. She invited me," implying that it would have been rude to turn her down.

Meanwhile, he enjoys the attention, he gets some practice, and maybe, just maybe, they'll find themselves alone and she'll touch his hand or he'll lean against her and all of a sudden he'll know: "Oh, this isn't just a friend."

Young Romeo: Heading for Heartache?

Q: Erik is eight, in third grade, and "in love" with a little girl in his class. It's all very sweet. He tells me that she is the prettiest girl in the school and that she loves him back. Yesterday, getting ready for school in the morning, he changed his shirt three times before finding one that was just right—he is trying to look his best for this little girl. Now Valentine's Day is coming up and he wants to use his allowance to buy her a really big box of chocolates. The little girl is a great kid, and it would appear that she enjoys his attention, but she's got a million other interests. The whole thing is so sweet I hate to say or do anything to break the spell, but is it normal for a boy this age to have such a crush on a girl? How can I help him understand how crushes come and go, so he won't be so hurt when this little girl loses interest? And what about the gift? The school discourages children from picking out personal "sweethearts"—and rightly so, I think. But this was something spontaneous.

MGT: As Marlowe wrote and Shakespeare repeated, "Who ever loved, that loved not at first sight?" It turns out that our Hero, our Romeo, is in third grade. I love stories like this. I wish there were more of them, but I am afraid our culture alerts boys too early that loving gestures are uncool or unmasculine or weird or stupid. I am sure that many boys find girls pretty and might wish to make such a gesture yet are stopped by some sense that it is wrong. Many a boy might be ready to transfer the powerful loving feelings he has for his mother and grandmother to a beautiful friend at school. Something stops him. He intuits that the gift will not be well received, that adult disapproval at school might ensue, or other children might tease and giggle and humiliate him. God forbid he might try to kiss the girl. Despite the fact that Sebastian the crab encouraged Prince Erik to "Just kiss the girl" in a Walt Disney movie, if your Erik tries it, he could end up being suspended or sued.

Your loving son believes that the rules of cool are going to be suspended for Valentine's Day and that he is going to be able to show his loving side and will find approval from a little girl, from teachers, from the world. Well, I think some romantic utopian social engineering is called for here. A little theater perhaps. "Send in the clowns"? In this case we have to send in the facilitators.

This is a situation where I think a call between mothers is appropriate. I think you should call the girl's mother and let her know that Erik wants to stop by and give her daughter the box of chocolates. Express your surprise, and reassure the mother that your son is no Lothario, no Don Giovanni. He is a simple eight-year-old romantic. With a friendly gesture on your part, the mother can forewarn her daughter to be gracious. Perhaps they can have a little gift to reciprocate. Erik can make his presentation to his ladylove without an audience to jeer him. She can be prompted to accept his loving gift. Being eight, he doesn't really have a plan for what they're going to do afterward. They're not going to run off to Vegas. If he is a normal boy he is not going to make excessive demands on her for extra time at school. He understands the meaning of Valentine's Day and wants to participate. He is going to grow up to be the kind of man who buys his wife jewelry and beautiful slips for her birthday, instead of giving her a new vacuum cleaner.

Teen Son Smitten by Gorgeous Girlfriend: Mom Not So Keen

Q: My son is sixteen and going out steadily with a slinky vamp of a girl. He's a smart boy, with a great future ahead in college and beyond, but lately I'm terrified that he's having sex with her and she's going to get pregnant on purpose to hold on to him. I just know that if I suggest she's not a good thing for him, it'll just drive them closer together. How can I handle this?

MGT: Here we have the return of Samson and Delilah in modern form. The seductive woman and the strong but innocent boy who is going to get his hair cut and lose his powers—or his college education, in this case—as a result of her sexual charms. I guess I have heard of it happening, the innocent boy and the seductive siren, but hey, he could lash himself to the mast (to change myths) if he didn't want to sleep with her.

I do understand that it is comforting to think of him as the innocent and her as the vamp, but I believe that you are not actually as worried about this girl as you are about your son's judgment. And you are dismayed to sense that there is a private part of your son's life that he has not been eager to talk about to his parents. I don't mean to be rude, but I doubt that he is innocent. The average age of first intercourse in the

United States is sixteen years old. That means half of kids
have had sex before the age of sixteen, and half wait until after sixteen. If he is having sex with this girl, he is just on
schedule. He hasn't been seduced early, nor is his life likely
to unravel because of it. He probably has devoted a lot of
time and thought and energy to getting her into bed (or
choosing someone who would take him to bed), and he is
probably very pleased with himself if he has succeeded. And
in his mind, it has nothing to do with going to college.

Also, I do not know many sixteen-year-old girls these days
who are planning to have the boy they are sleeping with
be their lifelong partner. Sixty-eight percent of high school
graduates go on to college these days, and more of them are
girls than boys. Most girls these days are planning to go to
college and expect that they will sleep with a number of guys
in college before they settle down to marry.

The hard part for you is that he is growing up and changing and you do not know whether he is behaving responsibly.
That, I believe, is what is actually "terrifying" to you. So you,
or his father, need to talk to him. You need to know more
about the life he is actually living, and you need to know
more about how he sees his own future. He might say something mature and reassuring. He may let you know, in very
direct and blunt ways, that he can handle the situation.

Have you asked him if they are having sex together? Do
you have evidence that they are having sex together? If you
have strong reason to believe that they are, have you asked
him whether he is using birth control? Would you consider

buying him condoms? (After all, the parents of sexually active girls take them to doctors to get them birth control pills.) I had a middle-aged friend who found used condoms in the bathroom wastepaper basket, left there by his college-age son. He was both disgusted to find them and reassured that his son was having responsible sex. I know someone whose son brought home a case of genital crabs that necessitated everything in their house being disinfected and washed. Now *that* leads to some open family conversations while father and son sit in the local Laundromat washing all the sheets in the house. It is a hard corner to turn in your relationship with your son, but everyone is on a more adult and mutually respecting level once the conversation has taken place.

How about his girlfriend? Do you know her? Have you talked with her? Do you know her plans for the future? How does she see her life and her college possibilities? Have you told her of your hopes for your son? Do they differ dramatically from her family's expectations of her? Instead of focusing on her makeup, her slinky clothes, and her spectacular figure, try to learn something about her inner life. You may find yourself very reassured.

Finally, how about her parents? Do you have a relationship with them? Have you said to this girl's mother or father, "I think they are very much in love," or more boldly, "I think they are passionately involved with each other"? The other parent might say, "Yes, I think they're pretty serious about each other, and it worries us. We hope they don't think about getting married too young. We're hoping she will go to the University of Michigan and major in business." Now wouldn't that be reassuring?

Why Does My Twelve-Year-Old Son Talk Like a Sexist?

Q: When can you expect your son to show some signs of being a feminist? Right now at twelve he seems like a budding sexist, but I sense in some ways that's just the first developmental stage of being attracted to the opposite sex, especially in a sexist world. Should I intervene? Is there a way to intervene? Or should I just hope he'll grow out of it?

MGT: Twelve is not a very feminist age for boys. Actually, fifteen isn't a very feminist age for boys, either, and sometimes thirty and fifty aren't really feminist ages for boys. Giving up the feeling of being superior to women, or wishing to dominate women, is difficult for men and boys because this is a patriarchal culture and the promise of superiority is implicitly made to them by a lot of cultural symbols and messages. They don't want to give up what they believe to be their entitlements.

At twelve, when most girls are cognitively, sexually, and academically more sophisticated than most boys, it is difficult for boys to think of them as downtrodden or in need of equal rights. Indeed, most boys would like to feel a little more equal to girls in seventh grade. But they don't. So they gather in groups and whisper sexist things in order to bolster their egos and irritate the girls.

But you're right; sexism, in a sense, is part of really coming to terms with girls, of acknowledging the reality of their lives. Boys and girls have really been living in different cultural environments since second grade. They have been playing by different sets of rules: boy rules and girl rules. When heterosexuality appears on the horizon, boys have to come to terms with what girls really want. And when they start being in relationships with young women, they have to take feminism seriously.

It is for that reason that the most outspoken feminist young men are in college. As one college man asked his friend, "Do you know why you and I are such advocates of feminism?" "No, why?" "Because the women we want to sleep with are all feminists." A cynical remark, perhaps, but not without a grain of truth. Women who sleep with men without asking for respect often do not get it. The men—or should I call them boys—realize that they are not going to be asked to change the boy rules. It is heterosexuality with young women, love for them, an internal sense of justice, and, ultimately, professional competition that turns boys into truly feminist men. It is in depending on a woman's skill, competence, and wisdom, either in a love relationship or a work situation, that really compels a man to reevaluate all the stupid things he said in seventh grade or thought in high school.

The boys who are most ready for feminist thinking—no

matter how Neanderthal they appear in seventh grade—are the ones who were raised in feminist households, homes in which boys have seen their fathers respect their mothers, where work has been shared, sisters and brothers have not been too gender stereotyped (I believe some is inevitable), and principles of equity and justice have reigned.

One last thing: as a young teacher in the early seventies, I tried to teach a book of feminist essays to a class of tenth graders. The boys found it preachy and irrelevant. To my surprise, I found the tenth-grade girls weren't very interested, either. They were far more interested in looking good and getting a date with the handsome, high-status athlete in the class.

Three-Year-Old Cross-Dresser at Preschool

Q. I am a former elementary school teacher and now run a day-care center. We have a three-year-old boy who comes four days a week. He always wants to play in the dress-up corner, he usually puts on a dress, and when the children play pretend, he always wants to be a girl. Whenever there is talk of a Disney movie, he wants to be the girl: Cinderella, Ariel in *The Little Mermaid*, Belle in *Beauty and the Beast*. Now, I am used to the fact that some boys at this age want to play with girl things from time to time. He's not the first boy we've ever had who has put on a dress. However, we have never before had a boy who was so persistent about it. This boy seems to wish that he were a girl. His mother has expressed some worry about it and asked me what I think about her son. I don't know what to say to her.

MGT: An extremely small number of boys express a wish to be girls from early in life. They identify with girl characters, want to play with girl toys, want to play "girl" games. These boys— often called "sissy boys"—hold to their wishes in the face of intense disapproval and criticism from their environments.

Unless such a boy comes from a troubled family, in which, for instance, a mother wanted a daughter and therefore dresses a boy as a girl and tells him that he is a girl, it appears that the drive to identify across genders comes from a psychological source we do not yet understand. Often their parents try to discourage them, punish them for playing with girl toys, and certainly shame them through their own fear and disapproval. What is amazing, in a psychological sense, is how and why such boys are able to hold on to their cross-gender wishes even in the face of almost universal condemnation.

These boys have been intensively studied. Research finds that a high percentage of these boys turn out to be one of three things. A very few are transsexuals, who feel they have been born into the wrong body; a number turn out to be "cross-dressers" (with either a homosexual or a heterosexual sex life); and some are simply and happily gay. A small number of such "effeminate" boys also turn out to be heterosexual and grow up to make relationships with women. Here is the problem for psychology and for you: you can say something to this mother about statistics, but it has no meaning for her son. No one can predict what his life holds for him.

What her son needs is to be loved, appreciated, and protected. If his parents are upset by his play and want to try, they can redirect his play toward more conventionally masculine play. They can say explicitly, "This is what we'd like you to play with, son." It won't affect a boy who is possessed of a driven wish to be a girl. It will work to steer some boys away from what is really an early feminine identification, a phase for some boys.

What is an early feminine identification? Almost all boys identify in the early years with their mothers. Freud felt that it was a natural first stage for all boys. Those are the adults with whom they spend the most time; those are the people whom they love the most ferociously. Small children love what their mothers do, and how their mothers look, and are identified with them. When she is sad, they are sad; when she is happy, they are uplifted. Why wouldn't boys, out of love, imitate their mothers? Many do. And it isn't destructive at all to their masculinity. Helping your mother in the kitchen, wanting to learn to sew, putting her necklace or high-heeled shoes on, all of these are expressions of love in little boys. Parents get unreasonably frightened of these moments of cross-gender identification. They are nothing more than a boy saying, "I love my mom and I think she is wonderful and she looks fabulous to me. See?"

At some point most boys begin to self-identify as boys, and

they try to be cognitively consistent. So they say to themselves, "I am a boy, and therefore I do boy things, and I make sure that I don't do any non-boy things because it would be inconsistent with being a boy." Nineteen out of twenty two-year-olds will name as their favorite toy a gender-stereotyped toy: truck or action figure for boys, doll for girls. The power of culture to teach boys and girls is so great, the gender identity of girls and boys is formed early. It is actually formed before they learn the difference between boy and girl genitals. Shown a picture of a naked boy holding a doll, two-year-olds will say he is a girl. What a girl *does* is more important than her body difference to another child.

The role of culture in forming identity is so huge that it is all the more impressive when a child defies cultural definitions of gender in the way that "sissy" boys do. It is hard on parents who had expected a typical boy or girl. It may be a psychological and spiritual struggle for a family to raise a boy who is effeminate.

What you have to do with this mother, and with her family, is to show her how to enjoy and love her son, even though he is different from most boys. Perhaps he is particularly imaginative or funny or kind. You need to be honest, both about the feminine nature of his play, which should be described in a matter-of-fact way to his mother, and about the strengths that make him shine among other children. The problem with most parents is that they will overfocus on their child's particular difficulty and start to forget to appreciate the whole child. This family is less likely to be freaked out by their effeminate boy if you and your staff take him in stride and love him as he is.

My best wisdom as a psychologist is this: virtually no parent ever gets exactly the child he or she hoped for. Some people give birth to intellectually gifted children who are temperamental or depressed; some give birth to wonderful athletes who are unkind to others; still others have children who have slight learning disabilities or significant neurological difficulties that can be a real burden to their families. Children always stretch you in ways you didn't expect. If you accept the challenge that your children bring into your life, you will grow. If you fight what they are, you will risk warping their personalities, you won't enjoy your own children, and you will fail to grow yourself. Share this message with his parents.

Eighth-Grade Boy's Behavior Makes Parents Wonder:
Is He Gay?

Q: Our son is in eighth grade and we are hearing from his school principal, a loving and straightforward woman, that he is starting to dress and act in ways that suggest he is gay. His teachers have made comments about his being "very different" from other kids. He once wore platform shoes to school, and another day he went with makeup on. How can we tell if our son is gay? Is he trying to tell us something? And if he is, how can we talk to him about it? He has never said anything about it.

MGT: I believe that if the principal of your son's school has overcome the social discomfort of talking to parents about this subject, then it is quite likely that your son is gay. If it were a borderline case, educators would take a wait-and-see attitude. My guess is that the school personnel are picking up a lot of messages from your son that he is ready to be seen and known. On average, most homosexual boys know that they are gay by the age of twelve. Some have always known that they are different from other boys; some know it as young as age five, but don't have the words for it. Other men do not come to grips with it until adulthood, but the average is age twelve. An eighth grader is typically thirteen, so it is a natural time for a boy to begin to announce who he is. (It is also a time when all adolescents tend to declare their autonomy and do things to outrage their parents. Imitating gay rock idols is one way of driving parents out of their minds. I'll address that issue at the end of this answer, but for the moment I am going to answer it as if he were gay.)

If your son is gay, you are going to go on a long journey with him, which will involve many conversations, and the early ones are going to be fraught with tension and peril. If he is gay, and doesn't consciously know it yet, you risk holding up the mirror to him prematurely and shocking him. If he is gay, and is aware of it, but is not ready to talk to you about it, then you risk throwing him off balance. More than anything, however, I think the chances of hurting his feelings, making him feel bad, saying the wrong thing that he will remember forever are increased if you haven't worked through your own feelings about the possibility of his being gay.

Before you start talking to your son about his being gay, you have to talk to one another and to some of your closest friends. You have to look deep into your own hearts and at your own prejudices. You may believe that you are not homophobic, you may think of yourself as accepting of difference in this world, but I doubt you wished for a gay son. Not many people do. Accepting that a son is gay involves some grieving for the daughter-in-law and the grandchildren you may never have. Although adoption is a possibility for some gay couples, more than likely you will not get a chance to dazzle and amaze grandchildren with fun vacations, birthday surprises, and family stories. Instead, you will have your son and his lover visit and share a room in your house. Or they won't visit, and you will be lonely. Being the parents of a homosexual son, inevitably, you will share in some of the homophobic prejudice that he will experience. Some of your friends might distance themselves from you because they are unable to understand or now will feel uncomfortable with him in a social situation. In short, if he is gay, your life has been changed. And you had no say in it. You will be subject to feelings of bewilderment, self-doubt, anger, and ignorance. If you practice a religion that disapproves of homosexuality, you may be thrown into conflict with your own faith. Some of this your son can help you work through, but some of it you have to do on your own.

I suggest that you go talk to a family friend who is gay and use him as a consultant. Ask him whether he believes your son might be gay, ask him about himself and how he came to understand and accept his own homosexuality, ask him about how his own parents came to a peace of mind on this issue. Ask him whatever you want to ask him. If you have no such friend, ask the school psychologist, social worker, or counselor for help in finding a trustworthy advisor. What you will get from the conversation is the experience of talking to a gay man about his sexuality and his life. That will be the best preparation for talking with your son.

Indeed, when you tell your son that you did some psychological preparation and homework, he will be respectful and impressed.

If I were you, I would buy some books on the subject. Become knowledgeable about the struggles of boys who are gay. Leave them around the house. They will be a signal to your son that you are trying to learn. Their presence may give him an opening to speak directly to you.

When you feel psychologically ready to discuss it with him, when you have gotten past the "ohmigod . . . not this . . . what will we do" hand-wringing stage and have confidence that you can speak calmly and intelligently with your son, then look for an opening. If he comes down to breakfast with makeup on, don't treat it as a joke, but ask him directly and honestly. Being thirteen, he is likely to reply to something vague with something equally annoying. If you ask anxiously, "Are you trying to tell us something?" he is likely to reply, "Yes, Mom, I want Fruit Loops rather than Shredded Wheat." And then what will you say? (Much of the conversation of all thirteen-year-olds is designed to make parents look and feel dumb—no matter what their eventual sexual orientation.) No, say something like this: "Your father and I feel that by wearing makeup to school you are trying to let people know that you are gay. We've read that this is one way that boys bring up the topic of their sexuality with their parents and teachers, and that's how we're understanding your decision to wear makeup to school."

Not even the most sarcastic thirteen-year-old is going to be able to toy with that observation. He might say, "Mom, I don't want to talk about this now." Or he might say, "Christ, Mom, you and Dad get totally worked up about nothing." And if he says that, you need to say, "We just want you to know that we've thought a lot about this and we love you. If you are gay, we can understand it, and we're ready to accept it and to support you in any way you need." Then let it go! Very few thirteen-year-olds are able to sustain a serious conversation over breakfast under the best of circumstances.

Let him go to school and know that you will get back to the conversation again.

Three nights later you may be watching the news together and there will be a news item about the "Don't ask, don't tell" policy for gays in the military. Say something empathic about the plight of gays in the military. Say something politically supportive of public efforts to address the issue. Go on the record with your son as being non-homophobic and having some political courage. Then turn to him and say, "You do know this is a family that is not prejudiced against gay people, don't you?" Perhaps he'll only say, "Yes," and nothing more. But you have made contact on the issues.

Conversations like this will also press a boy to acknowledge that he is not gay, if in fact he is straight and just trying to experiment with his identity and outrage the adults in his life. If he says, "Oh, Dad, all rock stars wear makeup and everyone thinks they're gay!" you can say, "Yes, many are straight and just being entertainers, but many of them are really gay. Theater and rock music are places where gay people can go because they know they'll find acceptance there."

If you open this door from time to time, you will be giving your son the certain knowledge that his parents can bear the reality of his life, that his parents are not clueless, and he will know he is loved because his parents are obviously making an effort to reach out to him. What more can a parent do?

Attractive College Athlete: Lonely or Gay?

Q. My son is a tall (6'5"), handsome, varsity athlete at a Division I college. Naturally, girls get interested in him, but he gives them no encouragement whatsoever. He doesn't seem to want to get involved in relationships at all. He didn't have a girlfriend in high school, never talked about having a crush on someone or being in love. When I asked him about girls, his excuse was always that he was focusing on athletics and getting a scholarship to college, which he succeeded in doing. Though he is kind and affectionate with me, he is extremely private. He seems very lonely to me and he does not give anybody a glimpse of what he is thinking. I have begun to wonder whether he is gay, but I don't know how to ask him the question. If I were wrong, it would be such an insult to him. If he is gay, it will destroy his father.

MGT: Your description of your son could very well be the life story of a gay man who also happens to be a superb athlete, or should I say a superb athlete who happens to be gay. I have heard similar stories in my therapy office. Many gay men live secret lives for many years until they feel safe enough to have a public relationship and "come out."

Research cannot yet give us a definite answer as to the number of gay men. Because of prejudice and homophobia many men will not admit to their homosexuality, even in an anonymous interview. However, most recent scientific studies suggest that 3 to 5 percent of men are gay. All of these gay men, when they were boys, heard a huge number of homophobic slurs in school. It has been estimated that boys in ninth grade hear twenty-five antigay slurs a day, regardless of their sexual orientation. Every boy knows that his masculinity is constantly and cruelly monitored by other boys. If he is suspected of being gay, he risks severe rejection. Every boy knows that prejudice against homosexuals is the last prejudice that is held by a vast majority of American adults. (Prejudice against blacks, Jews, and other ethnic groups is no longer acceptable to most Americans.)

A boy who is gay is psychologically at risk, not because he

is mentally ill—both the American Psychological Association and the American Psychiatric Association declared more than twenty years ago that homosexuality is not a mental illness—but because of the severity of the prejudice he will face in life. Every gay boy is some mother's son and some father's son. The love and acceptance they find in their families is often critical to their eventual happiness and self-acceptance.

Any high-visibility athlete who is gay, however, faces an unusual struggle. People often believe that athletes are super-masculine. They are so competitive, so muscular, so "tough." They appear to be the embodiment of manliness. That is not only the perception of the public, it is often the belief of people in the sports world. A talented gay athlete undermines that belief. If you can accomplish a tremendous amount athletically without being heterosexual, then it means that athleticism and masculinity are not synonymous. Many people will be upset by having that assumption violated. Women athletes have been more open about, and the public more accepting of, their homosexuality. Tennis players like Billie Jean King and Martina Navratilova have publicly acknowledged that they are lesbians. So have women swimmers and skaters. However, things remain difficult for men.

The great Olympic diver, Greg Louganis, acknowledged in his autobiography that he was gay and has said in media interviews that that was the single bravest act of his life. Former major league baseball player Billy Bean hid his homosexuality throughout his baseball career but, after quitting the game, announced in 1999 that he was gay. He told reporters that he had been unable to come out when he was in baseball because he was afraid of discrimination from his teammates and the club management and of adverse national publicity. In the end, it was the death of his secret lover and partner that made him want to live an honest public life.

If your son is gay, it is only sane for him to fear the prejudice of his teammates and his coach. He has to anticipate that other men will suddenly be nervous in the shower with him. There is no doubt that comments, gossip, and fear will follow him if he comes out to his teammates. The best he can hope for is that he has a tolerant coach and a loyal team. Since your son hasn't come out, if he is gay, I have to conclude that his fear keeps him from letting anyone know the details of the life he is living. If he is gay, he is either having secret relationships or he is waiting until his college career is over before becoming emotionally involved with another man. That is a long time for any young man to defer his intimate and sexual life.

What can you do? I would talk to your son about your sense that he is lonely. I would tell him that you have wondered if his loneliness arises from his having to hide part of himself. Tell him you have wondered whether he is gay and that you hope he is, because if he is not, he must be terribly isolated, which worries you even more than any of the hardships of homosexuality. (As a psychologist, I am aware that I am in the minority in the United States, but I am more worried about the effects of severe isolation than I am about homosexuality.) Reassure him that you understand that there are many different ways to live a life and find love in life. Say whatever you can to give him your acceptance in advance. I believe that if you put your emotional cards, your hunches, on the table, you will make it possible for him to open up to you.

The most worrisome part of your question is your assertion that his homosexuality would "destroy" his father. It may be that his father has felt masculine himself by producing such a tall, handsome, athletic son. It may be that his father is homophobic. No son wants to lose his father's respect and love. You may even fear that his father will turn his back on him. That is enough to keep your son from "coming out," and if that is the obstacle, he is facing a long internal struggle. He will need your love and support in order to find the courage to let his dad really know him. If you suspect that is the obstacle, that's what you'll need to talk about with him. If your son confides to you that he is gay, and you know that his father is not prepared to handle this news in a loving way, then share with your husband what you know now about the importance of a parent's acceptance. He needs to know that a refusal to accept his son's homosexuality will not prompt his son to change sexual orientation. It will only lead to conflict and loss. He needs to hear that a father's love and acceptance are what every boy desires and deserves. And he needs to understand that he can be an inspiring figure in his son's life, but only if he begins by accepting the reality of his son's life.

Early, Casual Sex: Is It Really "No Big Thing"?

Q: Judging from the media and the way kids talk, sex is "like no big deal" anymore, but I can't go along with that, especially with AIDS as an issue for anyone who is sexually active in any way. I have trouble with two issues and how to talk with our fifteen-year-old son about them. One is the casual way sex is portrayed as part of "coming of age," as if it's an accepted rite of passage of every kid over twelve. If someone isn't going to wait until marriage, then I think at least they should reserve sexual intimacy for a close, loving relationship. It was called premarital sex when I was younger, and I did that, but it was after I'd graduated from high school and was out in the world, and it was in a relationship that seemed headed for marriage. All that said, I feel like a hypocrite if I say to keep sex for marriage. There are so many willing teenage girls today. How can I persuade our son to resist the social pressure, and even his own desires, to have early, casual sex and wait to make sex part of a deeper relationship? Doesn't all this have some effect on a boy's emotional life and growth?

MGT: I appreciate the honesty and the conflict in your question. For those of us now in our forties and fifties, who were in college when the sexual revolution was launched, the sexual minirevolution of our children is something of a dilemma. We "did it" earlier than our parents thought right and our children are "doing it" earlier than we did. Can we say that we got it right and our children are wrong? We, the adults in this country, have created a media and TV world soaked in beautiful, seminude bodies (*Sports Illustrated* swimsuit edition, *Baywatch* and MTV's *Spring Break* concerts) and shows that feature casual premarital sexual relationships (*Friends* and MTV's *Real World* and *Road Rules*). Practically every magazine in the front of the grocery store features a beautiful body and the promise of a story inside that gives advice on how to have better, more exciting sex. What kind of impact did we, as a nation, expect this to have on our children? Ours is a relentlessly stimulating culture that promises kids that sex is fun, sex is a game, everybody's doing it. Why wouldn't they try it early? After all, everybody else is doing it—or it looks that way.

The average age of first intercourse in this country has been falling for twenty years. It is now midway through the sixteenth year. That means that approximately half of kids have had sexual intercourse by the age of seventeen. If the small amount of research and anecdotal evidence is to be believed, there is a lot of oral sex going on in the years before intercourse that is not defined by kids as having sex. And yes, boys will say, "It is no big deal." So, too, will many girls. However, boys say all kinds of things are "no big deal," even when they are. Sex cannot be dismissed that easily. What I see is that kids try to make sex into a casual game, and then they discover that it cannot be played in a casual way. They discover what we all discover: the heart and the body are connected. The body always follows the heart and the heart follows the body, even when you try to keep them separate.

Let me address the issue of AIDS and then move on to the emotional aspects of sexuality, which is really what your question is about. Kids can contract a mortal illness now from having unprotected impulsive sex. One-quarter of all high school graduates in this country leave high school with some variety of sexually transmitted disease, most of them less serious than AIDS; nevertheless, they are chronic diseases that can affect their fertility. It seems to me that we have to educate kids early and frequently about the nature of AIDS and other sexually transmitted diseases (STDs) and we have to teach them about the importance of protected sex. To give them anything less than a complete education is to put their lives at risk.

In my graduate school training, I read the American psychiatrist Harry Stack Sullivan, who wrote that early sexual experiences "coarsened" a boy's personality. Throughout my career I have watched and listened to see if that observation was true, and I have to say that I have not seen that to be the case. It is a boy's definition of masculinity and his attitude toward women that determines how "coarse" his approach to sex will be. If he has been taught that getting laid is central to his becoming a man, and if all of his friends see it that way, he is likely to engage in exploitative sex. If he has seen a disrespectful or unhappy relationship between his parents, he is going to re-create that type of relationship in the world; con-

versely, if he sees that his parents have an equitable, passionate relationship, he is going to look for a girl who fits that
model.

What I have seen is that teenagers, boys and girls, have
flipped the order—the previous generation's order—of things.
They have oral sex before intercourse, and they are willing to
"hook up" with several partners before settling down and
having a serious relationship. Many of them have made sex
into recreation, and by defining it as a game, they have partially rewritten our sexual scripts. They expect to experiment
with sex early, and they say it "isn't sex." They expect to have
deep and meaningful sex in the context of a loving relationship sometime later. Our teenagers are becoming more like
European teenagers in their patterns of early sexual experi-
mentation. In all respects, boys think of themselves as readier
to have earlier sexual experiences than girls do, but that is the
result of boys needing to prove their masculinity in some way.
It is also nothing new. The research literature on sexual behavior has always found that a greater percentage of boys
have earlier sexual experiences and they have "done it" with a
smaller percentage of girls.

I still talk with boys who want to wait, to have the "first
time" be very important. I talk to boys who want to wait for
some time because they want to be sure they are really in
love with the person with whom they first make love. They
want to demonstrate that they are good and reliable partners.
They may also be anxious about getting to know girls or anxious about sexual performance. I also work with boys who are

college bound, who do their homework, and are committed to their varsity teams. They don't have the free time for relationships or a lot of sex. You cannot do everything well in high school and they know that. Research shows that adolescents who participate in meaningful activities, whether it be varsity athletics, drama, debate team, marching band, or youth group at church, have lower rates of early sex, and lower rates of early pregnancy and STDs. If you want to slow your son down in the sexual arena, it would be helpful to him to have high academic expectations and long-range goals.

Our sexual expectations are formed by the behavior of our peers. If by sophomore or junior year in college a boy has not slept with someone, he is likely to become quite desperate and self-critical. In his own mind, he has fallen behind the group. Since I believe that people's sexual scripts are written for them by their friends, it is likely that kids will tend to have sex at around the same time as the other young people they are with. That peer pressure is a hard thing for parents to fight.

If I, as a psychologist and therapist, have reservations about the present trend toward sexual experience at younger ages it is this. Younger children are emotionally immature; a fourteen-year-old is far less emotionally steady than a twenty-one-year-old is, and being immature, he does not read the feelings of other people very accurately. That means that two younger teenagers can more easily hurt each other's feelings without knowing it. And they have fewer resources for protecting themselves from the very powerful feelings of happiness, obsession, abandonment, and loss that sexual experiences create.

My wife, Theresa, and I once worked as the counseling team for a coed boarding school. She decided to leave the school a couple of years before I did. I asked her what she would and wouldn't miss about the job. She replied, "In the last three years, I've heard kids in therapy describe more lousy sex than I'd ever heard before. I won't miss that." I, too, have heard a lot of hurtful, unsatisfying sexual experiences described. I listened to a girl in therapy say she wanted to "re-virginize" herself so that she could start over feeling innocent again. When kids embark on an early sexual career, what they cannot imagine—and the media images will never prepare them for this—is that good sex takes practice. That is something that you can tell your son.

I believe in honesty. I believe in being down-to-earth. If you want to counter the culture and tell your son the truth, let him know that the best sex is to be found in a committed relationship. Sex reaches its highest level of passion and its greatest depth of fulfillment with someone you really trust. Furthermore, according to recent research, the adults in the United States having the most sex are married couples! Though I am not a priest or a minister, I know that human beings often find sex with a person they love and trust to be among the most psychologically nourishing, comforting, and sacred experiences in their lives. For some people, spirituality, love, and passion can become beautifully intertwined, and it is mind-transforming.

If you can describe, with some sense of enthusiasm, the kind of sexual experiences he is going to enjoy in his life, he may be able to hear you when you tell him that receiving oral sex in the back room of a party is the junk food of passion. It is hard to resist, but it usually makes for lousy feelings afterward. Fortunately, for many adolescents, crummy sexual experiences usually lead them to want to have a fully loving relationship. That is true for girls and for boys.

Masturbation: A Little Light on the Subject

Q. I'm not sure I want to know much about boys and masturbation, but is there anything I *could* or *should* know about it that would help me be a better, more understanding parent? I accept that if I open the wrong drawer in my son's room I'm likely to find a *Playboy* or *Hustler* magazine. I've heard that boys do it a lot, and so I won't open my son's door unannounced and I do respect his privacy. I presume some of that is fine, and too much is not, though I have no idea how I'll ever know whether he's engaging in too much, and I can't say I'd be inclined to confront him with that question. What would you and my son like me to know?

MGT. This is a tough question to answer with a straight face because I keep imagining a mother asking her son if he is masturbating the right amount or "too much." The boy would practically have a heart attack. The only appropriate response to such a question would be to shout, "Mom! What's the matter with you?" When I was an early adolescent, much of boy humor was devoted to the horrible thought that your mother would catch you masturbating. ("Has your mother ever caught you jerking off in the closet?" "No." "Good place, isn't it?")

Teenage boys masturbate a lot. It is almost a universal practice. An adolescent boy is getting five to seven surges of testosterone per day, and that means he is getting erections and feeling sexually excited on and off all day. If you measure a man's sexual life by ejaculations per week, he peaks at the age of 15 and his choice of partner is himself. Boys talk and joke about masturbation a lot. (One joke goes, "Research shows that 95 percent of boys masturbate and the other 5 percent are liars.") It is part of boy life.

Boys don't need instruction or discussion about masturbation. It happens quite naturally for them; if you remember your toddler son, he was able to find his penis and play with it without any instruction. If he could do that at two, he can certainly manage at twelve or thirteen. Your son cannot hurt himself. I guess he could make himself sore if he masturbated all the time, but that would be a self-limiting problem.

All boys need from their mother is the mother's calm acceptance that they are growing into men. If you can find some way to joke about it, that will let him know that you know he is growing up. The only time a mother needs to respond is when her son is very obvious about his sexuality.

One mother noticed that her son was somewhat secretively changing his sheets several times a week. When she asked him why he was doing this, he was a little embarrassed and said, "Well, you know, they get messy and stuff at night sometimes." She was sensitive to his discomfort with "messy" sheets and being quizzed about his laundry but really didn't want the extra work or the constant reminder of his sexuality every time she washed more sheets. Having been a parent who talked with her children about personal health matters from their earliest days, she was ready the next day, handing him a bundle of new tube socks with the advice that "a man once told me that clean tube socks work great, and you just toss them in the wash. That way, you won't have to explain yourself to anyone, and it makes life easier on both of us." That's about as much discussion as any mother would want to have about masturbation.

I worry about depressed, anxious, or lonely boys who spend a vast amount of time alone in a room. Perhaps they masturbate "too much," but their problem is really that they are disconnected from people and the relationship they have with themselves is the only gratifying one in their lives. I worry about boys with Obsessive-Compulsive Disorder (OCD) who develop hand-washing or showering rituals at this point in adolescence. Someone, probably a therapist, should ask them whether masturbating is making them feel horrible and guilty. But if a boy has OCD he is suffering from a serious anxiety disorder and should be in treatment and on medication for a host of reasons. His sexuality is only one part of it.

Finally, I worry about boys who get addicted to pornography. That can be a serious addiction and needs to be addressed as an issue. How do you define a pornography addiction? That is tough to do, given what is available to everyone on the Internet these days. I would say that when the consumption of pornography takes on a compulsive quality and crowds out other activities in his life, you should worry. When it occurs in a socially isolated and lonely boy, then it could be symptomatic. I know parents who received a $400 phone bill one month because their son called phone sex lines. Something like that reveals a level of compulsive need that overrides good judgment. He was letting his parents know that he needed some limits and attention.

What healthy boys need is privacy and for their mothers not to be horrified or excessively squeamish. If their fathers are horrified by the fact that their sons are masturbating, the fathers are likely to be suffering from serious amnesia about their own teenage years.

Speaking of
Feelings and Communication

Is Our Sensitive Boy a Sitting Duck for Bullies?

Q: My son is ten years old. He is sensitive, he is able to talk about himself, and we've worked very hard to keep him in touch with his feelings. How can his father and I protect him, or how does he protect himself, when other boys start to tease him? Won't he need to be tough? I mean, our culture isn't changing all that rapidly, is it?

MGT: No, I don't think our culture is changing all that rapidly, and I do think there is going to be a requirement well into the future for boys to look or act tough, especially in early adolescence. I do think that boys are going to tease and test each other and attack one another's masculinity in very superficial ways. That fact seems regrettable and inevitable to

155

me, not only because some boys cannot protect themselves effectively, but also because the demand to appear tough, even when they don't feel it, is a burden to all boys. I hope that the roles that are assigned to boys broaden in coming years. However, if it is going to change, it has to change with mothers *and* fathers *and* sons. We know from research that fathers are a major part of the problem. They treat sons and daughters very differently, using warmer and more emotional language with their daughters than they do with their sons, so boys grow up seeing a more closed and tougher father than do their sisters. In my experience, mothers bear some responsibility, often because they have bought the idea that boys aren't naturally sensitive, or aren't supposed to be. Why do I think mothers believe that sensitive boys are the exception to the rule?

In the last two years I have traveled around the United States. I've probably been in more than eighty cities in two years, speaking about boys, and very often I get a question from a mother about her "sensitive" son. She approaches me tentatively, even apologetically, and says, ". . . my son is very sensitive," in a tone that suggests unmistakably that her son is different from other boys and that difference is a source of worry. She hasn't thought it through, but what she is saying implies that the majority of boys are *not* sensitive, that they have tough hides and are not easily hurt. The assumption is false. In my experience, all boys are human, boys are sensitive, boys are easily hurt. To paraphrase Shylock's speech from *The Merchant of Venice*, ". . . doth not a boy bleed?"

When we assume that most boys are tough, or should be, and that most girls are sensitive, we are engaged in gender stereotyping at the most basic level. It is always a mistake to assume that other adults do not feel the same pain as you or that other boys do not feel the same pain as your son. What you have fallen for is the public mask that many boys wear. You have been taken in by what have been called their "masks of masculinity." You do not see them flinch, withdraw, get depressed. You don't see them cry at night in their beds, as many do. Millions of boys go home from school and say, "They teased me today," and are hurt. Your son is likely to be such a boy. What makes me sad is that not all boys can reach out for help in that way, that many boys will have to pretend that they are not hurt. They won't be able to report their life experiences to their parents because they are afraid that their parents won't accept a sensitive son, a son who is easily hurt.

I read a story once about a boy whose father kept encouraging him to fight at school as a way to prove his manhood. He didn't want to fight. He was sorry to let his father down, but he felt no need to fight. Then one day he got an allergy and his lip swelled up terribly. When his father asked him about it, he impulsively reported, "I fought a boy in school today." His father was thrilled, and when later the mother guessed the truth and tipped off the father, the father was enraged with his son. His son was a wimp *and* a liar! It is in part because they fear their parents' reactions, their parents' expectations for their manhood, that boys act the part of the tough, insensitive son. Playing the role often requires a boy to cut off parts of his emotional life.

The best thing you can do for your son is to have faith in his "sensitivity." Let's call it "emotional intelligence," the way Dan Goleman did, or "emotional literacy," as Dan Kindlon and I did in *Raising Cain*. Your son's emotional literacy is going to give him ways to understand the teasing that comes his way, it is going to help him anticipate threatening situations, it is going to help him "psych out" his tormentors. Yes, he will be teased in the "culture of cruelty," in which boys live during the ages eleven to fourteen. Yes, he will need to protect himself. But unless he lives in a very rough and brutalizing environment, where he will not be able to avoid physical confrontation, his emotional intelligence will be sufficient to keep him safe.

All you have to do is respect his need to appear strong at times, and make it safe for him to open his heart to you. There is a huge body of research suggesting that sensitive boys, emotionally literate boys, are going to have a much larger repertoire with which to meet the many complex and challenging emotional experiences in life, of which teasing is just one. Congratulations on raising a "sensitive son"!

Little Fish, Big Pond: Will He Sink or Swim?

Q: We live in a small community on the outskirts of a large city, and my thirteen-year-old son, Zachary, has always enjoyed being the "big fish in a little pond"—being recognized for his abilities as a student and a team player, though no star, in the park district recreation programs. The trouble is, when he started junior high this year, it was at a larger school that combines the students from a number of elementary schools in the area, and Zachary suddenly became a "little fish in a big pond." He didn't "make it" into the advanced placement classes at this school, and he didn't make the cut on the sports teams he chose to try out for, either. On top of that, his best friend moved away and he had never made a lot of other close friends, so he has no one at school who even notices whether he shows up for a day or not. He's never said a word about feeling bad about any of this; in fact, he's kind of tight-lipped about it all, but lately he's been doing really badly in two important classes. He fails to do the homework or says he did it but forgot to turn it in and now can't find it. Nothing we say makes a difference. The teacher says Zachary needs to be responsible for himself and his work and needs to suffer the consequences of his actions, and we agree to an extent. On the other hand, I feel like there are all sorts of things bothering him, but he insists there's nothing wrong and he acts helpless to change the way things are going. How can we figure out what's really going on, allow him to learn about responsibility, but help him in any appropriate ways to turn things around before he gets a reputation as a loser in this new school full of kids?

MGT: I don't think the issue here is responsibility, and he's certainly not a loser. Zachary is unhappy and overwhelmed by

his losses. He has had a serious loss of status, both academically and athletically, he has lost his neighborhood school,
and he misses his close friend. He has had too many rever-
sals of fortune in too short a period of time, and he cannot cope.

Please, stop and consider what name we would use to
describe an adult woman who had become psychologically
paralyzed in the way Zachary has. If a woman had had her
best friend move away, had been reassigned from her old job
in the company to a new and unfamiliar job, and had had her
beloved three-times-per-week aerobics class suddenly stop,
all in the space of a month, we would think: "Too much
change. That's a lot to handle." And if all of a sudden her
productivity at work had fallen dramatically, we would have
no problem in saying, "She's depressed." All of her friends
would be talking about it, encouraging her to get help, talking to her about her losses, empathizing with her distress.

When a child, especially a boy, suffers a similar number
of losses and has fallen apart in school, what too many teachers say is that he "needs to be responsible for himself and his
work and needs to suffer the consequences of his actions."
This kind of thinking makes me furious. Children don't just
stop succeeding for no reason at all. A responsible child
doesn't suddenly become irresponsible for no reason at all.
Every child has a life, and a story, and some solid anchors that
hold him or her steady. If all his anchors are pulled up, he
drifts. Who doesn't?

The key here is to understand that Zachary is doing the

best he can at the present moment, and remonstrating with him, or telling him what he ought to be doing, isn't going to help. He knows that he's not doing well. He is confused and ashamed. And that's the best he can do right now.

When I was working for my Ph.D. at the University of Chicago, I took a clinical seminar with a maverick psychiatrist, Alfred Flarsheim, M.D. One day he drew a simple diagram on a blackboard and I have never forgotten it. He drew what looked to be a very large H, two vertical lines with a horizontal line in between them. He pointed to the horizontal line and said, "That is someone's level of functioning when they come to see you." He then drew a dotted horizontal line about three inches above the first line and drew an arrow curving up from the solid line to the dotted line. Then he declared, "If someone comes to you and their level of functioning is here (pointing to the solid line), any damn fool can point up here (to the dotted line) and say, 'You should be up here. Pull your socks up! Do better!'

"Saying that to a person doesn't take any training or understanding," Flarsheim stated. "Anyone can do that. Teachers and parents do it all the time. If, however, you want to be a therapist, you have to understand that every person who comes to see you is doing the very best he can, given the present conditions of his life. No one gets up in the morning intending to do badly. We are all struggling to do as well as we can, given our economic, familial, and psychological pressures." Then Flarsheim drew a dotted line three inches below the solid one, with an arrow curving up to the solid line.

"If you want to *really* understand a person," Dr. Flarsheim said, "you have to understand what he does each day to get from here (lower dotted line) to here (solid line of present functioning). That's every person's courageous struggle."

At first I couldn't believe my ears. We're all doing the best we can at any given time? We have to understand how someone gets from very low down to somewhat low down, and we cannot ask him to do more? Was I listening to Dr. Pangloss from Voltaire's *Candide*, the tutor who declared that this was "the best of all possible worlds"? It took me a while to realize that Flarsheim wasn't saying everyone is doing fine. He was simply saying that everyone is doing the best they can at any moment, given the limitations of their lives. It was the simplest and without a doubt the most profound thing said to me in my training, and it has helped me to remember how to think like a therapist.

So, now we have to put Zachary on the horizontal line of our H and appreciate the fact that he is struggling every day just to function at the level of that solid line. He has to carry his grief and his depression to school and function at a reasonable level. He is doing his heroic best. Pointing up to some place above him and saying, "You should be here. You need to be responsible," is not going to get him there. We have to change the circumstances of his life. Without a change, he is not likely to get better anytime soon. Yes, some people—children included—spontaneously recover from depressions. In fact, most do. However, many do not. On aver-

age, it takes three years for a childhood depression to be diagnosed. And that is a lot of life for a boy like Zachary to lose
in a joyless daily struggle. No, we need to help him by helping to change the circumstances of his life.

What does he need? First, he needs empathy and open
acknowledgment of his losses. Second, he has to have the
sense that people are struggling creatively to help him. Third,
he needs his teachers to stop blaming him and calling him irresponsible. He needs at least one of his teachers to take a
special interest in him as a person, help him connect with
some compatible kids in cooperative learning projects, and
perhaps discover some other "Zachs" at his school equally eager for new friendships. Fourth, he needs a psychological
evaluation. And finally, depending on the psychologist's or
psychiatrist's diagnosis, he may need some therapy or antidepressant medication. It may turn out that Zachary does not
have, in the opinion of the professional who sees him, a full
clinical depression. But he is not happy, and time is a-wasting.
Let's get him some help, and some support and advice for
you as well.

Now, I could have answered this question by giving you
normative data about how most early adolescents in the
United States experience a loss of confidence when they
reach junior high school. Many of them suddenly feel less
special and less talented than they used to. It is a tough time
in the lives of children. Happily, self-confidence typically returns by ninth grade, though never as fully or in all the areas

of life where it existed before. This finding alone is reason to hate the whole idea of junior high school. (If I were in charge of schools, all elementary schools would be K through 8, and everyone would be able to play on a team. There would be no cuts until the varsity level in high school.)

I could have said that in time Zachary will make a new friend, will adjust to junior high, and will pull out of his funk. He might, but I do not believe in endless waiting periods for children in pain. That's why I am a child psychologist.

Little Boy Angry about Time-Outs

Q: Why does my four-year-old son get so angry when I try to send him to his room? For example, sometimes he runs around the TV room and jumps on the furniture and knocks things over. If I have spoken to him several times and he hasn't stopped, then I go into the den and stop him and tell him he has to have a time-out in his room. He cries and says he does not want to go. When I insist, he swears and throws things. His behavior going into a time-out is almost always worse than the misbehavior that got him the time-out in the first place. How should I handle this?

MGT: I know that time-outs are the modern recommended punishment. I have recommended them myself and have used them with my own children. But they do not work with all children, nor do they work for all children of all ages. I think your son may be too young for a time-out. It may panic him to be away from you when you are angry with him. The fact that his misbehavior escalates after you tell him about the punishment suggests to me that he is experiencing some separation anxiety from you. My best guess is that the idea of being in his room alone is more than he can bear at the age of four. How big is your house? How far away is his room? Does he panic when you give him some other kind of punishment?

Mastering anger is the big issue for four- and five-year-old boys. They very often greet our authority with confrontation, puffing out their chests or shouting in an effort to bowl us over. Their ferocious behavior often successfully hides the fact that they are scared. Boys experience the same need for attachment and nurturance that girls do at the same age. A time-out can be scary for a boy if he believes that he is being abandoned or that you have withdrawn your love. I have known boys who have been deeply frightened to be sent to their rooms; it feels like exile to them.

We have to be careful not to be taken in by the tough-boy mask that our sons sometimes show us. We have to understand that two things can be true at the same moment. A boy can be trying to frighten *you* and he can, at the same time, be quite easily frightened himself. The best book on boy anger is Maurice Sendak's *Where the Wild Things Are*. Remember Max? The little boy who dressed up like a wolf and told his mother, "I'll eat you up!" She sent him to his room and he then became totally filled with anger and went off to the land of wild things and said, "Let the wild rumpus begin." But when the monsters tried to make Max the king of all wild things he said "no." He wanted to be back home where people loved him best of all (and his dinner was still warm). Sendak beautifully illustrates my point about little-boy anger; they are dependent and furious at the same time.

Sometimes we get fooled by boy toughness and we give them punishments that are terrifying for them, but they cannot tell us how scared they are because they want to act tough. I think that is what is happening with your son. I would recommend that you keep him with you in the kitchen. Put him to work mopping floors, scrubbing something. Stay at his side and let the community service activity you have required of him absorb some of his wild energy. Boys of all ages respond to punishments that require them to do something. It calms them down. Perhaps I am only writing this because I wish that instead of having to spend hours in detention in school, as I did, I had been asked to dig post holes or wash kitchen floors. Doing something for his mother, a reparative act, mobilizes a boy's desire to please in a way that exile or detention does not. It brings out the best in him instead of the monster in him. Try it with your son.

No More Strong, Silent Types?

Q. How can we raise our sons to embrace the best qualities of traditional masculinity without adopting the idealized qualities of the "strong, silent type"?

MGT: I do not think that the image of men as strong or silent will ever go away, any more than the image of the "cowboy," the athletic "hero," or the "gentle giant" will go away. These are all traditional images of men that are prized in the culture. Culture does not change quickly, nor should it in this case. There will always be strong, silent men. There will always be the Joe DiMaggio who inspires us with his play, has great dignity, and has little to say. And such men will be celebrated in song, in art, and in prose.

The problem for boys arises when one single type of man is held up as the ideal to which all boys must aspire. When we accord one type of man status as the only truly masculine man, then we cast all other forms of manhood into doubt. What is a talkative boy going to feel about himself? What is a boy who is not physically strong likely to feel about himself? How can the dramatic boy feel that there is a place for him among other men when he grows up?

I was once interviewing an eighth-grade boy actor in Maine. Here was an incredibly appealing, talkative young man. He had switched schools to an accepting progressive school because he had been teased so ruthlessly at his previous school. He had also developed a philosophy about being a different kind of boy. He said to me, "Yeah, sometimes I have to go to a house in the neighborhood and watch wrestling and eat hamburgers, you know, just to get a dose of what other boys do, so they'll leave me alone." His observation is funny, but it is also a shame that a boy has to apologize for himself. And sad that he has to watch wrestling for remedial reasons. (In my opinion, no one should have to watch wrestling unless they absolutely want to!)

We have to show boys that there are many styles of manhood. In my life, I have run into many different men, some tight-lipped and stoical, some affable and funny, some tough and physical, others cautious and self-protective. I have met aggressive women and nonaggressive men. The diversity of men I have encountered has been fascinating and wonderful. Boys cannot feel safe as children and adolescents unless they know there is a place for them in the pantheon of men. There is, of course, but it is hard for them to know it when they are presented with just a few stereotyped ideas about men. We have to show boys, over and over, that there are many different kinds of men, and they will be one of them.

Speaking of
School

Pushing for Pride, Mother Laments Eighth Grader's Careless Bs

Q: My son is lucky in that he has always made good grades without putting forth much effort. But he is in eighth grade this year and has slipped from easy As to careless Bs. When I see his report card with those Bs and I know how little he puts into his schoolwork, it feels hypocritical to say that Bs are fine when other children making those Bs are working so hard for them. I don't want to seem like one of those parents who wants a straight-A child at any cost because I'm really not one. It's not the grade that bothers me—it's his lack of effort. I'd be satisfied if he worked hard and made Bs. I just want him to put some effort into his work. How can I encourage him to take more pride in his work without sounding like I'm just pushing for As?

MGT: Actually, I don't hear you pushing for As. That's not what comes across in your question. I think that for you this is a moral, not an academic, issue: your son is wasting his talents, intellectual gifts that other children do not have, and that offends you. I don't blame you. You are obviously from a family that values education and you consider your son lucky to have been blessed with what I call a "school brain," and you believe that he is morally obliged to use it.

There are not too many children in the world born with a natural "school brain" (for me this is different from IQ). Though he has one, a "school brain" is not enough. He also has to want to make school his own, he has to want his own education, and he has to see the point of it. And he's not there yet. A lot of middle-school boys are still struggling with whether or not this education is really for them, or whether it is just an adult plot to bore boys out of their minds. They don't know whether to really commit themselves to it, or do it as a game. Then again, some boys start to really want to succeed, but develop fears about testing themselves. What if they really try hard and don't turn out to be #1 in the class? There is the potential for humiliation there. A common defense against failure, a kind of psychological hesitation, is to not really give it all you've got.

The most common cure for what ails him is peer competition. It will begin to annoy him that some other child in the class, boy or girl, who is not as gifted as he is, is actually starting to beat him. That will get under his skin. The second most common cure is falling "in love" with a wonderful teacher. When he gets a teacher whom he really respects, and one who values him, it may be that teacher who says to him, "When are you going to really start to push yourself?" And that may be all he needs.

But you are asking me about the role of parents. You are asking me about short-term motivational techniques, and I'll try to give you some hints. But I have to tell you up front: they lack punch and staying power. What is really going to motivate him toward school achievement is whether he has parents who read, who use the skills they learned in school, who have educated friends. He has to be able to see that intellectual curiosity and achievement make a difference in life. That's what will motivate him in the long term.

In the short term, I would be honest with him about its being a moral issue with you. Don't confuse him with comparisons to other kids; don't talk about Bs or As in concrete terms. Talk about his effort. Don't harp on it, don't sermonize at length. Just tell him succinctly that you really experience it as a moral matter. Then let it go. Ask him whether he can think of anything that would motivate him to work harder. Can he think of anything you could do to help him work harder in school? If he suggests a $400 Burton snowboard, my guess is that you would also find that morally offensive, so tell him at the beginning of the conversation that a cash bribe is not on the table. But there might be something else he is interested in earning that you might find acceptable: a week at a sports camp, a visit from his cousin in California.

It is also only common sense to make certain that he does not have too many distractions around the house when he comes home from school. Limit the phone, computer, and TV in a reasonable way. There is almost no eighth grader on earth who has the self-discipline to limit his media appetite. (I have friends who "ground" their son by telling him that his punishment is "No screens for two days.")

I have seen many brilliant moderate-achieving boys in eighth grade wake up and start to really accelerate in tenth grade. Ultimately, people like doing what they're naturally good at. Coordinated people like playing sports because they come easily; verbally gifted people like crossword puzzles because they come easily; and bright children like school because they come to understand that they have a good "school brain" and they might as well use it.

Little Lies Something to Worry About?

Q: A counselor from our son's high school recently contacted me to say that our son had been missing certain classes on days when he had not been reported absent. When I asked my son about it, he said it wasn't true. But it was. I am very upset about the fact that he would lie to us—more than about missing the class. He's hiding something, but his grades are fine and he's never been in trouble before. We have no idea what this is about, and the guidance counselor didn't know either—he was just contacting us because of the marked absences. How can we talk about this with our son when he has already lied to us about it once? It doesn't feel right to just let it drop.

MGT: Didn't you ever lie to your parents? I thought all kids lied to their parents at one time or another, sooner or later. I certainly did. Lying is a form of personal power. It is a form of independent action. Very young children cannot lie to their parents because they are either emotionally transparent, or too guilty, or too terrified of the consequences. Little kids need their parents so much, and are so scared of disappointing them, that they cannot stick to a lie, even if they tell it. Often they confess in the most charming ways.

However, as a boy gets older and begins to think of himself as competent and adult, he may want to try out his personal power. There are many forms of personal power for an early adolescent boy. For him, the ability to take the bus on his own, to manage his money, to go on a plane flight without having to wear a tag and be escorted by a flight attendant; riding a bike uptown on his own, being dropped at a mall without his mother having to see that the other kid's mother has already arrived, are all signs of his maturity. But having done those things—all of which are approved of by his parents—he may want to try to take his destiny into his own hands. What could be more natural, and more cool, than skipping school? His parents didn't approve, he did it anyway, he lied to the guidance counselor, and they all fell for

174   Speaking of School

it. That's bliss for many boys. Just wait until they tell their friends!

it. That's bliss for many boys. Just wait until they tell their friends!

If you are having trouble remembering how satisfying it is to lie to adults, I recommend to you one of my favorite movies, *Ferris Bueller's Day Off*, which stars Matthew Broderick as the ultimate school skipper. He is so sophisticated, so clever, so grown-up. And the principal? He's a hopeless, earnest, clumsy, humorless sadist. Try as he might, he cannot catch Ferris Bueller, even though he knows that Ferris Bueller is lying to him. If that movie doesn't remind you why it is fun to lie to your parents and skip school, then nothing will.

Now, having seen the movie, you have to act like the principal. The problem is that as parents, you have to take lying seriously and you have to take a stand about school. You must talk to your son about his school skipping and his lying. There should be an appropriate consequence for his having done both. He should be consulted about what punishment he believes fits the crime, and he should have to serve the punishment in full. If he chooses something too inconsequential as a punishment, then you should decide on the sentence. Make it significant and stick to it!

You see, boys love to fool their parents, but they have contempt for parents who are easily fooled. No teenage boy can respect his parents if they are clueless. So here's what you have to do: (1) lighten up; (2) don't take his lying as evidence of deep character flaws; (3) punish him for lying; (4) be vigilant, check regularly with the guidance counselor, keep on the lookout for lying, and don't get fooled again in the future. Then go back to numbers 1 and 2, and keep a sense of moderation. If this was an isolated incident, then respond to it as an incident, not an indictment.

Fourth-Grade ADHD

Q: Jon is in fourth grade and hates school. He has been diagnosed with Attention Deficit Hyperactive Disorder, and school is a real struggle for him. His teacher this year doesn't seem to have any ideas about how to engage him in the work. He stays frustrated a lot, and recently when he got mad about something at home, his temper exploded and he smashed a window in our living room with his bare fist. We're worried about him, of course, and we talk and talk and talk with him like all the parenting books and magazines say to do. But his anger seems to come from very deep, and when it blows, he just loses control. What could possibly make him such an angry child at so young an age? If it's school, what are we supposed to do? We can't just not send him, and private school isn't an option for us. We tried him on Ritalin for a while and it didn't do anything for him, plus we've read so much about the overuse of Ritalin, and we really don't like the idea of medicating Jon. We'd rather help him learn to deal with life without drugs. How can we best help him?

MGT: I really understand why your son hates school. I think one of the difficulties of parenting a child with ADHD or any other learning disability is to appreciate how deeply they hate school. When you ask, "What could possibly make him such an angry child at so young an age?" the answer is not difficult to provide. Your son is dying the death of a thousand cuts—every day at school. And the reason is simple: ADHD is a real disability that doesn't go away. And he has a disability, and other children in the class don't have it.

A psychologist friend of mine once said to me, "For a learning disabled child, every day at school is a series of small traumas." How would that be for us as adults? None of us would go to a job where we felt incompetent every day. How would you like to have to go out on the court with a professional basketball team and have to play with them when they were running circles around you? How would you like to be a lab assistant in an organic chemistry lab without much training beyond high school chemistry? You would feel totally humiliated. And what would you do if you knew you had to face that humiliation again tomorrow and the day after tomorrow? You would put your hand through a window.

None of us would be able to get out of bed if we had to work side by side with people who did a task effortlessly when it was a terrible struggle for us. We would become enraged or depressed. That is the dilemma of the child with a learning disability.

Now, having described the dilemma of a learning disabled child with as much power as I can, I will step back and say that the reason children with learning disabilities don't go completely crazy in school is that all children have some learning differences, all children are struggling with learning new material, all of them are small folk in a world run by adults. That is to say, children with learning disabilities also have a lot in common with other children and that's why they are able to get out of bed and face a day. They also have the love and support of their parents, and perhaps they are good at sports, or they love drawing, or they are superb at Legos and Game Boy games. Their strengths and pleasures make life worth living. They also want to please parents and do school because their parents believe in it so much.

The trick with an ADHD child is to help him survive school until adulthood. Adult life is much friendlier to people with ADHD. He can then go out in the world and become a freelance photographer, a helicopter pilot, an emergency medical technician, an engineer, a surgeon, or a coach who never has to sit down and whose attention is riveted by the action of the game. There are tons of successful people out there with ADHD. It is school that is the problem. ADHD kids are at special risk for anger, depression, and antisocial behavior because they spend so much time doing a task that is so hard, and so much of what they hear from adults is "You have to try harder. . . . Can't you sit still? . . . Didn't you hear what I said? . . . Try listening next time. . . . Pay attention!" One study found that children with ADHD had negative interactions with adults 80 percent of the time.

You have to do a lot to protect a child with a serious case of ADHD. First, you have to be working in an alliance with the school. You need to know how his teachers see his school day.

Does he have an IEP, an Individual Educational Plan? Is he receiving special services? Does he have a teacher who knows him, understands his disability, and likes him? Does he spend any time with other children who struggle in the same way?

Second, I would urge you to consider experimenting with a few different kinds of medication for your son. One trial of Ritalin is not enough; it wasn't a fair test. I have seen medications work miracles for kids with ADHD. I have also seen kids not respond to medications. But I think it is worth a thoughtful trial. He may not have had the right dosage. Or he might respond better to a different stimulant medication to help him with his attentional difficulties. Ask your doctor about stimulant medications other than Ritalin. What concerns me the most, however, is that he might be suffering from a bit of depression. Depression in boys often comes out as anger or irritability. Your son's anger is significant. There are good medications that are used to treat both attentional problems and depressive difficulties. Most of these medications are relatively safe. I urge you to consult your son's pediatrician or get a referral to a child psychiatrist who has experience in the use of such medications with children. People talk all the time about the side effects of medication, but what are the lifelong "side effects" of not taking a medication for depression? What are the side effects of failing in school every day? I urge you to reconsider medication and I recommend to you the books *Driven to Distraction* and *Answers to Distraction*, by Edward Hallowell, M.D., and John Ratey, M.D.

Finally, you need a guide or a coach whom you can consult about these matters. You need a child psychologist or psychiatrist with whom you can consult from time to time, someone who really knows a lot about ADHD. It doesn't have to be regular weekly therapy. Far from it. But you do need someone to give guidance and support for you and your son through his school years. These children are often very smart, perceptive, and creative, and have a different vision of the world. Accept their gifts and help them grow. Good luck!

Teen Son and School Don't Mix: What Can Desperate Parents Do?

Q: Our son is flunking out of high school. Stan is a sophomore this year, and although he is a bright boy and does very well on standardized tests, he cannot seem to connect with the work, the responsibilities, and the consequences of the school world. He never has. He doesn't do drugs, he enjoys family times together, and he has several good, long-term friendships. But his grades and schoolwork are a disaster. A few years ago he was evaluated for learning disorders and there's nothing significant enough to be the cause of his trouble. We sent him to a highly individualized private school through junior high school, and it was a constant struggle. Now he's in an excellent public high school with devoted teachers, and the struggle continues. We've begun to explore vocational education options with him, but he's ho-hum about those, too. Stan is a high-level thinker in science and history—

he is a voracious reader and has taught himself in these areas. That's one reason his teachers have been so lenient, but it can't go on, and he certainly can't get into a traditional four-year college program with these miserable grades. We're out of ideas. Where do we go from here?

MGT: Your situation is a particularly tough one. I cannot pretend otherwise. Sometimes there are kids for whom school just doesn't work. It makes me wish Stan could go and work on a farm or a ranch for a while, where everyone got up in the morning and worked and all the work was useful. I bet if there were a crisis, or a Habitat for Humanity project that he could join, Stan would be a real help.

Stan needs a change in his environment, at home or at school or both.

As a former Outward Bound instructor, I can tell you that programs like these can be turning points in a boy's life. There is nothing like them for changing the environment, changing the assumptions, and making a boy accountable to his peers, not to adults. When you are out in a boat on the cold Atlantic, or rappelling off some serious cliffs in Colorado, you cannot afford to be not motivated. Other kids absolutely need you to be focused, on task, and fully involved, because their lives depend upon it. I've seen these kinds of outdoor experiences really energize kids. In recent years, these kinds of programs have become more widely available at more affordable costs, and some offer scholarships for children from low-income families, so there are options like these for nearly every child in need of them.

With respect to school, you are down to relatively few options. If Stan really is flunking out and the counselors at his high school are at a total loss, you'll need to be looking elsewhere. If it is feasible, you might send him to a boarding school with an outdoor or a farm program or a boarding school where many boys have faced academic failure in their old school settings. If that is not feasible, you might try a trade school or an alternative/therapeutic school where the faculty are trained and experienced in drawing out a boy's motivation. These schools don't have a great success rate, but they try hard, and with some tough cases. It would be interesting for Stan to find himself in an environment where there are many other amotivational boys.

There are many ways to skin the high school cat. I know a young man in Boston who left high school and is educating himself at home on a computer. That's right, he is home-schooling himself on computer and staying in touch with many other students in the Boston area who are doing the same.

Stan sounds like a sweet guy, but we also have to consider that he has some low-level depression or that there is an intergenerational family issue that is being played out here, one that is too subtle to be diagnosed from this distance. I would suggest that you see a family therapist—specifically a narrative family therapist—who could help Stan and your family "rewrite" the story of Stan's failure. He is living a "dominant negative story" and you are caught in the script as well. We have to figure out whether this script captures all the realities of his life.

Finally, you need to remember that life is long. Stan can go to high school and finish college in a year or two or five or ten. There are hardworking young men all over the world in Third World countries who are plotting and dreaming of emigrating to the United States, where they hope someday to drive a taxi and then maybe, just maybe, get an education. Their time line is very long, indeed. Perhaps they'll get a college degree in their thirties. Stan's developmental time line may be long, too, though we don't know why because we are fooled by his comfortable surroundings and his educated parents. And perhaps he won't be able to tell us until he is older. Until that time, if he has a job and is a loving family member and isn't doing drugs, what's the rush?

One problem may be that Stan cannot feel his own motivations because everyone around him is doing all the feeling for him. Everyone else is tearing their hair out, everyone else is generating options for him—including me, apparently. You see, I'm sympathetic with your plight. If it were my child I might be doing the same thing. If it were my child, I'd try everything. But in the end, a parent has to step back and say, "It is your life to lead. And there is only so much we can do, and we did it." I've just known too many people who have gotten thrown out of school or college and who later credit that experience as the "wake-up call" that got their attention and helped them become motivated to make something of themselves.

The problem here is that no one can predict what the right change in environment might be. Eight boring months working at McDonald's might be the right change in environment, too. So could a stint in a community program that works with disadvantaged youth. I know a man who said that the most important experience of his adolescence was a summer job emptying cans into a garbage truck. Working with uneducated, hardworking guys in the hot sun picking up people's garbage was a singular formative experience for him. He realized that he really respected the psychic discipline and physical labor that the job required, and he also felt keenly that he didn't want to do that for his life. It provided him with the motivation to go to college and to become a teacher.

So you see, who knows what the "right" environment is going to be? Especially without Stan's input. Perhaps he just needs to sit and think.

How Long Can Our Son Wait for School to Offer a Challenge?

Q: Alex is seven and bored already with school. He has been reading since he was three, loves science and literature, and basically has been self-teaching himself for years by reading, watching PBS, and talking to adults he meets wherever we go. He has a harder time with children and especially with school and the boredom he feels there. The school day seems very long and discouraging to him. He's not unfriendly to other children, or especially unliked, but he has no close friends his age. The school social worker said recently that Alex is so far beyond the norm for his age and grade that the teachers can't really modify the curriculum for him. She said, "What my hope is for Alex is that he can be patient and we can get him through to high school without doing any damage." Alex enjoys his home life and after-school activities. It's the emptiness of his school life that bothers me. I see him closing down at school and not being very interested in the work. How can I help him "be patient" when I'm losing patience with the system myself?

MGT: Exceptionally gifted children of the type you describe need special attention, not so much to arrange for skipping grade levels, but to provide them an appropriate opportunity to find challenge and the opportunity for growth through their school experience. Chances are that most of his peers and perhaps most of his teachers see him as one of the "lucky" ones for whom learning comes easy. In the current situation, though, your son is at risk for depression. The problem is that so many adults are dazzled by—or envious of—brilliant children that they can't empathize with them and therefore don't help them effectively.

I had a psychiatrist friend who was a genius. He had gone to college at fifteen and medical school at nineteen. He joked by saying that "being a genius means you're going to have a long psychoanalysis." Now why would it be that someone that smart would inevitably be headed for psychological pain? Wouldn't things be easy for them? Aren't they lucky? The answer is "yes" and "no," and your question illustrates the "no" part. Of course regular schoolwork is easy for a highly gifted child. But that also means that he may be profoundly lonely and bored a lot of the time.

Let's put ourselves in the shoes of a child like this for a moment. Have you ever spent a day with someone who doesn't read, doesn't watch the news, doesn't know what is going on in the world, doesn't have any sense of history? Such a person can be a warm and lovely human being and can do admirable things in the world, but at the end of the day you may feel desperate for more compatible company. Why? Because it is lonely to have to be with someone who doesn't share your frame of reference. You have to constantly adjust your thoughts and conversation to meet that person at a different, and possibly less interesting, level.

Now, imagine a child having that experience. Imagine a five-year-old boy having to adjust his interests to meet the intellectual level of another five-year-old. "Oh," he realizes, "this child is my age and looks like me, but he doesn't understand what I understand. I have to talk about something else. And I cannot tell him about my discoveries because he won't 'get it.' " Now imagine that the child at age seven realizes that he is smarter than a number of the adults taking care of him. That is very confusing for him. They are bigger, they are more experienced in life, they take care of him, and yet they don't understand what he understands, or even *that* he understands. They don't seem to know him at all. They ask him to do things that make no sense (why should he spend so much time on reading readiness skills at school when he is reading chapter books at home?). Who is he going to talk to? What if the adult he is speaking to doesn't understand what he is saying? It is lonely.

I love the story of the famous theoretical physicist who, as a child genius, walked into his mother's kitchen and asked whether it was true that God was everywhere. When she said "yes," he asked whether that meant when he came into the kitchen that he was pushing God out. Now here is a four-year-old who is grappling with the concept of the displacement of matter (theoretical physicists have an average verbal IQ of 160). How is it going to be for such a child if the adult to whom he is speaking does not understand the level of abstraction at which he is working? If a normal four-year-old walks up to his mommy and holds out a watercolor he has just painted, she says, "Honey, that's wonderful." The four-year-old future physicist needed his mommy to do that for him with respect to his abstract thoughts. She could not just say, "What an interesting thought, honey!" (though that's a start). She had to engage with him, so he felt that he could be understood. She had to ask, "Is God made up of solid material? Can two objects be in the same space at the same time?"

We're not all smart enough to do that. What his mother realized was that she might not be able to provide everything for him. He needed special schooling, where a boy with a mind like that can be with other children who share that level of intellect. The alternative is loneliness. The brilliant writer Susan Sontag reported that as a young child she sat on her bed, looked at her shelf of books, and thought, "These are my friends." Even as an adult she found that one of the few people to whom she could converse with ease was her son.

There is no reason in the world why Alex should have to "be patient" and wait years for his education to come to him. He needs to be with other children at his level. He should have an enrichment tutor. For emotional and social reasons you might want to keep him with children his own age. After all, he is going to have to live all of his life with people who are not as bright as he. But part of every day he should be with someone who can offer him an intellectual challenge. If he doesn't have it he'll die of loneliness, he'll get depressed. And from your question, I gather that has begun to happen. When you say "closing down," I think *depression*. An inadequate or inappropriate education can cause a child to become depressed. It is not the responsibility of that child—even a very smart child—or the child's parent to figure out what the school system lacks. You do, however, have to be an effective advocate for your child.

You have to keep after the school, seeking out someone who understands his case. He needs an individual educational plan, an IEP. He should have psychological testing and his IQ should be documented. Perhaps he has an IQ of 150.

By law, if a school cannot meet the educational needs of a child, whether he is handicapped or brilliant, they are obliged to pay for an education in a school where they can be met. In New York City, Hunter College High School is a "public school" which admits only children with IQs in the 99.5 percentile or higher. If there isn't such a school in your district—and there almost certainly isn't—he needs a special class that responds to the needs of gifted children. If the system cannot provide that, and keeps telling you to be patient, ask your school counselor, social worker, or psychologist for contact information for the resources serving gifted students in your area. Perhaps there is a private school that serves such children. A school that fails to provide an appropriate education for a child is ignoring the law, and you may want to talk with a lawyer. In my view, it is a crime in a moral and psychological sense for schools to not provide educational services for children with special needs, at either end of the intellectual spectrum.

Trombone Boy Ready to March to a Different Drummer?

Q: Hank has played trombone in the school band since he was in fourth grade and has enjoyed it very much. He's in eighth grade now and still seems to like it a lot but says he wants to drop it next year when he enters high school. In my opinion, that's the worst thing he could do—drop it when it's the source of such good times and socializing. It is "the group" that he hangs with socially at school. If he drops it,

I'm afraid that with the high school–level courses and home-work, he'll have a really hard time finding a whole new group of friends to feel part of. My husband agrees with me but doesn't think it's worth arguing about. Is there a useful way for us to talk with Hank about this or is it going to come down to just letting him do what he wants or making him do what we want?

MGT: I keep staring at the last sentence of your question, the part that says, ". . . is it going to come down to just letting him do what he wants or making him do what we want?" I think that is so often the bind that parents get into with their kids. Force the child or give up on something worthwhile? Is that the only choice? Though your question is about musical in-struments, it is actually about a much bigger issue: how to re-spect the growing autonomy of a child while at the same time guiding him toward intelligent choices for which he will be grateful later. But before I get into parenting philosophy, let me address your situation: To trombone or not to trombone, that is the question.

If every boy who started playing an instrument in elemen-tary school kept it up into adulthood, the homes of America would be crowded with pianos, French horns, clarinets, drum sets, and xylophones. They are not. They are full of TVs, com-puters, and lawn mowers. At some point in high school, after high school, or in college, the majority of instrumentalists—boys and girls—give it up. Girls often get back into touch with their elementary musical years through supporting their own children in their musical ambitions. For boys, the instrument is often dropped without much regret. Why?

Boys give up things in adolescence that they do not think are consistent with their masculinity or their sense of adulthood. If a boy wants to belong to a "cool" group and the cool group doesn't approve of instruments, he is very likely to drop it. The pressure of his social ambition and his identification with the group is quite strong. On the other hand, if he has a friend in high school who plays an instrument, or there is a bandleader whom he likes and respects who asks him to try out for the band, he may be persuaded to stay with it. You cannot predict either of those things.

What is interesting here is that your son is announcing his intention to give up his instrument almost a year in advance! What's that about? He's saying, "Mom and Dad, I hereby put you on notice that I am going to be a young adult next year and I am going to be changing the rules. So I am giving you fair warning. Get used to the idea. And start with giving up your love for my trombone playing."

Fair enough. He's made his announcement. He's also baiting you to find out if you are going to be able to handle his adult self. Don't go for the bait. I would greet such announcements with respectful acknowledgment. "Oh, well, of course things will be different when you are in high school. It would make us sad if you gave up the trombone, but perhaps that will be what you have to do in high school." End of discussion . . . for the moment. Don't get into a fight about it during eighth grade.

When the time comes for him to go to high school, I would let the band teacher talk to him. I would imagine that his trombone teacher might be in touch with the high school bandleader. I have watched teachers in high school—in those big, scary, lonely high schools—recruit boys to debate teams, math teams, wrestling teams, and the band. They need trombonists. Your son is going to fill a need and find a place in high school. He is going to be useful in ninth grade. Now that's worth keeping up an instrument for. But if you fight a lot about it in his eighth-grade year, he may have become totally entrenched in his position by the time he arrives there.

What if he decides not to tell anyone in high school that he ever played trombone? What if he wants to give it away that summer before high school? Here's your moment. You go to him and negotiate: "Is there anything we could do for you in return for your continuing the trombone for just six more months? We want you to be sure of your decision. We don't want you to do anything impulsive that might cut you off from an opportunity in high school. Would you be interested in going to Wyoming this summer with your aunt and uncle in return for keeping the trombone? Could we help finance that mountain bike you want? (And don't chide me about "bribing" kids. Adults trade and make deals all the time. Kids do it too. And parents can do it with children. I'll address the how and when in other questions.)

If I had to bet money, I'd bet that he'll give it up anyway. But that band teacher might get to him. His friend in tenth grade who plays the trumpet may say to him, "Hey, try out for band, some of the prettiest girls are in the band and they love guys who play brass instruments." Or it might be that your son will be persuaded by the respect and honesty of his parents' concern for him. You never know.

Avid Reader Is Underachiever

Q: Our thirteen-year-old son is an underachiever: his grades are up and down, he has trouble getting himself to study, and he seems so disorganized. He is always losing stuff. He's always been that way and he doesn't seem to be maturing. This year we have really cracked down on him, taken away his computer games, TV, and everything, but it hasn't seemed to make a difference. He's doing about the same in school. He's still up late at night doing homework at the last possible hour. What's odd about him is that he loves to read. He has read thirty-seven science fiction novels in the past year and he could tell you everything about them. What do we do to make him a more consistent student?

MGT: I am asked to address more of this type of question than almost any other. If I had a dollar for every disorganized, underachieving seventh- or eighth-grade boy I have been consulted about, I would be rich. Still, there are some important issues here and I take them seriously, even if I have heard the question many times in many forms. There could be a learning disability here; there could be excessive parental expectations at work; there could be an unhappy boy hiding behind these science fiction books. However, the likeliest answer is that what we have here is a normal thirteen-year-old boy. But to get to that conclusion, or to some more worrisome one, I have to ask *you* a set of questions, the answers to which will guide my advice. Since we're not sitting in the same room together, I'll have to walk us through a kind of decision tree until we get to an answer that is helpful to you. Here goes:

First, you say your thirteen-year-old is an underachiever. I need to know: compared to what? Is he an underachiever in relation to your academic hopes and dreams for him? An underachiever compared to other thirteen-year-olds? Compared to his own IQ? Compared to how you were doing in school when you were his age?

Second, has he seemed disorganized in comparison to other boys his age, or again disorganized compared with how you wish he would be? And if he is totally disorganized and at times frankly incompetent, may I be so bold as to ask: Are you still making his school lunches? Are you still doing all his laundry for him? Does he have regular chores to do around the house? Do you hold him to them? In other words, are you contributing to his incompetence by doing everything for him, and then not liking him for it?

Third, has your total involvement in his homework and your scorched-earth policy with respect to TV, computer, and

Game Boy made any difference? It sounds like it has not. Has it occurred to you that if a punishment isn't working, it is the wrong punishment? Are you beginning to ruin your relationship with him? Is he angry and not speaking to you a lot of the time?

Fourth and finally, when do you think a boy should become an independent, organized worker? If you are his dad, try to remember at what age you became self-disciplined, self-monitoring, and consistent about your schoolwork. If you are his mom, try to remember what kind of a student you were at his age, and if the answer is that you were perfect, try to remember what your brothers were like at thirteen.

Before I finally answer this question, I have to tell you that I have a personal reaction to this because at around the same age I was told—it seems like almost every day—that I ". . . was not living up to my potential." My parents told me, my teachers told me, my aunts and uncles obliquely referred to this lost potential of mine. (I loved the aunt who didn't seem to think I was going down the drain!) And I guess at the age of fifty-two, I am still struggling with that wasted potential. How the hell did everyone else know so much about my potential when I was thirteen, and who is authorized to tell me that I have lived up to it now?

Let's try to understand this boy. First, if he has been chronically disorganized *in comparison to other boys his age* for his entire school career, he may have a nonverbal learning disability. The executive function center in his right hemisphere may make it difficult for him to remember and track stuff that is easy for other children. That is a real learning disability. It is not dyslexia and therefore may not have been picked up by his first- or second-grade teacher, but it is nevertheless a real disability. You should ask his two wisest and most sympathetic teachers how he compares on these kinds of tasks with *other boys in his class*! If they say he strikes them as really different than other boys on these dimensions, I would recommend that you get him some psychological testing. He might have a subtle learning disability such as short-term memory problems, visual memory problems, or processing difficulties. Sometimes they are very subtle.

There is no reason—indeed it would be very harmful—to punish a learning disabled boy for things he cannot help. He needs more help in breaking down tasks, organizing home-work, etc. You need to get him help with study skills and how to organize a notebook. He can be taught to compensate for his brain "hard-wiring" difficulties, but reproach and punish-ment are not going to get him there.

Second, if you are still always making his sandwiches and doing his wash, he may not have had a lot of practice in orga-nizing himself. Parents often treat sons and daughters very differently with respect to completing ordinary tasks, and so their daughters grow up more competent. A teacher in Washington, D.C., once told me that when she was twelve, her mother asked her, "Would you please make a sandwich for your brother?" And she replied in exasperation, "Mom,

I'm twelve and he's fourteen! He can make his own sandwich." And her mother said, "But dear, he doesn't know
where anything is in the kitchen." And her daughter said,
"That's your fault, Mom, not mine." And the daughter walked
away, indignant, righteous, and *completely correct* in her
analysis of the situation.

If you are raising an entitled prince, who expects other
people to organize him, please stop doing it! Let him experience some of the natural consequences of being disorganized. Let him find his soccer shoes and shin guards right
before a game, and if he cannot, let him explain it to the
coach or perhaps he'll have to sit out a game. He won't forget
them again. Let him miss a bus. Let him get in trouble with
his teachers if he forgets his homework. Tell his teachers that
you are going to let him "fail" at some small things so that he
learns to manage himself and his time. The private schools in
New York forbid parents from faxing homework to school
that was left at home because if they allowed the practice,
some parents would be constantly "rescuing" their children
from the consequences of their own errors. Some parents
cannot stand for their children to actually experience things
in life. Please try to remember how you became an organized
person. I am sure that it didn't happen because your mother
or father reminded you of everything you had to do.

Third and finally, at a certain point in life your son has to
make a decision about what kind of student he is going to be,
and many boys choose not to be great students. It isn't an accident or an oversight, they didn't forget about school, they

are fully aware of what school involves, they are not de-pressed. They say to me, "I don't like school very much," or "I always leave my homework till late 'cause I hate it." They've made a deliberate, conscious decision to not get very good grades in school. Nevertheless, these boys tend to make hardworking and successful adults. As we pointed out in *Raising Cain*, many boys don't find school a boy-friendly place right from the beginning. Research tells us that girls do better in school than boys from elementary school through graduate school. Despite their failure as boys to do well in school, or as well as girls do, many men make quite a success of their work. Many boys are just waiting for school to be over so that they can do something useful!

It would be great if every boy—every child for that matter—achieved to his full potential in school, but it is never going to happen. Don't ruin your loving relationship with your son with unrealistic expectations. And here is the nub of this case. Try to remember that this thirteen-year-old boy read thirty-seven books on his own in the past year! I know many parents who would trade in their sons for a reader like him. Your son is educating himself, he is focusing on what he likes, he can remember details when he is moti-vated to do so.

My advice is, first, talk to his teachers and find out whether they think he is in the normal range of boy behavior. If he is, then stop taking everything away from him and being so dis-appointed and punishing in your attitude toward him. In-stead, start reading some (no need to read them all) of the books he's reading and find a way to appreciate what he loves so much. And finally, start buying him more books or become a regular at the local library. If there's one piece of active parenting you might do, make sure he gets a good night's sleep. A boy this age should be asleep by 10:30 P.M., whether his homework is done or not.

Speaking of
Teachers

Kindergartner Is Exhausting Teachers and Classmates

Q: One boy in my kindergarten class has a terrible time settling in to a school group and school routines. In group activities he pokes, pushes, and annoys neighboring children to get their attention. Sometimes I have to physically remove him from the group when he is too disruptive, and once recently when I did that, he pushed me hard and hit me. When I placed him in a chair by himself, he knocked it over and then overturned a table nearby. Outside at recess, when a teacher called him to come, he ran in the opposite direction instead. When I talked with his parents, I could see that his mother is exhausted by him and his father deals with him by spanking. What can we do at school?

MGT: My friend and psychiatrist colleague, Edward Hallowell, M.D., author of *Driven to Distraction*, taught me years ago that you could usually diagnose ADHD by how worn out the boy's mother is and how bad she feels about herself as a mother. So when I hear a description of a boy who is physically active, impulsive, and disruptive, and I hear that his mother looks exhausted, I have to think of ADHD. But to be sure, I would have to consult with you, the classroom teacher. Because of their extensive experience with many different children over a number of years, I regard teachers as the best source of diagnostic data on a boy with ADHD. I trust the clinical observations of teachers at least as much as—and often more than—I do mental health professionals. Mental health professionals who meet with a child in their office for an hour sometimes see only a narrow range of behavior. Most children can pull themselves together for a nervous visit to a doctor. Because teachers see children in many different kinds of situations over time, they have data on the extremes. They see the explosions. They see the frustration, the wild, out-of-control behavior on the playground. They see the child run in the opposite direction when he is called.

If I were sitting with you, I would do what I do with the teachers in my school. I would interview you about the boy. I would immediately ask three questions of you:

1. How does this boy compare, on the dimensions of physical restlessness and impulsivity, with other boys in this year's kindergarten class?

2. How does he compare on these traits with other boys from classes in the past?

3. How many years have you taught kindergarten? If you told me that this was the most active five-year-old you had ever seen, but you'd been a teacher for only a year, I would take your observations seriously, but I would check with a more experienced teacher at the school as well. As a first-year teacher, your "research sample" isn't big enough. If you told me that you had been a teacher for fifteen years and this was the most impulsive and reckless boy you had ever seen, I would sit up and take notice. In fact, I would consider that a trustworthy preliminary diagnosis, though I believe that it should be affirmed by a child psychiatrist or psychologist.

Teachers shouldn't diagnose children on their own. They aren't licensed to diagnose, and it gets them into trouble with some parents. A teacher who says, "Your child has ADHD and should be on Ritalin," should duck down quickly behind the desk, because some parent—probably a physician—is going to take the teacher's head off. What teachers can do brilliantly is describe behavior, give specific instances of it, and convey their sense of worry to parents. For example: "Your son cannot sit still, even though he tries, and he says whatever comes to mind in morning circle and cannot hold himself back even when one of the teachers sits next to him. He tried to hit me when I was separating him from the group, and the other day when I wanted to talk to him, he ran away from me. I am worried that he wants to control his behavior, but he cannot. Have you seen any of this at home?" Nine times out of ten a very relieved parent will say, "Oh, yes, we're just exhausted. What do you think we should do with him?" At that point you say, "Why don't you check with the principal (or other appropriate administrator) and get the name of a reliable child psychologist or psychiatrist who can provide a more specific evaluation and offer some suggestions."

But I digress. You asked me for advice.

I am going to answer this question as if this boy were suffering from ADHD. The only competing explanation I can think of is that he is just a very active boy who has been hit a lot at home, and he is bringing his anger and aggression into the classroom. There is research suggesting that very aggressive boys in kindergarten aren't "naturally aggressive," but rather are imitating the behavior they see and the discipline they receive at home. It can be both, and often is in the case of ADHD because the boy's overwhelmed parents have been hitting him—spanking, smacking, jerking him around—when they lose their patience and creativity.

In either case, this boy needs care in school and his family needs guidance. ADHD boys need four things: understanding, structure and clear guidelines in the classroom, support for their families, and evaluation for medication. In the classroom, you may have to provide him with structure that other children do not need. You or your assistant teacher may have to sit with him in circle. You may have to provide him with notice that transitions are coming up. You may have to put him on a point system, or a behavioral system with stars, and thereby reward him for self-control. The agenda for this boy needs to be self-control.

When he runs away from you and you catch up with him, you need to know what he expected. Did he think you were going to hit him? Why did he think so? Does his father chase him and spank him? You are going to need to introduce him to the idea that you do things differently at school than what he has experienced at home. Does he understand that? You may need to give him a place for time-outs at school. Is there an administrator who is willing to provide a safe time-out space until he can regain control of himself? Is there an administrator willing to discuss the possibility of evaluation and medication with the parents? Can you and the administrator work as a team on this one? You may need some support, too. However, if you handle this boy with understanding and structure, he may look like a very different kid at the end of the year with you. And you will have started him on the road to success in school.

It will be important for his parents to be providing a similar version of support and expectations at home, after school, and through the summer months. And you should assist at your school in helping prepare this boy's subsequent teachers with any helpful information that will enable them to continue to provide the most effective response to this boy as he grows and progresses through grade levels.

Charming Boy's Dark Side Expressed in Art

Q: I am concerned about a boy who is very charming around adults, mature and comfortable in conversation. He loves to write and act and has a great sense of humor. However, when I see his compositions for English class, many are dark, self-deprecating, and even sinister. Is he most likely okay and just more in touch with his "dark side" and able to articulate it better than most boys? Or does he need help? How can I tell and what can I do?

MGT: All children, no matter how optimistic and mentally healthy they may be, have to come to grips with the complexities of human life. They have to reckon with evil, with death, with their parents' imperfections, and with their own dark impulses. Everybody has the capacity for evil in them; everyone has fantasies of anger and revenge. Years ago, when I taught psychology to high school students, I asked them how many of them had ever, in an angry moment, wished their parents would die. One hundred percent of the class raised their hands. I once gave out a questionnaire at a high school that included a question asking whether they had ever thought about suicide. Forty-five percent of teenagers acknowledged that the thought had at least crossed their minds, even if they had never really considered it.

What kind of a world is it where children wish their parents dead and think about killing themselves? That's the world of children. Children quite spontaneously shout "I hate you" at their parents or "I wish I were dead." That's part of every child's emotional repertoire. In his famous book, *The Uses of Enchantment,* Bruno Bettelheim discussed why some fairy tales, especially dark and scary stories, have such an enduring hold on the minds of children. He said it is because the stories mirror the angry, vengeful, terror-struck thoughts that exist every day in the minds of children. Think about *Hansel and Gretel.* Their mother dies and their stepmother forces their father to take them out into the forest and abandon them. They then meet a witch who puts them in a cage and fattens them up to be eaten. They escape that fate by pushing her into an oven. What about *Cinderella?* Her mother dies and her evil stepmother treats her like a servant, showering her stepsisters with everything good. Fairy tales are grim indeed.

What about a modern fairy tale like Disney's *Lion King*— the most watched video of all time? In it, an evil uncle makes the lion cub believe that his father does not really respect him. Later he persuades the prince that he is responsible for his own father's death—by trampling. And what about *Star Wars?* Luke Skywalker learns that his father is Darth Vader, a Jedi Knight who went over to the "dark side." May I remind you that Stephen King is the best-selling novelist in the world? Is what your student is writing any darker and scarier than Stephen King?

Literature is the place where children can express and experience all of their dark emotions as well as their more joyful ones. Freud believed that people sublimate sexual and death instincts in artistic expression. That does not mean that art is therapy. Art has to be taken on its own terms, not reduced to psychology. However, it is the case that novelists and playwrights, painters, and filmmakers get to wage war, torture people, commit murder and rape and incest—all in the name of art. You know, we cannot teach Shakespeare to students in high school and then become worried when they write dark dramas. Do you remember how many people end up dead onstage at the end of *Hamlet*?

You describe your student as someone who loves to write and act. He is an aspiring artist. As long as he treats people well in school, seems reasonably happy, and is not signaling suicidal intentions through his English essays—something that many boys do—you do not need to be worried. If he discusses serious violence or suicide in his writing, you must talk to him about it. If not, I would simply talk with him about how powerful and disturbing you find his vision of life to be. Treat him as a serious writer. Have a personal response to his work and share that with him. "Your story was terrifying and very well done. I couldn't stop thinking about it. It surprised me because you are such an upbeat person." I bet that your student will then tell you something about his creative process that will be fascinating to you. Touching base with him about the sources of his writing will also reassure you.

Whether you believe him to be an aspiring artist or a more troubled boy, you should discuss the situation with your school's social worker or psychologist for any additional response that might be warranted. And discuss with his parents the tone and content of his writings. They may be able to offer another piece of this boy's story. He may be at home, just as you describe, a boy doing fine, who is simply captivated by the excitement of creating scary fiction. Or they may share with you that he has been more remote, angry, or sullen at home, has suffered some hurt or loss in recent months, or that they, too, have noticed that he has become suddenly obsessed with the dark side of life. If these details point to a troubled boy, then the need for more specialized help becomes clear.

Math Whiz Struggles with Fear of Failure

Q: In my freshman advanced math class, there is a boy who is clearly very bright and belongs in the class, but seems determined to sabotage himself by failing to turn homework in or finish problems on tests. At the same time, he is distraught by his bad grades and I have seen him wipe angry tears from his eyes when he gets back a paper with a low grade. I can't figure this one out. Can you offer some ideas to help me break him out of this self-destructive rut?

MGT: Oh, I know this boy. I have seen him in many forms over the years. He is yearning for success and afraid of failure. He is tied in knots because his performance in school does not live up to his intelligence or his image of himself as being a boy in control. The problem here isn't just math; the problem is his developing as a learner, developing strategies for dealing with frustration and feelings of ignorance. Math—even advanced math—is only one of this boy's worries. He is struggling to develop into a dogged, courageous student. Such students are made, not born, and there aren't a lot of boys in ninth grade who have developed into steady, resilient students. Their self-esteem and their personal discipline are too erratic for that.

What adults forget about school is how exposing it is to learn something new and how humiliating it is to make mistakes in public and to fail. Stop and think. When was the last time you were given an assignment to do in public that involved mastering material you knew nothing about? When was the last time your boss handed you back a report marked up with red ink? When was the last time you got a grade on top of a piece of work—in front of other people? I know a school principal who took a summer course in weaving on a big loom. She said it opened her eyes to how hard it is to be a student. There were moments when she just wanted to put her head down on the loom and cry.

Most adults avoid experiences of learning or of public humiliation. A few years ago my wife and I thought we would throw a big ice skating party at my school's rink. We thought it would be fun for everyone to skate alongside his or her children. On the day of the party we got call after call from parents saying that they hadn't skated in years, they didn't feel comfortable, they would drop their children off, but they wouldn't stay. It would be too embarrassing to even try.

Eventually only two adult couples out of twenty were willing to come and try to remember how to skate in public.

Children are put in embarrassing positions in school every day. It is such a routine that we forget how painful it can be. That's what school is about. This boy is smart enough to do the math; he has to learn how to support himself emotionally when he does it. You can help him in this regard.

I would suggest that you talk to him. Ask him whether he knows how smart he is in math. Does he feel smart in your class? If not, why not? What happens when he tries to do the homework at home? Is it too frustrating? Tell him that you see how much he wishes to do well. Tell him you have been a witness to his frustration. Ask him if there is any way you could make math more accessible for him. Tell him that you have seen other boys like him get the hang of advanced math by midwinter (if that is the truth).

When I remember back to my struggles in freshman calculus in college—how I avoided the homework, how long it took me to arrange for a tutor, how I struggled in the final exam—I have some empathy for this young man.

Concerned about Boys Unfocused in School

Q: I'm concerned about the boys who have a difficult time staying focused in the classroom during work time and are constantly socializing in disruptive ways instead. Specifically I'm thinking of a six-year-old student in my first-grade classroom and my own son, who is twelve. Through the years my son's teachers have talked with me about his potential, but also about the fact that he needs to focus and stay on-task better. I see the same qualities in my six-year-old student, and I see both boys feeling not so good about school. How can I help my first-grade student so he doesn't have the same problems in later years that my son has now? And how can I help my son?

MGT: Many boys have a more difficult time in school than do girls. There is a simple reason for this. By school age, three-quarters of boys are more physically active, impulsive, and developmentally immature in comparison to girls of the same age. On the dimensions of sitting, focusing, and self-control, boys are slower to develop (and a boy with ADHD is always going to have trouble focusing). That means that the things that are relatively easy for girls are going to be pretty hard for most of the boys in a class. That simple fact has powerful implications for boy performance in school because boys, like all human beings, like to focus on things that they are good at. It is hard to stay "on-task" when something comes hard; it is easier to stay focused when you love something or it comes easily. Chances are your twelve-year-old son has things such as video games or Legos that he can focus on with great intensity. But in the classroom he—and your six-year-old student—have trouble maintaining that focus, and they want to socialize instead.

For many boys, the school day feels longer and is more demanding than it is for girls. Even in prekindergarten, boys are more likely to get in trouble; they are more likely to be scolded for running, or wrestling, or being in the wrong place. While girls can sit in their chairs, boys are falling out of them. It can happen that boys begin to develop a conflicted relationship with school. They experience the environment as confining and the teachers as disapproving. Whenever I interview third- and fourth-grade boys, they tell me, "The teachers like the girls better." It is almost a universal observation by boys in school, and it is often wrong. They have many, many teachers who love boys and appreciate their energy and boldness. However, they have had many more restraining comments made to them in the classroom than the girls, and boys notice the discrepancy.

I wish you could talk to as many adult men about school as I have. Many of them report that school was a misery. These are men who are now successful and *very focused* on their jobs. Why is it that men can be so focused on their work, and yet had such trouble focusing in school? First of all, they grew up and developed self-control. Secondly, they feel in charge of their work and they are rewarded for what they do. Finally, many men find jobs that allow them to be physical. Adult life is easier for a man than was school. Imagine your restless boy who cannot focus in school. Now picture him piloting a plane, driving a UPS delivery truck, working on a construction crew or supervising one. Things are moving fast, events command his attention, he's there by choice, and he is in charge.

It is a mistake to assume that just because a boy cannot

focus in the classroom, he is wasting his potential. He may be fulfilling his potential on his computer or Nintendo game, or on his soccer team. He may be developing focus outside of school. Until a boy develops more self-control, the classroom needs to be as engaging and "hands-on" a place as you can make it. There have to be breaks for exercising and socializing in school. And finally he needs empathy. A boy needs his teacher to understand that school may be a struggle for him. What would be most helpful is if you as a teacher and a mother can have the confidence that he will learn to focus in school in time, and that school does not always predict how successful a man will be in his work life.

Boy "Cutters" Need Attention

Q: I am aware of several boys in our high school who "cut" themselves and one boy who has been self-mutilating his arms for several weeks. These boys are not part of a gang or the same circle of friends. They come from seemingly well-adjusted, well-educated, and emotionally giving families. What is this about and how can I do something to help them?

MGT: Cutting is a very serious psychiatric symptom. Any boy who has been self-mutilating his arm for several weeks is making repeated calls for help, though he will resist help when it comes. The only adolescents who cut with regularity are the ones who are suffering from serious depression, forms of disassociation, and personality disorders. Though you have said that this is not a group phenomenon in your high school, I would have expected that such symptoms were part of a group contagion (I will try to explain later why it can happen to separate individuals who are not part of a group). If one student starts to cut himself, other less disturbed individuals might join because it is a group phenomenon, though it probably does not mean the same thing to members of the group as it does to the habitual cutter.

The problem is that one disturbed person, especially a charismatic or challenging kid, can "set the standard" for apparently courageous behavior that is in fact desperate. That is, a "cutter" who cuts in a desperate attempt to feel something, because his internal experience is so barren and devoid of feeling, can inspire others with his apparent daring and courage. Every teenager—even from the best family—has a small or not so small part of himself or herself that feels alienated and misunderstood by the adult world. He feels that way from time to time just because he feels young, frightened, and unequipped to face the world. The developmental requirement of moving away from your family and transforming your relationship with your parents is a demanding one. The expectation in American culture—constantly reinforced through TV images—that young people should be cool and self-sufficient as soon as possible can lead to profound loneliness and alienation. All you have to do is watch the videos on MTV to see how much mainstream teenage culture is about feeling alienated from the adult world.

Adolescent boys are still in need of adults, but they hate

themselves for being so. In an effort to become adult they often isolate themselves from the adult world, and then suffer from lack of intimacy and support. They can become profoundly lonely. Teenage boys often flaunt their loneliness through self-destructive behaviors that seem to say: "I'm out here in danger, and there is no one to help me except me. And I don't know how and I'm not sure I care!"

It is very hard for me to believe that the cutting in your high school is not a group phenomenon, to some degree. It may be that school gossip has spread around the community and that every alienated boy yearning to be recognized hears that the cool way to express distress is cutting. Suicide gestures, eating disorders, bulimia, and the more common alcohol and drug abuse behaviors spread in communities in the same way.

I think you have to turn to the administrators and the mental health professionals in the school. If parents are unaware of cutting behaviors, they should be made aware. I believe that the school psychologist or social worker should be speaking with the boys and their families, and should be working to get them into psychotherapy. I would also work on a preventive basis, having a speaker come to the school and address the issue. Having such educational talks has helped teenagers to recognize the seriousness of eating disorders among girls; they could also help with cutting behaviors that seem to be spreading in your school community.

Boys Who Need Therapy: Is Anybody Listening?

Q. In my twenty-two years of teaching, I have seen many boys who I thought could use some psychotherapy. I have referred a number to therapy through the school counselor, or recommended it to their parents. Very few of them have gone to therapy and even fewer have stayed for any length of time. Why is it so hard to get boys into therapy? Is there an effective way to get boys to try therapy and perhaps to remain until they get some benefit from it?

MGT: From the time they are little, boys receive messages from our culture that being tough, independent, bold, and successful is what makes a boy masculine. By contrast, girls receive the message that it is important to maintain relationships with people by opening your heart to them. The different social training of boys and girls accounts for why adult women are overwhelmingly the consumers of psychotherapy. Boys and men often believe that by going to psychotherapy they are admitting that they are unsuccessful. And they imagine the process is going to crack them open and reveal them to be confused and weak.

Men and boys often react to psychotherapy with anger and impatience. In the movie *Analyze This*, the Mafia chief, Robert De Niro, insists with the help of a gun that the psychiatrist, played by Billy Crystal, help him get rid of his anxiety attacks. He is outraged that a big strong guy like himself could suffer from paralyzing anxiety. The humor in the situation, of course, comes from the fact that gangsters do not generally seek therapy. For a psychologist like myself, however, the movie was reminiscent of doing therapy with most men and boys. Many boys I have seen feel (a) angry about having psychological symptoms; (b) upset that talking doesn't seem to change things immediately; (c) worried that someone will find out they are in therapy; (d) impatient to get out of therapy before they start to feel dependent on the therapist. You have to address all those feelings over and over in order to help a boy stay in therapy. Very often he does not stay long enough to give you a chance to address his fears about the process.

Research tells us that a boy is four times more likely to be referred to a school psychologist than is a girl. That has certainly been the case in my career. When I have worked in elementary schools I have been sent boys with learning problems, behavior problems, and undiagnosed depressions. When I have worked in high schools, generally my clientele has been girls who have volunteered to come see me and boys who have been sent by the deans or by their advisors following disciplinary or academic problems. Beneath a boy's disciplinary problem there is almost always one of four things: an undiagnosed learning problem, an unseen depression, problems with substance abuse, or a tragic family situation.

Now that I work in an all-boys' school, most of my referrals come from the deans, advisors, or coaches and most of my boy clients are initially resistant to therapy. It helps some of them and it helps me that they are *sent* into therapy and required to stay there for a certain number of visits. I am very grateful that my school uses its natural authority with boys to send them into therapy. I could not work without that force propelling them my way. Boys often stay to talk with me because some teacher whom they admire believes it would be good for them. I ride on the coattails of the relationship they have with another adult. A boy who trusts another adult takes me on faith.

In order to keep boys in therapy, I try to involve the family as soon as possible. Adolescent boys often feel misunderstood by their families; they are angry that their mom and dad don't "get it." If I meet his parents, then a boy and I always have something real to talk about. In my opinion, family therapy is the most powerful way to get a boy engaged with a therapist. Mothers have told me that their sons "never talk," but in a family therapy session, with the parents articulating their worries about their son, he will always talk. Boys like to be expert, they like to set the record straight. After a good experience in family therapy, in which the boy has felt understood, he may want to stay and do some individual work with the therapist. Families can always negotiate with their son in order to get him to come to those initial meetings: "We need you to come to family therapy because we're going to get the therapist's advice about how much to let you use the family car. If you want to use the car, you should be at the meeting to give the therapist your opinion." I have seen parents ask their sons simply, "This is very important to me. Would you please come to therapy three times as a favor to me?"

Boys often experience the adults in their lives as having

the problem, not themselves. This phenomenon is called "externalizing" (in contrast to girls, who are generally "internalizers") and it is often morally upsetting to adults; they want the boy to "take more responsibility." I actually do believe that the boy experiences the problem as coming from outside himself, and so to have some of the other characters in his life come into the therapy session addresses his world as he sees it. I have done a modified version of couples therapy with a boy and the teacher at whom he is angry. It helps a boy to have the real person there.

I would like to say that there is some magic kind of therapist for boys, that there is a certain kind of therapist whom I can describe for you who works for boys. There isn't. Doing therapy with boys is never as easy as therapy with girls, for all of the reasons I outlined in the first paragraph. However, there are some therapists who seem to have a high rate of success with boys. Some combination of traits of being matter-of-fact, having charisma, forthrightness, a sense of humor, and, most especially, a manifest liking for boys can make a man or a woman—and I have known many women therapists who were sensational with boys—the right therapist for a boy. Boys are very clear in their assessments of therapists. They describe therapists whom they don't like as "stupid," "dorks." If teenage boys like their therapists they will shower them with praise, saying, "He's not too bad," "She's pretty clued in," or the highest praise of all: "She's pretty cool." An adult thus described will have a higher success rate with boys than other people. Once you find such a person, hold on to their name and send boys to them.

Bold-faced Lying to Teacher: What's He Thinking?

Q. Why would a boy lie to his advisor about some troubling behavior that he had already admitted to the Dean of Students and been reprimanded for? Even in the face of several eyewitness accounts from other faculty members, he lied. What could he possibly be thinking?

MGT: I happen to know that this question comes from a woman teacher, and typically only a woman would ask it. No man would have to ask me this question. Men know intuitively why boys lie, yet straightforward, in-your-face lying remains something of a mystery to women. Girls and women believe in a cycle of transgression-confession-redemption and closeness. Women think that the story of wrongdoing should go like this: you commit a sin, you are discovered, you feel terrible until you tell someone about it, you feel much better, you tell other people, everyone forgives you, and you feel much closer. That's why a woman would ask a boy about a crime to which he has already confessed. The woman wants to give the boy a chance to go through the confession-closeness part of the cycle with her. She imagines that he will feel better after the conversation.

From the boy's point of view, that's the dumbest thing in

the world. He's already confessed. Telling it again is only going to humiliate him; telling it again is going to make him feel
bad all over again. From his point of view, asking him to talk
about behavior he has already discussed with the Dean of
Students and for which he has been reprimanded is utterly
pointless. No matter what you say, he hears you saying, *"You
really screwed up, didn't you? That was pretty stupid, wasn't
it? A dumb thing to do, even dumber to get caught. What a
total turkey you are."* What is that voice that he hears? It is,
of course, the voice of his conscience, the voice of his own
disappointed perfectionism, but it sounds like the voices of
the boys group in eighth grade. Boys get teased incessantly
by other boys, and are made to feel small and ashamed for
any little thing that they do that is wrong or not cool. That
voice is then internalized and becomes a built-in critical re-
flex that boys cannot avoid. Have you ever heard boys re-
proaching themselves on the sports field? They get angry
with themselves, they shout at themselves; if they could,
they'd kick themselves in the ass.

The secret to the psychology of men and boys is to understand how much shame they feel for anything—large or
small—that they do wrong. Feelings of shame and inade-
quacy go to the heart of their feelings of masculinity, so the
stakes are very high. And yet, being boys, they get into trouble over and over for little things. They are too physically active, they stand on the desks, they throw things out the
window, and they don't do their homework. By the time a boy
is in high school he is accustomed to a cycle that is very dif-

ferent from the girl cycle. His cycle goes like this: do something stupid, try to hide it, get caught, feel even more stupid, get punished, get teased, get asked about it again and again, feel more and more ashamed.

Boys want to tell the truth. They are not natural liars. They just fear the feeling of shame more than they fear losing their relationships with adults. That's why they will lie in someone's face. They are less concerned about the impact on the other person of being baldly lied to than they are about the humiliating inner feelings they are going to experience. That is why it is such an achievement for boys to live under an honor system, or for men in the military to absolutely tell the truth. When a man can say, "That was me, sir. I did it," that is the greatest proof of emotional courage. For most men it requires courage to be able to anticipate the shame and sense of isolation they are going to feel, and to tell the truth anyway.

I see a need for the moral training of boys at home and at school. They need to be taught how to act with emotional courage, and they need some step-by-step instruction without shaming. Talk with your student, but open with an acknowledgment. "I know that you've already talked with the dean, and I know you feel badly about this. Would it be okay if I ask you one more question about it?" If he nods "yes" as if he means it, then proceed with your question. If he nods "yes" in a way that suggests he actually means "no," then I would say, "Well, you may be feeling too raw right now. Can we talk about it in a few days?" That gives him time to prepare himself.

Proud Boys Struggle to Deny Learning Disabilities

Q: In my work with boys who have learning disorders, I have found that by middle school, many of them insist that they don't need special help anymore, even though it is clear that they do. They seem determined to take the "I can do it myself" stance, and nothing—not even bad grades—seems to change that mind-set. It seems hopeless to keep trying sometimes, but I don't want to give up. On the other hand, I feel ineffective. Is it too late to help these boys?

MGT: The hardest thing about a learning disability is that *it really is a disability*; it doesn't go away. The second hardest thing about a learning disability is that it is mostly invisible. I have seen many parents struggle for years with the fact of their children's disability. I see that they hope it is temporary, that it can be completely tutored away as if it were the result of poor teaching in the early grades, or a developmental lag that will resolve itself. If adults can engage in a psychological struggle with the reality of a learning disability, why wouldn't children do the same? Why wouldn't they engage in prideful denial, wishful thinking, and displays of not caring—for example, not being upset by bad grades? They do.

No child wants to be learning disabled. It is tough on them all, boys and girls. If I look at it just from a boy's point of view, it is hard on his self-image, self-confidence, and his feelings of competition. It may affect his sense of strength, which is part of his sense of himself as masculine. He may feel that

being learning disabled makes him stupid, babyish, and incompetent. A boy wants to read as easily as other boys read,
just as he wants to be able to run as fast as any other boy on
the soccer field. If he is learning disabled, he is never going
to read with the ease of other children. That is going to make
him feel wounded and angry.

Now why do boys become angry and resistant about having learning disabilities around middle school, when they
have been willing to accept help in earlier grades? There is a
developmental explanation. It is around fourth grade that all
children begin to get a realistic sense of their abilities. If they
haven't been as good as other children reading out loud in
first or second grade, they hold on to the hope that they will
catch up. Certainly we encourage small children in that direction. "You'll get the hang of it soon," we say. "It takes a
while to get good at this." We reassure children constantly
that if they stick with it they'll get it. However, by fourth
grade they are coming to understand that they won't ever get
it as easily as another child. The concept of the permanence
of cognitive abilities—i.e., there are kids who are brilliant at
math and others who are lousy at it—emerges with development. How a child feels about that discovery depends on his
psychological strength and resilience. It is never easy for any
of us to resign ourselves to being "not as good" in anything. It
is that much more difficult for children with learning disabilities to accept that they are stuck with being lousy at something that most other children do well, or at least better than
they do.

I asked my daughter, Joanna, to read your question and answer it. An eighth grader, she has a language disability and attends a school for children with learning disabilities. She read it and said, "This is a tough one. It isn't too late to help them, but you have to help them without them knowing it." I agree with her. The supports for these children need to be invisibly in place, a respected part of the regular routine of school. Everyone should treat extra help as an ordinary part of childhood for most children, even if there are differences in the amount of help a child receives. By middle school all children hate being different, and children with disabilities feel that as strongly as any child. That is why Joanna fought ferociously against being pulled out of class for special tutoring. She didn't want to be seen as needing special attention. That's why a school designed exclusively for children with learning disabilities can be such a boon for these students. Everyone gets help. Special needs are the norm.

You do not say whether you are a mainstream teacher or a special education teacher, but I assume that you are a mainstream teacher. You give grades to children, and your students with learning disabilities are certain—even if they are wrong—that their grades are likely to be lower than anyone else's. Many boys defend against low grades by not trying and not caring. They seize negative control of the situation. It is around this time that it is important to read about the life outcomes of learning disabled children; it is important to have adults with language disabilities talk to the children about how they compensated for their troubles.

You might encourage others in the community to take this task to heart. I know of a fast-food restaurant across from a large Midwestern suburban high school, where the owner has created a permanent bulletin board display of famous or accomplished people with learning disabilities. These are faces of rock singers, TV and movie stars, and other adults that children recognize and admire—including the owner of the restaurant. Every day hundreds of students see that display and, whether they struggle with learning disabilities or not, the message they get is an important one: people with learning disabilities are everywhere and, like everyone else, they can grow up to be valued, successful adults.

Getting back to your classroom, the answer to your question is this: It is not too late to help these boys, but you have to get past this phase of denial and resistance. You have to keep giving the children help, making it as much fun and as routine a part of school as assembly, P.E., or recess. Stick with it and don't catch their discouragement from them. You need to have faith in them, even when they have lost it in themselves.

Speaking of
Social Anger and Aggression

Lunchroom Banter Serves Up Social Cruelty

Q: I volunteer in the lunchroom at our junior high school and I've been disturbed by some of the lunchroom banter I hear, especially among the boys in one particular group. They are a group of "popular" boys, and I'd think they wouldn't feel the need to put down other kids, but they are very vocal in the way they tease some of the "nerdy" kids or others who simply aren't in their group. They'll tease these other students about anything and everything, and it hurts me to hear them do this and watch the others suffer the stings of those insults. Why do they feel the need to do this and how could someone here do something to improve the situation?

MGT: Early adolescence is a tough time for boys because their teasing of one another is incessant and at times truly hurtful. In *Raising Cain* we called it the "culture of cruelty" among boys, and it is at its peak between seventh grade and tenth grade. When you ask boys about the constant insults, they often dismiss it as teasing, having fun, nothing serious. But when you work with boys in therapy they are much more honest about it. It can be extremely painful.

One teacher, recalling middle school, said to me, "It was kill or be killed every day." He wasn't talking about actual fights, though that is a reality among boys in many schools; he was talking about the psychological experience of being a middle school boy. You have to be constantly on your guard.

The most painful aspect for boys is that they attack each other's masculinity constantly, and the leaders are very often the popular boys who are in a power position that allows them to define what is cool and what is nerdy, what is masculine and what is not.

Why does this happen? There are two reasons: one biological and the other cultural. Many social scientists believe that patterns of boy behavior at this age are analogous to social dominance patterns among animals. Young male elk spar constantly, chickens have a "pecking order," wolves create a hierarchy with high-status males and low-status males. Young male chimps fight and wrestle until they establish a dominance hierarchy in which every young male knows his place, whom he can beat and whom he cannot beat. There is research to suggest that boys create the same dominance hierarchy patterns. Because we are human, the patterns are much more complex, but what you see in the lunchroom is fairly straightforward: the high-status males rehearsing their contempt for the lower-status males.

From a psychological point of view, what is happening is that boys are trying to define masculinity. Masculinity is a social construction, it is not a biological given, and it is very hard for boys to define. Furthermore, from the beginning of their childhoods they have understood that you have to pass some tests to become masculine, but our society does not actually provide the tests, and the criteria for becoming a man are uncertain. And so the way boys define masculinity is in the narrowest and meanest possible way. They enforce on one another an extremely stereotyped version of the male ideal. Size, strength, and verbal cruelty are considered good; anything tender, compassionate, thoughtful, or artistic is considered feminine and dangerous. Without a clear definition of male, boys build themselves up at the expense of others. They are creating tests—tests of physical prowess or verbal cruelty—to prove they are masculine and to demonstrate that other boys are not as masculine as they are.

The difficulty with masculinity is that it is a fragile concept. You can lose it easily by failing any test. In the past when I have asked high school boys what it means to be a man, they have said, "You have to be ready to fight at any time." Many boys believe that for a period of years in high school. A lot of energy goes into posturing, threatening, and especially social cruelty.

Do boys everywhere experiment with social cruelty? In my experience, they all do, but setting makes a huge difference. Families that homeschool their children tell me over and over that they do not see this kind of cruelty in their children. There is no doubt that putting kids in junior high schools increases the peer pressure and teasing among boys. There is less of it, much less of it, in well-staffed neighborhood schools or well-staffed smaller private schools. The key phrase is "well-staffed" and by that I mean not only plenty of teachers and support staff, but a watchful, supportive, responsive staff that is alert to this kind of behavior. Intervention by trusted adults—parents, coaches, and caring teachers—can make a real difference. If a teacher or coach takes a stand against teasing, it diminishes, though it never disappears entirely.

The constant tension in working with early adolescents is allowing them some space in which to exercise their autonomy, while at the same time monitoring the group so that they do not brutalize each other with verbal cruelty. It is an unending task in middle schools and junior highs. From the point of view of a psychologist, it is the most important thing that adults can do for boys because if boys receive too much of this teasing, hazing, and intimidation, it can traumatize them. All men have gone through this treatment. Many men remain guarded, wary, and friendless because of the ferocity of the teasing they received when they were in middle school.

On the offending side, if boys are in the position of dishing out insensitivity or cruelty routinely with no negative consequences, then they learn to be bullies, if not with their fists, then with their social clout. It's bad training.

The actor Dustin Hoffman said in an interview that all of his life he had been trying to recover from the cruelty he experienced in middle school because of being small and an actor. He said it with real feeling. I have heard many men say this. When I asked a group of men whether they thought some of the hazing and teasing they received had helped strengthen them, they said "yes." When I asked them whether they would like their sons to go through what they did, the men said, "Well, maybe 50 percent of what we experienced." I understood them to be saying that boy life is twice as cruel as it should be for good mental health. That boys do not thrive with all the teasing they receive in junior high and high school. We need to have smaller schools with lower student-teacher ratios. We need to not accept cruelty as an inevitable or necessary part of turning boys into men. We have to keep boys safe in schools, on teams, wherever they gather in groups. If we do, they will become more loving and compassionate men.

Managing Anger: Everyday Strategies and More Spackle

Q: Our house is "decorated" with fist-size holes and other damage from the times our son has lost his temper and kicked a door or wall or put his fist through a wall. He is not violent toward other people, but when he gets very frustrated or angry, he hits things, slams things down, or kicks the wall or door. It didn't do much damage when he was five years old, but he's fifteen now and our repair bill is going up. Neither my husband nor I are physical in this way, so we don't know where he's picked this up, but we know it needs to stop. How can we help our son find more acceptable ways to vent his anger?

MGT: Over the past two years I have asked the men in my audiences of parents and teachers how many of them hit or kicked walls when they were growing up, and it is always a majority that raises their hands. This must be a very common form of male expression. Boys and young men need to signal how incredibly angry they are and they need to let us know that they *could* hit someone if they wanted to, that they are fully capable of—as they put it—"really doing some damage to someone." However, they also want us to know that they can control themselves and not take their anger out on people. So the compromise is the wall. Fair enough.

There are two things that concern me about your son. The first is that you say the walls are "decorated" with damage. Has this become a habit of which he is proud? There is a time to begin to get control of this impulse, and fifteen is not a bit too early. We do not want him to become so accustomed to hitting things that he damages the walls of his dorm in college or frightens people outside of his home.

I knew a young man in college who, in his distress over his

breakup with a girlfriend and his frustration with her refusal to talk to him, went and pounded on her locked dormitory door. She was inside and extremely frightened. She called the campus police and when they arrived he was in big trouble. Though he later said he had never intended to hurt her, and did not even do much physical damage to the door, his explosive behavior terrified the people around him. Whether he meant it or not, his actions communicated a threat to the girl and everyone around him that night. He wasn't venting his anger in the privacy of his own home, with understanding, accommodating parents there. In the outside world, his angry, aggressive behavior was taken at face value and he had to deal with a dorm full of frightened students and the campus police. Though he was not a violent person, the college held him accountable for his behavior and asked him to take a year off.

You need to talk with your son about the way he handles anger and your concerns for him and others. If he is making a habit of these angry displays, he is headed for trouble in the "outside world." You need to help him develop some more self-control.

How can you do that? Start by asking him straight out if he is able and willing to get a grip on this behavior or if he needs help to do so. Ask him in a calm and lucid moment, and explain why it is important. If he is ready to give it up—and most boys do want to manage their anger in more acceptable ways—then give him help to do so.

Steps in managing anger include recognizing the feelings that lead to anger, stalling the impulse to act in anger (the old advice to "count to 10" is good advice), and finding other ways to express anger or defuse it. Can you review with your son those times that he has felt angry and has been able to restrain himself? Under what conditions is he able to identify his feelings and when can he not do so? Once your son understands the sequence of his own mounting feelings, ask him to come up with a few specific strategies he feels are practical for him when he feels anger building. Can he walk away, walk on the treadmill, take a run around the block, or go for a swim? I always start by asking a boy what has worked for him in the past when he has been able to control his temper and build from there.

Let him know that from now on, if he damages property at home, he deals with the consequences. If he puts a hole in the wall, he's going to have to repair it and make reparations for any upset or inconvenience to others.

For the damage already done, buy him some spackle and paint and present him with the tools and the opportunity to make repairs. If he balks at the task, then hold off some other privilege—such as using the car, or being driven somewhere he wants to go—until the work is done.

Most boys don't want to live as angry young men. They'd rather feel in control of their emotions than feel out of control. If the situation doesn't improve, talk with the school social worker or psychologist for additional help. I'd like to see your son get the help he needs at home or from school rather than get matters explained to him by a police officer, the hard way.

Bully or Bullied: Finding the Roots of Aggression

Q: Jim is just eight years old, but already he's getting a reputation as a boy who hits first and talks later—if at all. He is constantly getting in trouble at school, and his teachers tell us we need to do something about it, but what can we do besides tell him he shouldn't hit other kids? The other kids are no angels, and when they tease him or cross him in some way, he feels justified in putting them in their place. My husband doesn't seem to think this is a big problem. He says Jim will outgrow it. How can we tell if this kind of bullyish behavior is just a phase?

MGT: Your son is either a bully because he wants to push people around and be "top dog," or he's pushing people around because he's been bullied and is striking back. There's a difference between a child who is regularly hitting as a strategy, and one who is regularly hitting after being teased. It's important to know which feelings are prompting him to hit other children, and here's why. If he is at the bottom of the social pecking order of boys in his class, and he is being teased or humiliated in the many ways boys do this to each other, then he is rapidly becoming a rejected, aggressive boy. He is reacting angrily to the rejection and cruelty he feels from his peers. That's not just a phase; it's a position he can get locked into in school, and it can be very damaging for his adjustment to school and for his personality.

If, however, your son is already considered a "popular"

boy, one of the leaders in his circle of friends, or one of those with a fairly high status in the pecking order, then it is likely he's choosing physical aggression as a bid for greater popularity. He needs to know that it's a losing strategy.

The research literature on children's groups shows that children eventually turn against children who use aggressive methods for solving problems. An aggressive child may impress people and have a following for a short time, but ultimately the group moves away from him and isolates him for the simple reason that they're scared of him. If this is your son, I am worried that he will have a lonely life and fewer and fewer friends. Another recent study shows that 30 percent of popular boys in the class are aggressive and do antisocial things—act out in negative ways, tease, or treat others harshly—but that the vast majority of the popular kids, 70 percent, represented students who use "win-win" social strategies for solving problems. So if your son is using aggression to gain popularity, he's using a low-percentage strategy.

The key to solving the aggression problem lies in identifying what it is your son is experiencing about school, home, or himself that makes him want to respond this way. Boys don't take an aggressive stand at school for no reason at all. I can't tell what the source of that anger is, based on your description, and perhaps you don't know either. But it is important to find out what his perception of boyhood or school or the social climate is that makes him think this is a way to solve problems. Many other children don't solve problems this way.

If you aren't sure what your boy is so angry about, you find out by looking at what's going on in three places: home, school, and his inner life.

You begin by talking with him—if he will talk to you about his life at school—and to school personnel. Your son may tell you all about it, about the humiliation he feels every day at school, or about his ambitions to be one of the top guys in the cool group. If he won't divulge much about his school environment or feelings, ask his teacher. The teachers know, and if they don't, they can make a point of watching carefully to see whether your son is lower or higher in the social pecking order.

Aggression at school is often a mirror image of something happening at home. Ask yourself about his experience of life at home: Does he experience you two parents as harshly critical of him? Do either of you routinely shout at him? Do you have expectations of him that are so high he is never able to meet them? Does he feel he's always being clobbered by an older brother? Could it be internal—an ambitious boy who cannot accept that he is okay as he is?

You can't understand aggression until you have the answers to those questions. Once you identify what is fueling your son's aggression, you can take steps to change what's going on. Enlist the teacher's help again. Tell your son that the adults in his life are cooperating to help him solve his problem. If he is reacting to what he perceives as a group threat against him, then the teachers need to be aware that school doesn't feel like a very safe place for him.

If you and his teachers understand the social situation and

communicate that to him, it will help him feel understood and that is inherently therapeutic. He may also need more focused help than that—counseling at school, perhaps in a friendship group or, in some cases, private therapy. Your son is young enough to respond quickly to helpful changes in the school or home environment. But boys of any age will benefit from the same process of discovery—identifying the source of emotional experience that is prompting the aggression, and changing it.

While it is true that many boys have fights at some time in their childhoods and many men remember the one or two or three times they fought in school, it is often not a cherished memory. It is a very scary memory that gets turned into a chestnut of a story, polished and retold until it shines. Underneath the shine is fear, because fights are scary and should not be a normal part of the school day. It is worrisome if a boy is engaging in fighting as a strategy to maintain his popular status; it is equally troubling if a boy is fighting because he feels so rejected.

Are Schools Overreacting to "Idle Threats"?

Q: A boy my son knows was recently suspended for making idle comments about "blowing up" some kids who tease him at school. I know this boy and just don't believe he ever would have done such a thing, but other parents I know have said nothing in his defense. I think adults—and now kids, too—are overreacting to the kinds of things kids have said for

238 Speaking of Social Anger and Aggression

years about people who bug them. How can we do a better
job of identifying the kids who are likely to do something like
that and the ones who are just letting off steam with macho
threats?

MGT: The way to better differentiate between boys who are
actually aggressive and potentially a danger to the community and those boys who are just engaging in macho "trash
talk" is to actually sit down and discuss things with the boys.
You need to find out what was going on inside the boy's mind
when he made his threat. In order to do that, you have to
take all threats seriously, at least at the start. If we dismiss
boys' threats as meaningless or say, "he's really a good kid;
he'd never do a thing like that," we deprive boys of the sense
that people are listening to what they say, and for some boys
that is an invitation to up the ante.

Since the shootings at Columbine High School and the
prior shootings in Pearl, Mississippi, and Springfield, Ore-
gon, educators in schools have been jumping all over boys
who say threatening or aggressive things. Suddenly educators
seem to have lost their sense of perspective and their sense of
humor. They appear to be overreacting, as you say in your
question. I have a different point of view. I think that educators were underreacting in the past. I welcome the change.
It is important for us to take verbal aggression seriously
because a school climate that permits a great deal of verbal
aggression is ultimately going to tolerate higher levels of
physical aggression.

Look at what happens when two basketball players start trash-talking at one another in a basketball game. First they make passing comments, then they hurl insults, then they get toe-to-toe and nose-to-nose, and then they start pushing and ultimately fighting. If the referecs don't get in between the two players early on in these exchanges, the likelihood of violence is increased. It is the same in any other sport; it is the same in schools.

In my view, one of the problems in schools in the United States is that teachers have become discouraged about their own effectiveness in addressing behavior problems in children, and they have begun to doubt that parents and the wider society will support them, so they do not confront the small problems. In my experience, if you do not address the little things, they soon start to grow. When you are willing to accept a high level of rudeness, and you do not step in until it becomes "serious," then things do become serious. As a society, we have been willing to accept a very high level of verbal aggression among boys and to think of it as harmless and normal. The problem with normalizing boy anger is that you then have to believe that boys saying "I'm going to get you" or "I'm going to kill you" or "You'd better watch out" is perfectly normal. If that is reasonable, then what is unreasonable?

Once you have accepted that a verbal death threat is normal, it is logical to think that all boy threats are intrinsically harmless, unless proved otherwise. In other words, to get your attention, an angry, potentially violent boy has to do something that is physically violent in order to get your full attention. One of the reasons that certain schools have a reputation for peaceful, responsible social behavior by their students is that they address all childhood forms of aggression immediately. Children's anger is taken seriously and met with a moral response. For that reason, children learn how to control it or express it in more civilized ways.

In this country we believe so strongly in individual rights and we have such a fear of "imposing values" on other people that we can become paralyzed about how to create a moral environment for children. Because of the debate over church and state, and the conflict between the rights of the state and the rights of the individual, American schools and educators became conflicted about the business of moral education for about twenty years. I believe society has paid a terrible price for the moral vacuum that has existed in many schools. I don't think that the reintroduction of prayer in public schools is the answer; that is largely a symbolic solution and it gives clout to those who would use their own particular religious beliefs to dominate others. What is needed is an environment that teaches respect and supports the natural moral authority of adults. As Tom Lickona argues in his powerful book *Educating for Character*, a moral school can be based on universal principles such as respect and responsibility.

If you have a school that holds children to the standard of respect and responsibility, then you have moral grounds for suspending a boy who has threatened to "blow up" other kids. At the same time, you also have grounds for speaking to the boys who were teasing him, because what they were doing does not qualify as respect either. Would those boys continue their harassment of a boy if they faced suspension?

We have had a twenty-year increase in violence among young people in the United States. Homicide is the second largest cause of death among teenagers in this country. If this society is going to cut down on boy violence, we have to meet it in all of its manifestations. We cannot rationalize death threats and then be surprised when boys actually do kill each other. We cannot turn a deaf ear to death threats, even from "good kids." Boys need to use different words when they need to "let off steam."

Aggression: Can We Look on the Bright Side?

Q: I hear a lot about aggression being a bad thing, but I think sometimes you have to be aggressive to be a leader or a person who gets things done against the odds. If it weren't for aggressive boys and men, we'd have had nobody willing to fight for our country in generations past. In fact, we wouldn't even have the country we know as the United States today if some aggressive men hadn't kicked some butt a couple hundred years ago. Some very aggressive men become highly valued as top management at big companies. I think aggression has gotten "bad press" and that it's time we recognized its value and let boys be proud of what comes naturally. What do you think?

MGT: Well, I have to say that I disagree with your premise. I am sitting looking at a newspaper and headlines that celebrate aggressive responses in business, sports, politics, and other realms. World Wrestling Federation TV shows are among the highest rated in the country; they consist of extremely large men slamming one another, jumping on one another, and throwing each other out of the ring. Last month I watched the Super Bowl, the most watched sporting event in the United States, and if I recall correctly, twenty-two men dressed up in pads and helmets did their best to knock each other to the ground. Whenever a defender broke through the line and sacked the quarterback, the crowd cheered, the announcers expressed approval, and the player himself pounded his chest like a gorilla. The whole game was very aggressive and, I have to say, I enjoyed it thoroughly.

No, there is a lot of aggression in our society and a great deal of approval for it. If a boy were looking around, he could find plenty of aggressive models. Why is it that you experience people as thinking that aggression is a "bad thing"? I think you are actually talking about parents, teachers, and child psychologists like me. We're the ones who worry about whether there is too much aggression in our society because we worry a lot about whether children are safe in one another's company. And we worry about whether children are going to learn self-control. We worry that the second leading cause of death among teenagers is homicide, and that 95 percent of those murders are committed by boys. I think it is impossible to work with boys and not worry about the aggressive models they see.

There is a difference between activity, aggression, and violence. When it comes to boys, people often confuse these three things. Very active boys are often accused of being aggressive when they are not. At times, real boy violence is rationalized as just being natural aggression, the inevitable result of testosterone, when it is not. We need to understand the difference between the three, and to teach our children the difference between them. Human beings are naturally aggressive; it is a part of our nature. I also believe that some human beings are more aggressive than others. Because that is so, a civilized society has to protect the less aggressive members of its society from the more aggressive members. You should not be able to get ahead in society by killing people, for example. We love movies like *The Godfather*, which are about murderous people, but we do not actually want these people for our neighbors. We don't want to be their victims. We want a society that protects us and regulates aggression and violence.

Boys are more active than girls and they certainly enjoy a kind of physical interaction that girls do not. They like to wrestle and they seem to enjoy a kind of competition that most girls do not. Beyond those simple observations, however, I can only say that boys get incredibly mixed messages about aggression right from the beginning of their lives. Their preschool teachers say, "Use your words, not your hands."

We take our boys to Sunday school, where they are taught to be kind and moral. They then watch certain famous athletes and superstars break all the "rules" and realize that such behavior is considered entertaining. They watch hockey players high-stick one another and commit illegal checks that injure other players. They are told not to harass girls, but when they do, very little, if anything, is done. And they are often left alone to tease and torment other boys. Many of them have fathers who tell them to settle their conflicts with other boys by hitting back. Many boys are in intense conflict about their own aggressive impulses, and too many of them commit violent crimes in their late teens and early twenties. Is that the result of the glorification of aggression in our society?

Many adults rationalize boy violence as inevitable, the result of a biological destiny for boys. Whenever I hear those arguments, I always counter with this fact: in 1996, there were two handgun murders in New Zealand, fifteen in Japan, and thirty in Great Britain; that same year there were over ninety-three hundred handgun deaths in the United States. The boys and men in New Zealand have testosterone, and so do the men in England. This statistic standing alone suggests that violence is culturally mediated. It is perfectly apparent to me that we are an unusually aggressive and dangerous culture.

We have to decide how much our "aggression" is necessary to us. You believe that we have to have boys and men ready to become warriors. I would argue, based on historical writing like Stephen Ambrose's *Citizen Soldiers*, that all men will fight in a just cause. Peace-loving men will fight to support a moral mission like World War II; most men won't fight effectively to win a war that is unjust. You argue that aggressive men succeed in business. I think there is a lot to support your point of view. But it is also clear that scientists with new discoveries, creative thinkers, gifted engineers, and talented team builders also succeed in business. How much genius is responsible and how much credit we should give to aggression is, I think, open to question.

Boy Violence: When Connections Count

Q: Every time there is a school shooting or other violence by boys reported in the media, we see a lot of stories about how the schools are trying to do different things to identify dangerous students before they do damage. But I have a hard time relating all this in any useful way to my own son, who is thirteen. I know he's not building bombs in our basement, but he complains sometimes about teachers or other kids being unfair or mean. I figure that is pretty normal stuff, but how can you tell when it's something to be concerned about? If boys are reluctant to talk about their feelings, and our son is, are there signs that we as parents can watch for to tell us if he—or a friend—is seriously troubled enough to hurt other people?

MGT: Boys do not suddenly explode in violence for no reason and without any warning signs at all. Please remember that after the shootings at Columbine High School, numerous students described gunman Eric Harris as an angry boy, a scary boy. Someone you didn't want to go near. Please remember that Eric Harris had written threatening messages on his Web site and that some folks in town had been sufficiently alarmed that they had reported it to the local police, who clearly felt that there was nothing they could do. There were many warning signs from at least one of those boys. The problem is that the people closest to them did not recognize the seriousness of the signs, or chose to deny them, and others, such as the police or neighbors who had reason to believe they were dangerous, did not feel empowered to intervene in their lives. In almost every situation of boy violence that I have read about, someone was worried about the boy before the violent incident took place.

The secret to stopping boy violence is not to develop better checklists for identifying potentially dangerous boys; it is for adults to be emotionally connected to all boys, so that when something is going wrong emotionally with a young man, someone senses it and does something about it. We have to have smaller high schools, where everyone feels accountable for knowing the students. At the boys' school where I work, we—teachers, coaches, administrators, nurse, and psychologist—are all so connected to the students (sometimes annoyingly so, from their point of view) that we know which boys we are not reaching. If we aren't in emotional contact with a boy, we redouble our efforts and notify his parents repeatedly that we are not connecting with him. If he then does anything scary, there is both a disciplinary and a mental health response.

But I am talking about schools, and you are asking for advice as a parent. Are there things a parent can do? Yes, absolutely. First of all, you have to watch for signs of angry or violent behavior. Has he hit people? Has he gotten into fights? Has he ever hurt anyone? If he has hurt someone, did he feel or express remorse? Does he collect guns and knives? Does he say threatening or cruel things to people? Is he fascinated by brutal and dangerous characters from movies or TV?

Second, you have to look for signs of poor mental health or social trouble. Is he withdrawn and sad much of the time? Does he like school? Does he have energy for a job or extracurricular activities? Does he have friends? Does he get invited to participate in weekend activities with other kids? If he is lonely, sad, angry, or isolated, he could be suffering from depression or some other mental illness, and should be evaluated.

Third, you have to look for positive signs. The absence of these can be as worrisome as the presence of negative signs. Does he spend time with the family? Even though there may be occasional conflict, does he have a good relationship with his brothers and sisters? Does he have fun when his cousins or his uncle come over? Does he want to do things with his father or you, such as fishing, watching TV, or following a local sports team, that he used to do when he was younger (a person's love and loyalty for his local sports team or his family should not disappear when he becomes an adolescent). Is there a trustworthy adult outside the family whom he respects and whose company he seeks? Does he have a part-time job? Does his boss like him?

Though many adolescents begin to develop a life outside the family and are not as much a presence there as they used to be, they should maintain a good relationship with some adult somewhere. If there are almost no positive signs in your son, you should be worried.

Fourth, I believe that most parents—unless they are mentally disturbed themselves—know in their gut if their child is troubled and dangerous. It is not unusual for adolescents to talk less than they used to with their parents. However, a dangerous or potentially violent teenager is unusual, and he acts in unusual ways. A loving parent will see that her or his son is acting differently than other boys and will be worried. The only question then is whether that parent has the courage to ask for help with the child from relatives, teachers, guidance counselors, ministers, and even police officers before something terrible happens.

Speaking of
Boys in Trouble

Golf-Cart Boy a Local Hero

Q: Last summer a ten-year-old boy in our neighborhood stole a golf cart from the golf course and took off driving down a major city thoroughfare. Eventually the police pulled him over and that was that. Fortunately no one was hurt. The problem is that my son, who is nine, speaks about this boy and his prank as if he is some kind of hero. I don't want to say anything bad about the boy. I don't think he's a bad kid, but what he did was wrong and dangerous, and really pretty stupid. How can I help my son understand that this is not a kid to emulate?

MGT: You're right, of course. It is dangerous, it is wrong. But I am sitting here smiling a big smile. Why does it make me grin whenever I picture this boy driving down the street in his golf cart? Why do I, like your son, kind of admire this boy? Why do I, vicariously, get a kick out of what he did? You see, I was mostly a very "good boy" growing up. I was cautious and paid attention to what adults said. I was an altar boy in church and carried the cross in the processional and tried to sit still through the entire service. If I broke even a small rule it made me anxious, so I didn't break too many (in my own defense, I did break some—I don't want to give the mistaken impression that I was a total goody-goody).

But in my own mind, I wanted to be bolder and freer. Have you never had the impulse to jump into something and drive away? Have you never been drawn to a golf cart? Just for a little spin? They look like fun, don't they? Have you never had the momentary thought, "The door to that police car is open and the motor is running, I could get in and drive away!" Can you imagine the look on the policeman's face?

Boys are more impulsive and physically restless than girls. By school age, three-quarters of the boys in a class are active and developmentally immature in comparison to girls of the same age. That's boys. That's the way they are made. Their physical approach to life makes some of them—not all of them—into risk takers and it turns the rest of boys, the cautious good boys, into the admirers of risk takers. For boys, the game is all about pulling the chain of the serious people. And who are the serious people in every boy's life? His parents.

Let's take James Bond, for example. In all the James Bond

movies there is a scene where the secret service technical guy, named Q, is showing James the car that is outfitted with all the whizbang devices: rockets, shields, machine guns, fins for going in the water, etc. And he says, without a smile (just like a parent), "This is the only one of its kind, James, you need to be very careful with it. Don't take any chances with it." And it makes us laugh, because you know he is just going to wreck it. He is going to be utterly, charmingly, wildly reckless. That's what we love about James Bond movies. He's the biggest boy of them all!

Now, does this mean that your son is going to steal a golf cart? I doubt it. Does this mean your son is going to do something dangerous and reckless? If he isn't a risk-taking sort of guy, I don't think he is going to start now. You would know by the age of nine whether he is or he isn't. If he is, you have to rein him in. You have to keep an eye on him. But I'm imagining that your son is a pretty steady, good boy. Now why does he admire the golf-cart thief? Because he's yanking your chain. Whenever he voices his admiration, you get serious. Your brow knits and you look worried, just like Q. And for a moment he gets to think, "Can you imagine the look on my mom's (or dad's) face, if I did something like that? She'd go crazy." And just that feeling makes a boy feel more powerful, more boy, and momentarily very happy.

Home Alone: Too Much Freedom at Thirteen?

Q: I am a divorced, single mother, who works full time to support myself and my thirteen-year-old son, Mark. We've been on our own since he was five. We moved to a new neighborhood about a year ago, and in the past few months I've begun to have problems with him around some after-school issues. We had an agreement that he wouldn't spend more than an hour on computer games in the afternoon, or use the Internet without my permission, but I've discovered that he's been going on-line without asking. I also believe he's playing games for more than one hour. On top of that, I discovered him experimenting with fireworks in our backyard one day and when I confronted him about it, he hid the evidence and denied it. I'm angry about his lying and about the Internet use, and I'm worried that he's headed for bigger trouble. His father is a deadbeat and nowhere around, and they have no relationship. I can't quit my job to stay home. What can I do?

MGT: I think that Mark has shown that he cannot handle three hours by himself every day. He has shown that he cannot resist the temptations of being home alone. The appropriate consequence is that he needs to get an after-school job, or join an after-school sports activity. He has to be somewhere where he checks in and out with an adult who knows where he is. You should talk to his school guidance counselor and get the names and types of programs that would suit him. Someone good at the school will work with you on this.

The issue here isn't lying, particularly. It isn't even illegal computer use. At the school where I work, we assume that virtually every boy in the school, given the opportunity, would try to download pornography off the Internet. We assume that the vast majority of boys would, given the opportunity, slip off campus, smoke dope, or drink alcohol. That's what most boys do when they have the time and the means. That doesn't mean they are going to turn out to be criminals. Far from it. It means that they are trying to do things that make them feel grown-up and we have to keep them young and focused for a few more years.

If you don't already know how to search his computer to see what he has been seeing and downloading, ask at the school office for the name of someone who can teach you how. You should know what he does on the computer and he should know that you know how to gain access. Anybody sophisticated with computers can teach you how.

Once Mark works for a semester, or does a winter sport, or performs some community service, he should be able to earn back your trust. Until then, he should have something to do after school. His choice, as long as it is adult supervised.

This is the toughest kind of problem for a single mom. My heart goes out to you. I just don't want you to think that this is necessarily pre-criminal behavior. It is not.

Mailbox Vandalism and Lessons in Justice

Q: Our fifteen-year-old son was walking home from school one day with some boys from his class, and one of them kicked down a mailbox. The home owner reported it to the school and the boy got into big trouble—but so did our son, even though he didn't kick the box down. How can we teach our son to respect the law when it treated him unfairly?

MGT: Adolescent boys between the ages of twelve and seventeen commit the vast majority of public vandalism in the United States. When boys are together they have—to use the jargon of psychology—a "disinhibiting" effect on one another. That is, the presence of a group can encourage boys to do stupid and reckless things. Sometimes the encouragement is overt, with conscious planning or with boys shouting to one another, "Yeah, do it. I dare you!" Sometimes the encouragement is subtler, with boys giving approval or being impressed by the antisocial acts of one boy.

I don't know your son, and I am sorry to be so suspicious, but I always wonder what role the group played in licensing one boy to commit a reckless act. What were the boys saying to each other just before one of them kicked a mailbox down? What was the mood of the group? Anyone who lives in a rural area knows that teenage boys regularly play "mailbox baseball," that is, knocking mailboxes off their posts with a baseball bat from a moving car. They do this to show they are strong, have no regard for rules, and are willing to risk getting caught by the police in order to demonstrate their toughness. Boys are often looking for tests to pass in order to prove their manhood. Committing small crimes, getting drunk, taking drugs, and having early sexual experiences with girls are some of the classic ways that boys demonstrate their strength in this and many other cultures.

Because the pressure to do these things is so strong among all boys, in the schools where I consult, there is always some presumption of collective guilt when boys are together and antisocial acts are committed. I am sure that this philosophy of "guilt by association" is wrong at times. Sometimes innocent boys are caught in the net with real troublemakers. When that happens, the innocent boys are outraged. However, the problem for teachers and administrators is that boys will rarely tell what really happened. The boy code of honor requires that boys never explain what went on in the group or what led up to the vandalistic act.

When teachers and administrators try to get to the bottom of these incidents, they are enormously frustrated in their efforts to discover the whole truth. Boys lie regularly and systematically in order to keep adults out of their lives. In the end, it is very difficult for a school to be just. School administrators are often left with this option: punishing the group or punishing no one. Other schools have tried to create a legal system that is more analogous to the courts. And such systems soon run into the same problems as the courts: long time delays before a decision is reached, adversarial proceedings, arguments about the nature of evidence. In some of the schools where I work, disciplinary hearings have become so legalistic that there is no quick justice in schools anymore. Most of the "crimes" that are brought to the attention of schools do not require the same level of protection as can be found in the criminal courts. If there is a true crime, it should be handled by the police and the courts. If it remains in the schools, I think everyone—kids included—has to understand that the judgments are going to be an approximate kind of justice.

For adolescents, who can often be intensely idealistic, this kind of justice is disillusioning. However, I am of the belief that learning that justice is not perfect is also an important life lesson. Sometimes life is not just, but it is often merciful. My guess is that the "trouble" your son got into will not harm him in the eyes of his teachers, coaches, or college counselor. If your son is generally a good guy, everyone will know that he was caught up in a group phenomenon and a group punishment. No one is going to hold such an incident against your son in the long run.

I believe you should encourage your son to understand the complexities of justice. I think you have to talk to him about questions of judgment. We all know that if you are caught riding in a car where someone else is drinking or smoking marijuana, you can be prosecuted for the crime. It is important for adolescents to know that when you are in the presence of a crime being committed, you may be implicated. That's a life lesson, too. I hope your son will learn from his experience. Encouraging him in his outrage at the legal system is not helpful to him. I hope you will use his unfortunate experience as a teaching opportunity. Talk to him about the difficulties and complexities of administering justice. He may need some distance from these events before he can fully understand them.

Underachieving High Schooler, Parents Projecting

Q: Our son is a senior in high school, and his laziness at school and at home is driving my husband and me crazy. He's a bright kid and has no reason to do poorly in school, but he has been blowing off his academic work for the past two years. He does the bare minimum of what's required and gets much lower grades than he could. When he learned to drive and got his license, he immediately got several speeding tickets and was put on probation. Now he could drive, but he is so negative, uncooperative, and unresponsive that we've taken away his car privileges because it's the only thing left that we can take away. He used to have friends who were go-getters, but over the past few years he's turned instead to a group of other boys who are clearly unmotivated. He's been hanging with them after school, smoking and doing nothing. We're worried because at the current rate we fear he has the notion that he'll just live at home with us after high school while he "thinks about what he wants to do with his life." We feel that he should get a job now since he's spending so little time on homework and might benefit from seeing what kind of work will be open to him if he doesn't get a college education. One thing that makes us even more concerned is that, although my husband is a very hard worker and a good, kind, and successful man, his brother is the model of a failure—lazy, never left home, and living now at age thirty-five with his mother. One of the teenage cousins in the family—a boy my son is close to—just flunked out of a state university despite being very smart. And my own father was an alcoholic, a lame father, and a failure at making a living as well. My husband and I are desperate that our son not follow in the footsteps of these miserable male family role models. We feel like we're caught in our son's rebellion—against what, we don't know, but we're definitely losing the battles and the war. What can we do to bring about some positive change and help our son get on a more promising path?

MGT: You are right to be worried about your son. Something changed in his psychology a couple of years ago and we do not know why. It is not usual for a good student hanging out with a productive group to suddenly change the way your son has. In terms of high school, it is pretty late in the game and he has lost a lot of time. Luckily, life is long and he can continue to grow and develop. But before that can happen, we have to figure out why he has just been stagnating in his life these past two or three years. There is a mystery here and you need to figure it out. You are on the right track in thinking about a job for him, but first we have to check on a few things, namely, drug use, alcohol abuse, depression, and hidden learning problems. Finally, there is an intergenerational family issue that has to be addressed. After we check on all these other things, it may be that we will discover gold in family therapy.

This is very much the profile of a boy who has been smoking a lot of marijuana in high school. Most kids get bored without a job, without a car, without doing a lot of homework. When they don't get bored, and just continue to float through high school, one has to suspect that there is drug use going on, because one of the leading symptoms of chronic marijuana use is lack of motivation. Have you checked his eyes when he has returned from an evening out? Have you ever found a "bong" in his room? Have you smelled smoke in his room? Do you talk with the parents of these other boys? Are they aware of drug use among this group? I imagine that you have been so disenchanted with his social group that you haven't reached out to the parents of the other boys in it. It is time for you to start. You need to take your concerns to other adults in the community. Have you spoken to your son's guidance counselor or advisor at the high school? Someone in the school should have an idea about this group. There are a significant number of boys who smoke weed before high school every morning. Your son could be one of them.

I don't want to imply that marijuana is the only villain. Alcohol is the usual "drug of choice" in high school. One-third of American adolescents abuse alcohol weekly. That is, they get seriously drunk at least one night a week. Pretty soon their whole focus is on whether they are going to party on the weekend. They often drink on afternoons during the week.

You have a history of alcoholism in your family and genetics seems to predispose some people to alcohol. How much does he drink? Has he ever come home drunk? Have you found empty beer cans in the trash? What do other parents say? You need to know. Please start asking.

It sounds as if your son went through a change in tenth grade. Was there also a change in his mood? Is your son's mood sad? Does he take much pleasure in life? Does he get excited about seeing relatives or old friends of the family? Or is his affect—his demeanor—quite flat? If you never see much change in mood, and he is always "down," he is likely to have a chronic depression. Many people think that normal adolescents are chronically grumpy, uncommunicative, and disinterested in life. Nothing could be further from normal. Normal adolescents have higher "highs" and lower "lows" than adults do. That is, they tend to feel things more acutely than we do (we're boring by comparison). Is there a history of depression in the family? Is this the pattern of the under-achieving uncle or cousin? Has anyone ever suggested your son is depressed? It seems likely to me that he is. The average adolescent depression isn't diagnosed for three years because people label it as "normal" for teenagers. What has happened to your son does not sound normal to me.

One source of depression in high school is hidden learning problems. In my work at a high school, some of the most frequent difficulties that I encounter are undiagnosed non-verbal learning disabilities. Usually, verbal learning disabilities—often called dyslexia—are diagnosed in elementary school because the first-grade teacher sees that a child has trouble learning to read. However, there are *nonverbal* learning difficulties that can remain undetected during elementary school in a child with above-average intelligence. These affect the executive functions of the brain: organization, processing speed, memory, and sometimes visual-spatial and math ability.

Your son might have arrived in high school and as the conceptual and quantitative demands of his courses increased, he might have felt overwhelmed. Like most boys, he would have felt ashamed and not wanted to tell anyone. These silent and hard-to-identify learning troubles often haunt boys in ninth and tenth grade. The teachers are baffled as well. They say to me, "He's a talker, but he's so disorganized. He can't get his homework in!" If the adults are confused and the boy ashamed, he is likely to feel as if he is defective and he will start to avoid things; he will become invisible in high school. It sounds as if this has happened to your son.

Finally, there is an intergenerational family mystery at work here. Why is it that someone in each generation of your family has turned out to be a total non-producer? We have identified alcohol and depression as possible suspects. What are other people in the family doing to "enable" the drinker or the depressed person? Does the family need a non-contributor? If so, why? Does having someone to look after serve some purpose for the caretakers in the family? I don't know for sure, but it sounds to me as if there might be some family collusion in this history of non-performance. It is worth looking into.

I need to return to your suggestion of a job for him, perhaps as a lesson in why college is important. I'm less interested in a job as a moral teaching than as a direct source of self-esteem. I do think that a job is often the most effective antidepressant that a teenager can take. The structure, the limits and demands (you can't perform at a job when you're smoking weed), and most especially, the paycheck can really help a young man's self-respect. I encourage you to support your son in getting a job. He needs to feel effective in the world. I would make his use of the family car contingent on his earning a paycheck. If he wants to stay at home after high school, it should be on the condition that he has steady work.

I would suggest that you talk to a number of other adults about your son, starting with his guidance counselor and ending up with a family therapist. You need to get a lot of consultation. My guess is that a few years ago your son—like so many American teenagers—invited you out of his life. As a result, you have felt disqualified. When the Carnegie Commission on Adolescence interviews late adolescents, age nineteen and twenty, and asks them what would have been most helpful to them during their adolescent years, they say, "More parental involvement in my life." The tragedy of teenagers is that they drive their parents away, their parents don't have enough information about them, and then the child fails to thrive. It is never too late to help your child.

Not So Sweet: Smoking at Sixteen

Q. We have suspected that our sixteen-year-old son is smoking cigarettes at school, and recently he admitted to us that he does. My wife went nuts over this and acts as though he has been doing drugs or something. I don't want him to smoke but I think it's just a phase and not a big thing to get worked up over. How can we respond to this in a way that makes the punishment "fit the crime"?

MGT: In your question you say that your wife has reacted "as if" your son had been doing drugs. You imply that cigarettes are fundamentally different from drugs. I don't believe that they are. He is inhaling a kind of drug. Nicotine is an addictive substance and it is more powerfully addictive for the young smoker than for an older smoker. The research is quite clear that the earlier a child smokes, and the more he smokes at a young age, the more likely he is to develop smoking as a lifelong habit. That is why it is very optimistic and perhaps foolish to expect that his smoking is just "a phase." I am in your wife's camp with respect to the seriousness of your son's smoking habit.

On the other hand, I do not think it will help him if you treat cigarette smoking as a "crime" deserving punishment. If he is buying them, he is, of course, breaking the law, and the person who is selling him the cigarettes is also breaking the law, at least in many states. However, when parents treat

smoking as a crime and become the police in their own
house, it usually turns into a battle of wills that the boy wins.
It becomes an issue of autonomy for a boy and he becomes
highly motivated to stay with it in order to prove his independence from his parents' judgments. Such a battle can make
family life terrible.

You should do two things. First, as a health matter, you
should restrict his smoking, so that it does not threaten the
lungs of anyone else in the house. Second, you should discuss
with him whether you can offer him any incentive to not
smoke. The former is both common sense and the law in
many communities. Smoking isn't allowed on airplanes or in
airports or in many restaurants because the research is clear
that breathing secondhand smoke is a serious health risk. By
enforcing these rules, you protect nonsmoking family members. You also make smoking difficult and uncomfortable by
forbidding it in the house and punishing infractions of that
rule. If he wants to continue smoking, he will have to do it
outside in the rain or in winter weather. It may not stop him,
but it may help him to cut down.

As for offering him an incentive: it is my experience that
no one gives up an addiction without a powerful reason. It
may be that if you wait, a girlfriend whom he wants to kiss
will tell him she hates the smell of smoke on his breath.
That's a powerful incentive for him to give up smoking
(though I've known dedicated smokers who would dump
such a girlfriend), but you cannot count on this happening.

He might find a girlfriend who smokes, and then they'll support each other's addictive habit. You should be proactive.

My advice would be to try incentives for not smoking. I have known parents who have negotiated incentives for a no-smoking pledge such as more driving time in the family car. Others have used cash incentives to good effect. And others have offered special trips or other purchases they know are longed for. I think such deals are more effective than punishments for the simple reason that behavioral psychology has conclusively demonstrated that rewards are more powerful than punishments in changing human behavior. Some people think of this as bribing your children. I disagree. I always remember that B. F. Skinner, the father of behavioral psychology, used to say that everyone criticized him for his mechanistic theory of rewards and punishments, but he wondered how many people would show up for work if they weren't given a paycheck. We all respond to incentives. I think of it as putting your money behind your beliefs, and there is no shame in that.

Drinking: How, When, and Where for a Sixteen-Year-Old Boy?

Q. We recently were surprised to discover that our son, who is sixteen, drinks an occasional beer when he goes out with friends or at some of their homes. In more than one situation, the parents actually offer it to them! Our son told us, "It's no big deal. I use it a lot less than other kids and I never drive when I've been drinking." When we expressed our displeasure with one of the parents who provides it at his home, this father said that he'd rather the boys drink at home "where it's safe" than feel they have to sneak around to do it. His position makes some kind of sense, but we really don't want our son drinking or hanging out in a group of boys who are drinking at home or anywhere else. Are we being unreasonable with our concerns? These aren't "bad" kids and we don't want to keep our son from his friends. How can we handle this situation diplomatically?

MGT: Sixteen-year-old boys do things to demonstrate that they are daring young men and independent of their parents. Given our culture's definition of masculinity and the multitude of messages they receive that drinking is part of the rite of passage from boyhood to manhood, it is not surprising that your son is drinking occasionally with his friends. The vast majority, something over 80 percent, of high school seniors have had a drink by the time they graduate from high school. The ironic fact is that your son and his friends are, in a sense, making themselves dependent on a father who seems excited to break the laws and prove himself to be cool. But this is lost on most boys in the early going. (Kids like to feel cool and be protected. That's why they go to malls.) They don't respect him and will tire of him soon enough.

I understand that you do not want him to be drinking anywhere. I understand that you cannot sanction what the other parent is doing. You have to remember that your son has grown up in a culture that defines drinking as grown-up, and especially as masculine behavior. If your son is successful in school, participates in extracurricular activities, treats his family well, and has some goals in life, then he is going to have a hard time understanding why his drinking is problematic. You will need to explain that underage drinking is illegal, and that this is a matter of respect for the law, for the safety of himself and others, and for parents. If you drink alcohol at home and still meet your responsibilities, it is going to be even more difficult to make the case to him. Then you will be thrown back on the law, or respect for parents, or some other principle. The problem here is that part of the appeal *is* breaking the law. As the French playwright Jean Cocteau observed, "The joy of the young is to disobey."

I think you can disapprove of his drinking and still not choose to go over him with a fine-tooth comb when he returns to the house. If, on the other hand, he comes home drunk, or you suspect he has been driving drunk, or getting into a car with someone who is drunk, then I would throw the book at him. Warn him in advance what the punishment will be, so there are no surprises, and if he violates your rules, take his car keys away for a month. If he is doing badly in school, I would pick that as the battle. All of the teachers I have worked with in high schools know that kids drink and accept that as a fact of life. What the best teachers do is challenge students to make them accountable. So do coaches. So should you. When I have worked in boarding schools, the dorm parents are aware that kids will attempt to drink in the dorms. The dorm parents work to make it as difficult as possible for kids to do that without being caught. So should you.

There is a ritualistic drama that I believe should go on between adolescents and their parents. They play their role and we play ours. They will always win, because they have more energy and ingenuity than we do. They are going to grow up and drink and have sex and spend their money the way they want. That's what adults do. All you can do is slow them down to give them a chance for their judgment to mature.

Speaking of
Sports

Baseball Player Plays Safe

Q: Our son is eleven and has been on the park district softball team for several years. We are concerned because he can't stand to lose, which means he goes into a funk whenever the team loses or even when he makes a mistake. We've also noticed that more and more he tries to play it safe rather than take risks to score, even when it would make sense to do so. How can we get him to just enjoy sports and not be so tied up in winning or playing it safe all the time?

MGT: You can get your son to not care so much about sports just as soon as American culture stops measuring a boy's masculinity by his participation in athletics. Until that happens—and I'm not holding my breath while I wait—your son is

going to feel what many boys feel when they step on the athletic field, i.e., that they have to prove through their athleticism that they are strong boys who will become formidable
men. I believe your son tenses up in baseball because his
manhood is on the line and he is entering a very self-
conscious stage in life.

Every boy is defined by athletics, whether he likes it or
not, whether he is good at them or not. Coordinated boys
who like sports enjoy very high status in boy circles; they become the early leaders of the pack in elementary school.
They organize the games at recess and have the right to ex-
clude boys who aren't good at games. Most boys want to play
with the athletic set and most do, even if they are not gifted.
It is only the timid and the very uncoordinated who avoid
such games from the beginning.

Boys of moderate ability are in a bind, however, and I
am imagining that your son is in that large group of boys
clumped around average. As time goes on, it becomes apparent that they are not as naturally athletic as the top tier of
boys are. When they are younger, in first and second grade,
they just want to run, to work off energy, and to be included,
and they will participate without self-consciousness. As the
years go by, they will begin to measure their abilities more
realistically against those of the truly gifted boys. It is around
fourth grade that boys "get it" that they are not likely to suddenly become good at baseball, for example, even if they
earnestly wish to be.

This more realistic self-assessment is painful for boys. It is hard for a boy to realize that he is not going to be good at math, or in social studies, but neither of those areas of expertise affects his standing as a boy. It is very likely that in a boy's mind, in your son's mind, baseball really counts in his self-esteem. His caution is then understandable. He is protecting his self-esteem by playing a cautious game of baseball. At least he can't screw up too badly; at least he won't make a fool of himself.

Better to stay on first than risk stealing second and get thrown out *in front of everyone*. What if your teammates and your coach don't approve of the risk you've taken? What if they think it was a bad strategy? Then you'll look like a dork! Then you will be responsible for the team's losing!

At eleven a boy is also beginning to picture himself standing alone in the world. He is no longer surrounded and buffered by his mom and dad and his brothers and sisters. As he begins to define himself as grown-up or "on his own" he suddenly becomes more psychologically alone than he has ever been. That feeling is going to be accentuated in a sport like baseball, where you literally stand alone at the plate or out in the field.

I don't know if you have tried it, but I assure you that standing at the plate waiting to bat is one of the most solitary experiences in life. Hitting the ball is one of the more difficult athletic feats there is (remember that very great hitters only get a hit 33 percent of the time). Many boys get quite anxious at the plate and remain anxious while they play baseball, knowing that they are going to have to return to the plate and try again. They may feel self-conscious about their throwing arm and worry that they will mess up on a crucial throw. Once you get started worrying about your performance in baseball, there is so much to occupy your mind.

There is also the developmental issue of wanting so much more than you can actually deliver. Learning to live with who you are and what you can actually do is an achievement of adulthood. Until you make peace with your limitations and come to fully enjoy your strengths, you may always be in something of a struggle with yourself. Boys of this age are often full of dreams, and tormented by their perfectionism. Does that sound like your son?

I am imagining that your son is slightly anxious much of the time he is playing baseball, and that is responsible for his caution. Please watch him and see if my theory is true. See if he starts to tense up as you drive to the field. We know he goes into a funk if his team loses. Watch for his relief if his team wins. Winning and losing may all feel to him like a referendum on himself and his personal value, his worth as a boy. All you can say is, "I'm sorry that you can't enjoy sports more. I know that you wish you could be better and always win. We just want you to know that we love watching you play. You always make a tremendous effort. You always contribute to your team. That's all any boy can do. We hope you can make your peace with that."

Afraid Son Will Get Hurt in Football

Q: My son loves football and wants very much to play. He plays on his town team and looks forward to being on his high school team. In his mind, he is going to be a star. He lifts weights and follows the NFL; he seems to know everything about football. Still, during games he gets thrown around. He is very coordinated but he is not all that big, nor is his father. He is never going to be massive and strong like some boys. I know I'm not the first mother to feel this way, but I worry a lot about his getting hurt. If he ruins his knees or receives a head or neck injury, that's going to be with him all of his life. I just cannot see that football is worth it. What should a mother do when her son is dedicating his boyhood to an aggressive and dangerous pastime that just doesn't make sense?

MGT: The problem is that you are asking a psychologist a philosophical question. I have no special training in philosophy. What in life is worth risking life and limb for, and how do we weigh the risks? Yes, he is likely to receive some injury if he plays football. It is likely to be a small injury, not a disabling one. Still, it is a risk. Everyone perceives risks differently. For the sake of argument, let me propose the following: you and I both know that thirty-five thousand Americans are killed in car accidents every year, yet we get up in the morning and drive around town and think nothing of it. Carpooling is far more dangerous than football. I know schools where kids have been killed on the way to school in the morning, and I have never known a child who was killed in a high school football game. There are many dread diseases and accidents that present a greater threat to your son than the chance that he will be seriously and permanently disabled in a football game.

I know disease and accidents are involuntary and football is a choice. You are not forced to put yourself in harm's way by playing football. Then why do boys do it, and why do some mothers enjoy it and others eventually come to accept it? And why have I, as a psychologist, come to appreciate the role of sports in boys' lives? Why have I come to respect football, my least favorite sport when I was a boy? If I can answer those questions, perhaps I can be of some help to you.

The reason I have come to appreciate athletics in the lives of boys is that sports are an antidote to the biggest problem facing American youth, which is uselessness. Our prolonged period of education, our long adolescence, comes at the cost of having our children feel that they do not have much to contribute to society. They are not useful. No one wants what teens produce, because it is not the adult product. Workbooks, homework, grades, the whole school catastrophe, none of it has any meaning for a wider society, and the outcome is never in doubt. You can get an A, a B, or a C and only your teacher and your parents care, but it doesn't really make a difference in their lives. We keep them in school and away from jobs that they could do. Cynical economists have said that high school and college are designed to keep teenagers out of the workforce, so they do not steal jobs from adults, so that we have low unemployment. I do not know whether that is true, but I see that teenagers who work mature more quickly and have more self-respect than kids who do not work.

Sports occupy a space somewhere between school and work. Sport requires a dedication and effort and produces a clear outcome: a win or a loss. Sports allow boys and girls to do something beautiful, exciting, and inspiring. Their accomplishments can be seen, measured, and even filmed! Also, athletics allows boys to do something that their mothers and fathers cannot do. Perhaps the parents played sports earlier in their lives, but now they are too slow, too fat, and too preoccupied to play an exciting game of anything. Adolescents, however, can be wondrously fit and can throw themselves into sport with an amazing intensity. How satisfying to be able to do something your parents cannot!

Sports give boys a chance to have contact with men. They have precious few male teachers in the elementary school years. The dominant experience of the American boy is being without a father. Sixty percent of American children will live at least part of their childhood without a parent, and the missing parent is usually the father. Coaches supply a lot of the male presence in boys' lives. One high school boy said to me, "I've loved all my coaches. Other kids have had lousy coaches, but all of mine have been awesome, even the ones who yelled."

The lives of American boys are often isolated. Boys don't get a lot of physical touch in our society because of our societal homophobia. Teams give boys a community, a lot of physical contact, and a sense of intimacy with other boys. They learn to know each other's strengths and weaknesses. In a well-led team that has no cruel hazing, your son will find a community to which he can devote himself.

Sports command boys' attention. It gives them an experience of being focused that they may never get in school. It lets them know what they are capable of achieving when they are motivated. It brings out the best in them. Just listen to boys and men discuss sports and you will discover that these are conversations about idealism, character formation, psychology, and love. Yes, love. Have you ever heard men discuss Joe DiMaggio or Carlton Fisk? Life is all there in sports, in one huge incomprehensible package.

The only thing that can spoil athletics for boys is a bad coach, and there are a number of them out there. But if your son gets a good football coach, you are going to see what it does for him. You are going to appreciate the dignity and pride he will enjoy as part of the team. I wager that if he continues to play, watching his games will be one of the things you look forward to the most. You may never love football, and you will hold your breath at moments during the game, but you will love that your son loves it. And you will have a

picture on your refrigerator of your son in his uniform, looking handsome and strong.

Hockey: How Much Is Enough?

Q: Last year we moved to a town north of Boston where
hockey is the big sport. Our ten-year-old son loves hockey
and played with the youth league. We were excited about it
until we learned that if he wanted to play, he had to play a full
schedule, and those boys had a fifty-three-game schedule,
starting in October and ending in April. I really enjoy watching my son play, and as his father, I appreciated his dedication and commitment, but our family had no life on weekends.
There were practices at 6 A.M.—sometimes at 5:30 A.M.!—
and games in the afternoon. We were often driving long dis-
tances to other towns. That was taxing, but the part that
really bothered me was that there were far more games than
practices. I thought the boys could get as much out of practice as they did out of games, but the games seemed so important to all the other dads. The schedule seemed to be for
them more than for their sons and I began to question the
value of the sport. What do you think? How much hockey is
enough for a ten-year-old?

MGT: I consulted a high school senior hockey player (Ian
Spechler from Texas, formerly of Massachusetts) about your
question and he was in complete agreement about the practice

vs. game ratio. He said, "When you are ten years old, you don't need to be Wayne Gretzky, you need to learn how to play hockey. Practices are more important than games at that age." From what I can see, the practices are every bit as much fun as the games for ten-year-olds. Furthermore, boys get much more skating time at practices than they do in games. It is no wonder that they prefer practice. Most of them are not yet developmentally ready to compete all the time; they just love to play and skate and be with their friends. The need for that quantity of competition comes from the fathers. The danger here is that a father will unwittingly exploit a son's enthusiasm and eventually the son will burn out on the sport.

When you see the energy and enthusiasm that boys bring to their teams, it seems impossible that they will tire of it and come to hate the sport. Yet for every boy who ends up playing a varsity sport, there are many boys who started out playing on town teams in that sport and really enjoyed the companionship and the exercise. Why do most of them eventually drop out? There are a number of reasons: realism and pride and identity are three. Overinvolved fathers are a fourth reason. Reality is the chief reason, because the town teams lead to high school teams, and boys come to realize that they are not going to be able to play for their high school. High school teams cut, and it becomes shameful to like a sport that you cannot play at the junior varsity or varsity level. That's why so many seniors stop playing a sport in their senior year; it hurts their pride to be playing at a junior varsity level in their final year. They would rather sit on the bench for a varsity team than play lots of minutes in every junior varsity game.

However, many boys who are capable of playing at the varsity level also give up the sport. As a psychologist, I have spoken with a number of them who have left their varsity teams. One of the reasons that they quit is that they feel their lives have become one-dimensional. The sport, be it hockey or football, overshadows everything else. "I want to do other things," they say. They want a girlfriend, to be in a play, to play in a band, to get an after-school job and earn money for a car. Fair enough.

Finally, however, they come to feel as if their fathers see them only as athletes. As one boy said to me, "All my father cares about is that I play hockey. That's the only thing about me that he's interested in." That son had to drop off the hockey team in order to demonstrate to his father that he was independent, and that he wanted to be seen for himself. (Let me make it clear that I am not bashing hockey; it happens to be the high-status sport in the Northeast, where I live. In Maryland it is lacrosse, in Florida it is baseball, in Texas and Louisiana it is football, in Indiana it is basketball. These are the sports that are so highly valued that they bring peculiar social pressures to a boy.)

Is it a bad thing for boys to play hockey and provide entertainment for their fathers? Isn't anything that gets fathers and sons together going to be good for their relationship? The answer is yes and no. Since American boys in general spend so little time with their fathers I am hesitant to criticize fathers who get up at 4:30 A.M., support a team, drive their sons to games, and cheer them on. Yet balance is important, and a father who fails to maintain a sane view of his son's athletics risks burdening him. That's what I think has happened in your town. A few zealous fathers have created a monster hockey schedule. They have lost perspective. It is hard for me to imagine that ten-year-old boys can play such a long season in a joyful way.

What you have to do is support your son for the sport, but make it clear that you support him only because he loves it. Express your honest skepticism about the size of the schedule and the motives of the organizers. Send a letter to the organizers with your thoughts—and mine, if they are of help. Your son needs to know that you are capable of making independent judgments so that he can do so as well. He needs to know that you are not as invested in hockey as the most fanatical coach in his league. That way your son can say if he finds the schedule too demanding. He can tell you if he is not enjoying it. You see, in his mind he may be playing hockey partly as a gift of love for his father. You have to reassure him through your attitude that you will love him whether he plays hockey or not. That is the only way he can make a true commitment to the sport.

The ideal sports father is one who gets enormous pleasure out of watching his child, a father who doesn't critique his son's performance constantly, and is always a bit worried that it is taking too much time from studies, from the family, from the development of other interests. It must not be all about hockey. I would like to see a father use the time in the car driving to games to talk about school, about teachers, about his son's friends, about what is happening in national politics. With a balanced father like that, a son can know whether *he* really loves the sport for the joy of it.

Basketball Coach a Stand-in Dad

Q: My husband became ill and died when our son was eleven. Our son is now fourteen, is starting high school, and has gotten involved in athletics—basketball. The coach is a very kind and supportive man, but I feel my son looks upon him as a father figure and spends way too much time involved with basketball as a way to be around the coach. I wonder if maybe he is confusing his interest in basketball with his emotional need for his dad. Also, his grades are suffering because he spends so much time playing basketball at school and practicing shooting hoops with the neighbor boys at home. I love my son and don't want to take this sport away from him, but I am worried about him. What do you suggest?

MGT: I am very sorry for your son and for you that he lost his father when he was so young. I guess it is better to lose a father at age eleven than at age six, but the truth is that it is tough anytime. The loss of his father shattered many dreams and plans he had, that he wasn't even conscious of having, because he took his father's presence for granted. His dad's death is a serious loss that will be with him forever, in large and small ways. In psychology we used to think that a successful grieving process could completely heal even a parent loss, but we know that the best that we can hope for is that a child mourn and find people who can partially replace the loss of the parent.

The most important thing to a grieving child is to have an adult—in this case his mother—who understands the magnitude of his loss and can talk to him about it occasionally, especially at anniversary times such as his birthday or the anniversary of his father's death, or at moments of developmental change: the transition to high school, the first girlfriend, the first high school basketball game, his wedding, and other times when he naturally would have wanted his dad to see him and take pride in him. As his mother, you will sense these quiet eruptions of feeling and yearning in him over the years to come. He might express them as grumpiness, anger, envy of other people, or blaming of you (the surviving parent always gets some anger for not being both). If you can connect these feelings up to his missing of his father, you will be helping him to understand and work through his grief.

The healthiest and best thing that any boy can do after losing his father is to find a father figure and invest in him much of the love, respect, and idealization that he might have had for his father. You are fortunate that he is investing in his

coach. He is lucky to have found a caring man in his basketball coach. His coach is lucky as well. It adds great meaning
to a man's life to provide something that a boy so badly needs.
Over my years as a therapist, I have played the role of father
figure to many boys who had lost their fathers and couldn't
seem to find any "natural" substitute for their dads. When I
was doing therapy, I wished that I could have been in a more
natural and fun situation with a boy, such as fishing or playing
basketball.

For what it is worth, it is my understanding that Larry
Bird, the great Boston Celtic basketball player, worked out
his grief over the suicide of his father by going to the gym
and throwing hoops for hours and hours. Not many boys are
going to turn out to be a Larry Bird, but I think for many
boys, a physical expression of grief is natural and expectable.

As long as you feel the coach is of good character, please
don't interfere with your son's relationship with him. Support
it in any way you can. Take your son out and buy the coach a
present at holiday time—nothing so big that it embarrasses
him—or invite the coach and his wife over to dinner at your
house. Encourage your son to show his love to his coach. Tell
your son that his father would have liked the coach, and tell
him why you think so. That will help your son avoid feeling
an internal "loyalty conflict" between his love for his dad and
his affection for his coach. As for his grades, I suggest you enlist his coach in encouraging your son to keep up his schoolwork. That's what good coaches do for all boys in sports

anyway, recognizing how rare it is for a boy to be able to make a living playing sports. Go talk to the coach, and thank him for the attention he is showing your son. Tell him how much it means to both of you. Caring coaches, teachers, clergy, neighbors, and uncles are a godsend for fatherless boys. They deserve our recognition.

Speaking of
Boy Fun, Games, and Laughs

What's So Funny about Body Parts, Etc.?

Q: As the mother of two boys, age fifteen and eight, I have to admit that I don't understand why boys find fart jokes and all scatological humor so funny. I've listened to this stuff since my older son was in a car pool in first grade and I'm bored with it. Boys never seem to tire of it. To tell the truth, my older son and my husband love reading Dave Barry together and when they fall on the floor laughing, I just bet it is some reference to a body part. It always is. I like to think of myself as a person with a sense of humor, but I don't "get it." Can you enlighten me?

MGT: Uh-oh. I have to answer this question in a serious, psychological way? You're asking someone who ranks Jim Carrey's

Ace Ventura: Pet Detective and Steve Martin's *The Jerk* among his top ten funniest movies of all time. Do you remember the scene in which Steve Martin's sharecropper father takes him out behind the barn to explain the difference between "shit and Shineola"? He points to the shoe polish can and says, "Son, this is Shineola." Then he points to a cow pie and says, "Son, this is shit." Then he repeats, "Shit . . . Shineola. You need to know the difference." Steve Martin says, "Thanks, Dad," and they start to walk back to the house. On the way, Steve Martin steps in the . . .

Oh, dear, I am hopeless. And so is my nine-year-old son. I took him and his two friends sledding today and they sat in the back of the car entertaining one another with a couple of truly dreadful dirty jokes, versions of which I heard when I was in elementary school. Do I need to tell you they were about body parts?

Okay, now that I have identified myself as being just like your sons and your husband, I will try to put on my psychologist's hat and give you a serious answer. I think boy humor is a mixture of biology, social training, and what I will call "antisocial" training or the desire to outrage adults. I think a woman's reaction to boy humor has to do with her life experience and social training as well.

Some things seem to be funny on a biological basis. Small children often laugh when they fart out loud; the sound is unintentional, it takes them by surprise, and it comes from the wrong end. Both boys and girls laugh at the phenomenon and when they are young their mothers often laugh or smile along with them. However, we know that from the earliest ages boys imitate sounds more than girls do. They imitate trucks and they imitate fart sounds. From very early they learn that making noises entertains other boys, and once they get that audience reaction, they are hooked. It is for this reason that one educational resource Web site designed for middle school children has a "Sounds" department which includes bird songs, heart sounds, and twenty different fart sounds. What a great way to get children interested in doing research on the Internet!

Humor plays a huge part in the boy social group. So much of boy conversation is about entertaining and therefore dominating a group. You can observe boys working very hard at trying to develop their joke-telling. To judge by the conversation over lunch at the all-boys' school where I work—and I'm describing the faculty table here—it does not stop as boys grow up. Psycholinguistic research tells us that conversation has different social purposes for men and women and these differences emerge early in the game. Boys are trained to be humorous for social impact.

We also know that doing something antisocial confers status on a boy in a group. Expressions of anger and efforts to outrage adults are likely to be met with approval by the boy group, even by boys who would not themselves engage in such activities. If a boy's aim is to outrage, then the disapproving face of an adult, be it his mother or a teacher, is exactly what he is looking for. The arrow has hit its mark.

Those are the reasons from the boy side. Why don't

women find bathroom humor endlessly enjoyable? Obviously, it is because they had different social training in their girlhoods. They have felt the disapproval of their mothers *and* the disapproval of the girl group when they have tried bathroom humor, and so they have given up on it as a way of making connections. Is that the only reason? Perhaps, but one woman I know had a theory that makes a lot of sense to me. She said that after raising three children and changing thousands of diapers (3 children $\times$ 5 diapers per day $\times$ 365 days per year $\times$ 3 years = a lot of diapers), perhaps body parts, poops, and farts lose their comic appeal. We will have to see whether, after a generation of fathers has been more fully involved in child rearing, dads still find "poop and privates" funny. I don't know of a cure for boy humor, and as for understanding, well, there is a deep gender gap here. My best advice is—lighten up!

Game Boy Dilemma

Q: My eight-year-old son is the only boy in his class who doesn't have a Game Boy. I don't want him to have one because it seems to take away from his healthy outdoor activity time. I worry that it's addictive, and I don't know what the long-term impact of playing it will be. But I also don't want him to be ostracized for not having one. When I try to talk to other parents about it they just say I should get him one. What do you think?

MGT: Some boys do use Game Boys and other electronic devices to tune out and to avoid human contact or fresh air and exercise. But those boys are the exception to the rule. For most, Game Boy and other electronic devices are part and parcel of an active, balanced life. I don't worry about boys unless their dedication to games seems to block out other aspects of their lives.

It's important to recognize that these games appeal to a boy's sense of mastery. They often play to the strengths of many boys: persistence, hand-eye coordination, hyperfocus, competition, and task-orientation in achieving various levels and goals. There is some evidence that Game Boy–type games begin the skill-building for careers with computers, so electronic games are not without their pre-professional aspects.

The most important feature of the games for many boys, however, is that they combat the worst feeling of being a child, namely, uselessness. We have to remember that as recently as 1940, two-thirds of Americans were either farm workers or they were part of a family being raised on a farm. Boys used to have a world of animals, equipment, tractors, and cars that they could master. They used to play an important part in the work and economic life of a family. If you ever speak with a man about his life on a farm, he will tell you how he drove a car when he was eleven or was able to run a complex piece of machinery. So many of those opportunities have been lost to boys in the present day.

Our boys are so sheltered and protected and are given so

few opportunities to venture out in the world and develop expertise. The Canadian biologist Farley Mowat describes in his autobiography, *Born Naked,* how he used to leave his house in Saskatchewan early in the morning and return twelve hours later after a day exploring in the woods and fields, even in the middle of the winter when the temperature was 30 degrees below zero. How many boys have a chance to express their autonomy and competence in that way? How many modern parents would allow their boys to go out and about like that? We're certain not many would. Still, boys have the impulse to master the world and to prove themselves.

A game is a little world that a boy can bring under his control. He knows where the monsters are hiding. Often he is faster and smarter at the game than his father is. That delights him and makes him feel competent. Having scores and levels allows him to compare his progress with other boys. If he doesn't want to go on the adventure alone, he can buy a connector wire and do the game with another boy. They will hunt, so to speak, side by side.

You say you're concerned that your son will be ostracized for not having this toy, but you don't say whether he is actually being excessively teased or iced out of his social group anyway. It's rare for a group of boys to label someone an outcast because they don't have a computer game. Boys pick on boys for other reasons, most having to do with social status in the group; having a Game Boy won't change that. More likely, the other boys are simply preoccupied playing their game, and your son has no way to join in. If your son isn't nagging you for a game, it probably isn't essential to him and he has found other ways to relate to his friends. If he is nagging you for one, find out why. If he thinks a Game Boy will make hostile boys nicer to him, he's mistaken. A Game Boy won't do the job. If he wants one simply so that he can play with friends, then it serves much the same purpose as a basketball or Legos when boys get together to play.

As for other parents, they probably react defensively when they learn that you haven't bought him one. Your parenting seems purer, more visionary, and perhaps they did not think the issue through carefully, so they feel reproached by your doubts. They want you to give in and stop making them uncomfortable. Don't worry about them. Consult your son about his experience in the group before you make up your mind. If you have any reason to believe he is suffering, the only two things to take into account are your values and his satisfaction with his life—and finding a manageable balance between them.

Paintball Gun for Thirteen-Year-Old Son?

Q: My thirteen-year-old son wants a paintball gun for his birthday in the worst way. Several of his friends have them, they play with them out in the woods, and I know my son has played with a borrowed paintball gun on occasion. I would buy one for him, but the idea of it makes my wife terribly upset. She thinks these guns breed violence. I think she is underestimating our son. He can tell the difference between play and reality. What can I say to convince my wife that this is a safe and reasonable toy for a boy his age?

MGT: I'd like to be able to help you here, but I am afraid you are going to be disappointed with my answer. I don't like paintball guns. I have been asked this question in many ways by many moms and dads, and I always hesitate because my answer is a combination of psychological knowledge and personal values. I cannot answer the question just as a psychologist. Psychological research can shed some light on the impact of pretend gunplay, but ultimately this question comes down to what kind of a stance you want to take in your family with respect to violence in our society and gun violence in particular. If you believe—as I do—that there is far too much gun violence in our society, if you believe that having close to ten thousand people die of gunshot wounds every year is a form of cultural insanity, then you have to ask yourself the question: "Am I doing anything to stop the culture of violence in the United States?" My belief is that if you are buying a paintball gun for your son, you are giving him a mixed message about violence.

I know many boys who love paintball. I know men who have played with them and said, "That is a total blast!" I know boys who are sane enough, well loved enough, and have good enough judgment so that they can use a paintball gun and never be led to gun violence. However, the psychological research is pretty clear that playing at violence has the effect of "systematically desensitizing" the participants to the experience of violence. Boys tell me, "Paintball is a game of strategy!" Indeed, it is. It is also a game that has elements of hide-and-seek, but isn't hide-and-seek. Ultimately, it involves sneaking up and shooting someone as if to kill him, and having the paint capsule create a fake wound on the victim's body. Just today a boy showed me the red bruise on his leg from a paintball birthday party. He showed it to me as if it were a badge of honor, a war injury.

We know that human beings do not ordinarily or easily kill other people. Killing does not come naturally. Killers go through a process wherein they are brutalized, taunted, then challenged to respond to any threat by killing, and finally celebrated for their violence. The process is brilliantly described in a book by Richard Rhodes entitled *Why They Kill*. One of the crucial elements in violence is seeing it. We know that children of fathers who hit their wives and hit their children are more likely to be aggressive in school and more likely to grow up and commit acts of domestic violence. All of this is well researched and well documented.

Where then do we draw the line? When do we say, "This is close enough to real violence that we shouldn't sanction it"? When do we say, "This might be okay for most kids, but it sends the wrong message and it might be harmful to a few angry or disturbed boys"? I know of a town where a bunch of boys went out with their paintball guns on a Halloween night and shot at people's windows at close range. They broke a number of windows. The police caught them and charged them with firearms violations under the town's regulations.

The boys' parents complained, "These aren't firearms." And the police said, "Actually, they are called guns and they were being used like guns to break windows. What's the difference between shooting out a window with a .22 caliber rifle, and shooting out a window with a paintball gun?"

I want to make it clear that I am not a Quaker or a pacifist. I bought my son a toy pistol and a Western holster and a cowboy hat when he was little. I bought my son a *Star Wars* light sword one birthday. He has had a number of lightweight Ninja-type swords over the years. For me, those are "pretend" and not close to real violence. The gun doesn't shoot anything, not even caps; the light swords and the Ninja swords were plastic, not even as dangerous as a stick in the yard. The line between pretend violence and real violence is not clear. It is in the eye of the beholder. For me that line is drawn in a way that excludes paintball guns.

Virtual Lives: How Much Is Too Much Time on Computer?

Q. Our son is thirteen, makes good grades, and has friends. We are concerned, though, that he plays computer games for too long. He can sit and play these games, some of them online with people from around the world, for hours, unaware of the time. We used to have a one-hour limit on computer, but we aren't always home, and even when we are, he plays until one of us notices that it's been way more than an hour. We admit that some of the games are actually pretty impressive strategy games, and it's hard to argue that he should stop playing these and go play Monopoly or Clue instead. How can we come to some reasonable rules about the time spent on computer games and some realistic way to get him to police himself in terms of time? Is there some basic idea we can keep in mind as we adapt the house rules regarding recreational computer use through these teen years?

MGT: Do you remember the musical comedy *The Music Man*? A con artist traveling salesman comes into a small Iowa town and gets the town folks all stirred up by telling them their sons are going to rack and ruin because they are spending time in a pool hall. "We got trouble, right here in River City," he sings. The boys in town, he predicts, are going to stop doing their chores; soon they'll be telling dirty jokes! His whole pitch is designed to get the people of the town to buy instruments and start a boys' band. A band, you see, will keep them from a life of "degradation." Much of the criticism I hear of computers and the Internet reminds me of *The Music Man*. Are our boys all going to go to hell because they spend so much time on the computer? I don't think so.

For one thing, all of the adults I know are spending more and more time on the computer these days, and they are very excited about it—myself included (I am writing this book on my laptop and sending the text out to my cowriter by e-mail). I know responsible grown men and women who are spending almost all day on the computer. Many of them are thriving in business because of their devotion to this new mode of communication. Why are we so worried that what is good for us is bad for our teenage sons?

The question to ask yourself is how do you hope he would spend the time instead? Do you imagine that he would spend the time playing the piano? If that were the alternative, then arguably that would be a better use of his time. Perhaps it would be healthier if he were playing basketball with friends in the neighborhood. But those are not the usual options for many children today. What if he is watching less TV because he is spending more time on the computer? A recent Stanford University study of Internet use found that of the people who spent more than five hours per week on-line, 59 percent were watching less television than they used to. Which is to be preferred?

I am always looking to see if a boy has a balanced life. How are his grades? How are his friendships? Is he physically active and fit? Does he treat people in his family well? Does he get enough sleep? Does he get to bed on time? You say that your son's grades are good and that he has friends. If you have answered "yes" to my additional questions, then what is there to worry about? Computers present some practical problems and they pose a large philosophical question.

On the practical side, many parents worry about their sons downloading pornography or that they might meet some creep over the Internet. Talk to your son about those two things. If he is fourteen, he has probably downloaded pornography already. I would be astonished if he hadn't. His classmates have told him how easy it is to locate. (Pornography on the Internet is generally more graphic than that which is available in magazines like *Penthouse* and *Playboy*, which boys have had access to for decades. I regret that, but it is a fact of life in America and a values discussion beyond the scope of this book.) Ask him about pornography, tell him what you think, and talk to him about pedophiles on-line. May I suggest that you do what Janna Malamud Smith writes that she did in a *New York Times* article entitled "Online but not antisocial":

> I recently told my 14-year-old that he couldn't put his computer in his bedroom and had to keep it in the family room. I didn't explain that I had made that decision because I wanted to keep an eye on what he was downloading, nag him when he has spent too much time online and pat his head occasionally, but I think he guessed. Yes, we all need to monitor this powerful tool.

Yes, we need to monitor computer use, just as we monitor everything in the lives of early adolescents, but we do not need to fear it. Incidentally, women educators are worried that girls are not spending enough time on computer in comparison to boys and that that is going to put them at a competitive disadvantage in college and graduate school. A vast majority of the students taking advanced placement exams in computers or majoring in computer engineering are boys. No doubt they are boys who spent a lot of time playing strategy games on their home computers.

There is a philosophical question that arises in connection with computers, and I do not have an answer to it yet. I don't know who does. We are, as a society, changing how we all, our children included, spend our time. Though I do not fear computers per se, life has shown me that every new solution brings with it new problems. The problem with computers may be that with children constantly interacting with a screen, something precious is being lost from their lives. Are children losing creative time, dreaming time, solitude, or time to be bored?

I think every parent has to remember what was most important in his or her childhood and try to provide that for his/her children. If computers become an obstacle to your children's having experiences that you believe they will treasure, then you should limit their computer time, because it is vital that parents feel that they are doing the right thing for their children.

To Scout or Not to Scout

Q: Our son was in Cub Scouts and has been in Boy Scouts now for a year. He wants to drop out, but we want him to stay in it very much because it is one place where we know he will do healthy, wholesome things and get to share some time with men who are good role models. My husband is out of town a lot on work. How can we persuade him to stick with it? We think he'll be glad he did.

MGT: Imagine that parents are given a limited number of magic "silver bullets," perhaps six, that may be used in the life of their son. These magic silver bullets must be saved for special circumstances: when you want to save his life, when you really want to make a crucial point, when you want to insist on something, when you want to change the course of his growing up in an important way. If you waste the silver bullet on a meaningless situation, it is gone for no reason. You use 'em, you lose 'em. Only rarely do you receive an extra silver bullet during the life of this child, and almost never during adolescence. It is best to think of them as absolutely finite.

Now that I have said that, is Boy Scouts something for which you want to use up one of your silver bullets? Perhaps it's that important to you. Your son will know when you are using the magic bullet. He will be able to tell that this issue must be vitally important to you, and your deep conviction may persuade him to give up some of his autonomy, his wishes. Your faith in Boy Scouts may help him to get over his doubts about the value of the enterprise. For a time, however, he will have to draw on your determination and faith in order to overcome his negative feelings about the Scouts. Knowing that you are that invested in the decision may make it possible for him to draw on your determination. He can surmount his objections by saying, "Okay, Scouts are so important to them that I will stick it out," but in the back of his mind he is thinking, "Next time they ask me for something like this, I won't have to say 'yes.'"

Obviously, these silver bullets are your convictions that something is very important to his life. I have seen parents use silver bullets to keep their adolescents going to church for a year or two longer than they might otherwise have done. I have seen parents use silver bullets on piano lessons or one more summer of camp when the son thought he was too cool to go to camp. Parents have used them to persuade their son to stay in a varsity sport he has come to dislike because it will help him get into college. Even if the boy eventually leaves the particular enterprise his parents cared so much about, even if he does not keep playing the piano, his parents' deep convictions leave an impression on him *and that stays with him for life*. In middle age he will say, "I stayed in Scouts because my parents really wanted me to. . . ." Or, "I went to church because it meant so much to my parents and it became vital to me." Or, "My parents were really passionate about music and I disappointed them by giving up the piano, but . . ." But what? What could he gain from seeing that his parents used a silver bullet on him that did not work? That sentence ends like this: "but I have taken their passion and principles into my work or into my family life. I have tried to honor their convictions in the way I have raised my children." He has a lifelong impression of his parents as principled, thoughtful people. He has the memory of his parents as willing to make a stand. That is worth having for your whole life.

Research on parenting tells us that authoritative parents

produce the most competent children, more successful children than those raised by democratic, directive, or "good-enough" parents. Being an authoritative parent is not easy. Authoritative parents have high expectations for their children and are highly responsive to their children's wants and needs. They listen carefully to their children, and they hold them to a high standard. If you are going to override your child's wants and needs in order to place a demand on him, it had better be necessary. If you do it all the time, for issues large and small, you are no longer an authoritative parent, you are a directive parent. The research suggests that he will not be as competent a child if you make the important decisions for him.

Are you aware that you can consult your son? You can tell him how very much Scouts means to you and suggest that you are considering asking—even requiring—him to stay for another year. Sound him out about whether or not this is a good place to use your silver bullet. He may have watched his closest Scout friend drop out, or his troop may include the boy who makes his life miserable at school. He may feel that at his school Scouts is not "cool" and a scout affiliation opens him up to ridicule he wants to avoid. His troop may not be as satisfying as he wishes it were, for any number of reasons. It may be that your image or memory of Scouts is quite different from the reality of it in his troop or in his life. He may indicate his level of feeling about the issue by saying, "Well, if it is that important to you, I might reconsider leaving." Or he might say, "Mom, can't you see I've hated the Scouts for a year and a half? I *have* been staying in because I knew it meant so much to you!" In the former, a silver bullet might be exactly what is needed. In the latter case, you might want to save it for another big issue. There will always be another big issue in your son's life. You don't want to have run out of parental magic when that time comes.

Girls, Boys, and Bedding: Coed Sleepovers

Q: Coed sleepovers are the newest teenage fad in our neighborhood. A lot of parents here say it's a safe, supervised way for the kids to have fun, and it keeps all of them from driving home late at night. I'm all for safety, but I am very uncomfortable with the idea of our fifteen-year-old son attending these parties. I know for a fact that often the parents don't do a very good job of supervising what's going on at all, and who could possibly supervise all night long? Our son says we're being old-fashioned and that it makes him feel like we don't trust him. We're open to new ideas, but this just feels wrong. Are we being overly protective or suspicious? If not, how can we explain our stand to our son without making trust the issue?

MGT: You are being manipulated by a master. Trust isn't the issue. Of course you don't trust him! Of course you are suspicious! Come on. He's fifteen. Honestly, what were you thinking about or doing in tenth grade? Okay, how about eleventh grade? How about twelfth grade? Whatever kids were doing senior year in high school when the presently middle-aged were those kids is what tenth graders are doing today.

If a group of fifteen- and sixteen-year-old boys and girls get together for the night at someone's house, and they spend a long time together in the cellar recreation room or in a bedroom upstairs, and parents don't check on them frequently . . .

What are they going to talk about?
   a. the grades they're getting in school
   b. existentialism
   c. sex (who is doing what with whom)

What are they going to watch on TV?
   a. "The News Hour"
   b. "Law and Order"
   c. MTV's "Loveline"

What kind of beverage is some teenager going to try to bring to the house?
   a. Poland Spring water
   b. root beer
   c. Coors beer

If there is a couple present who like each other and neither of them has their parents there, what will they try to do?
   a. help the host parents in the kitchen
   b. propose a game of Monopoly
   c. sneak off and "hook up"

If one couple sneaks off and leaves the others to think about what they're doing in private, what are the other kids likely to do?

a. all fall asleep immediately

b. gossip, gossip, gossip

c. start to pair off themselves

Well, you get my point. This is what young people do, and what they have always done. The question is not whether sex will happen, but when. And the "when" is, to a certain extent, under your control. At some point, your son will feel old enough, and you will respect his judgment enough, for you to let him go, not because you don't think something will happen. It will be because you think he's old enough and careful enough to take care of himself when something happens.

Have you talked to him about your family's values and sexuality? Do you know what he believes? Have you talked about these subjects together? Certainly, if he asks for your trust, you can ask him some questions in return before you give him your trust. Are a lot of kids in his grade having sex? How does he feel about that?

After this conversation, or without this conversation, do you feel that he is a responsible and loving person who is going to use good judgment? If the answer is "yes," let him go. If the answer is "no," keep him home for a while longer. Just be honest. Tell him you don't want him to start his drinking or sexual career this soon and you don't trust such parties to be sex-free and alcohol-free. If they were going to be dull, everyone could have stayed home in their own beds.

You are bound to hear otherwise about this. I know many teenagers who are quite vocal in their defense of these slumber parties, their insistence that "nothing happens," and their belief that they are more socially and sexually savvy than their parents were at this age and better equipped to deal with the pressure. I have heard from some parents who say similar things. But I also know, from talking with teens in school and in therapy, that although they wish desperately for the fun freedom of the moment, they often are relieved when their parents stand between them and this kind of good time. The peer pressure is on. There are times when parents need to be the ones to "just say no."

Using Stereotypes to Get Laughs

Q: My son, James, fourteen, has a great sense of humor and often delivers pretty good one-liners that make people laugh. I'm bothered by the fact that lately he's begun using foreign accents that add to the humor—but only because they play off stereotypes of people in certain jobs. I have let it go uncensored at times when he's with other boys and they're all laughing, because I know if I said anything they'd all turn it into a joke. But I'm really offended by this. I talked with James about it later, and he said he didn't mean anything by it, and that it was just in fun. How can I talk with him about this without sounding like a humorless, oversensitive spoilsport?

MGT: There are many definitions of what a parent needs to be. Being a "humorless, oversensitive spoilsport" is one of the chief jobs of parenting. "Wear your jacket. . . . Take your dishes to the sink. . . . Have you brushed your teeth? . . . It's time for bed. . . . Put down the Game Boy and come to dinner. . . . Are you wearing your retainer?" All of these are sentences that come regularly out of the mouths of parents, and all of them qualify as being "humorless" and are certainly capable of spoiling the sport of children. I am certain that you have been saying all of these things since your son was very little.

I am equally certain that you have gone through long periods of time when you have been at peace with being a humorless spoilsport (read "parent") and at times have felt very good about how consistently boring you have been. When your son thought that he could magically have his teeth become straight without wearing his retainer, when he thought he could function in school without actually going to bed at night, you stuck to your guns.

The difficulty here is that you now have a large son with a sophisticated sense of humor and an apparent capacity to monitor his own behavior. And you thought for a moment that your days of being a dreary drudge were over. You have been tricked! You thought you saw the light at the end of the tunnel of parenting, but it was only the train of adolescence coming the other way. You had a momentary lapse, really an attack of nostalgia (psychologists call them "regressions"), and you wished to return to the days before you were a parent. You wanted to get out of the role of being a spoilsport. You wanted to just be an adult in the presence of your grown-up son, who for minutes—sometimes hours—each day allows you to feel like your long-lost humorous self. Then all of a sudden he is telling tasteless ethnic jokes, imitating accents and doing a stupid skit in public for his friends, making fun of a grocery store clerk, for instance.

You think—actually, you are wishing—that by the age of fourteen, your son should be able to hear what he says and have perspective on it. You hope that he knows standards of good taste and believe that you shouldn't have to supply him with an adult viewpoint. As a kid might say, "Wrong!" or "Not!" Any ninth-grade teacher could have told you that he isn't there yet.

Indeed, if you work in schools you see that ninth-grade boys are still incredibly young at moments, especially when they are together in groups. Individually they can be dazzling adults. They can stun you with their maturity and their idealism. However, they cannot maintain any kind of maturity consistently, especially when they are competing for attention and popularity, which is what your son is doing. Boys often try to dominate the conversation through the use of humor. In the book *You Just Don't Understand*, the psycholinguist Deborah Tannen describes the way in which men use conversation, and especially humor in conversation, to entertain and to dominate. That's what your son has been doing. He has been successful in being known as a comedian. He has been gaining the appreciation of everyone around him. He has won your respect for his one-liners. He has an act and he's been getting applause for it, both from kids and adults. Who can blame him for pushing the envelope with his act?

Furthermore, he watches TV and goes to movies. He's watched *Saturday Night Live* and MTV. He knows that much of successful humor in the media is tasteless ethnic humor. He knows that Jim Carrey gets paid $20 million per film for imitating funny accents and making fun of people. He gets paid millions to memorialize a comedian who made a career out of playing "the foreign man" and an insulting, vulgar lounge entertainer. Why shouldn't your son try as well? Twenty million dollars is a lot of money.

What he lacks at fourteen is the experience that allows him to distinguish context and timing. What works on TV is often offensive in person (heck, a lot of it is offensive on TV, too, but it is more offensive in person). What works for an audience that has paid money to hear a stand-up comic at a comedy club doesn't work on your mother who is driving the car pool. Boldness, antisocial behavior, and shocking adults are high cards for fourteen-year-old boys. They appreciate a classmate who will disrupt the class, take on the teacher, and break rules in public. Such behavior raises their stock in the group. But it strikes adults as offensive and immature. So your son is going to have to make a choice between being the class clown and being respected by the adults in his life. You have to help him by sharpening that choice.

All of this goes to say that when you are present for an offensive display of humor, one that plays to prejudice and ethnic stereotyping, you have to say so. And it will make you sound like a humorless spoilsport. No way around it. But what if you don't say anything? Who will? And isn't it important that he hear from his mother that what he is doing is tasteless? He may choose to continue to do it, but at least he knows that his mother thinks it is offensive. He may try it out on someone else, and if they react the way you did, he thinks, "Ah . . . another person thinks it is tasteless. Not just my humorless old mother." And then, maybe, just maybe, he will stop. I believe that is why many eighteen-year-old boys don't tell the same jokes that fourteen-year-old boys tell. We call it maturity, but it is really the cumulative experience of having their humor strike adults as offensive. No boy wants to continue to tell jokes that fall flat with an important part of his audience, particularly that part of the audience he loves and respects, namely, his mother.

Speaking of
the Big Questions

Rich Hero Worship vs. Family Values

Q: Bill Gates is my son's hero, along with a lot of other rich guy celebrities and anybody with the everyday trappings of success. We are nowhere near rich and never will be, which doesn't bother us, but we feel our son is ashamed of us. How can we help our son develop a desire for personal excellence and contribution without the certainty of a big payoff?

MGT: You do not have to worry about your son's respect for Bill Gates. You don't say what your son's age is, but it doesn't matter. Whether he is ten or twelve or fifteen or seventeen, what is important is that he looks up to people. I know many boys who are so cynical about the adult world that they don't have heroes at all. I know boys who idolize so-called professional wrestlers, or the rock group Blink 182, all of whom have multiple lip rings and performed a music video in the nude. By that standard, your son's choice of Bill Gates is pretty conservative.

I think you are taking his admiration of a billionaire somewhat personally. You imagine that he is dissatisfied with his family's income. I do not think that is necessarily true. If a man admires the female scenery at the beach, does that prove he doesn't love his wife? If a woman longs for a weekend alone in the woods, does that mean she plans to abandon her family? Do fantasies prove that you have no moral values? No, of course not. We're all allowed our inner thoughts without everybody assuming that we're going to act on them. Just because your son likes Bill Gates does not mean he is going to turn out to be a ruthless, materialistic person in order to make big bucks. Nor does it mean that he does not appreciate and love his family.

Daydreaming, imagining the future, thinking you could be a big deal someday, all of these are important and healthy parts of boyhood—or should be! When you work with boys who struggle to find heroes, dream dreams, and imagine success, boys like those I knew when I lived on the South Side of Chicago and worked with children whose lives were scarred by poverty and violence, it makes you sad. When you realize that their greatest ambition is to be as powerful as the local gang leader, it makes you frightened. I am glad your son has a hero, and I repeat, Bill Gates is a pretty conservative choice.

I'll tell you what I like about Bill Gates as a hero. Here is a nerdy, not-so-handsome guy with glasses who has, with his own genius and ambition, become extraordinarily powerful. He gives every nonathletic boy who is interested in computers the right to dream that they can be "top dog." On a values basis, he is also an amazing philanthropist. With the decline of affirmative action in this country, Gates has done more to help minority children get a college education than anyone in the country.

When our children get to be around eighth grade, parents start to extrapolate somewhat catastrophically into the future. They look at their child's fourteen-year-old interests and project those into the future adult. You need to stop imagining that your son's values at the present moment are going to be his adult values. His present preoccupation with money and power is just a stop on his way to becoming a balanced adult who will appreciate his family's hard work and love for him.

Son on a Mission: Will He Come Home?

Q: My son is eighteen years old and graduated from high school last spring. He was a super-achiever in high school, a brilliant boy, who was accepted at an excellent university and was supposed to start there in the fall. But last summer he worked with a missionary group that traveled to a Third World country, and now he doesn't want to continue for a college education. He just wants to be a missionary. Not only that, he has become what I would call a fundamentalist with rather severe views of those outside this faith community of his, and not interested in building bridges with other faiths, as my husband and I have done in our lives. My husband and I are quite upset, first at the idea of losing him at this young age to life in a risky Third World country. And second, it is so hurtful to us that he could make a spiritual home with this fundamentalist denomination, when they show no respect or even tolerance for other religions. When we try to talk with him about it, he says he is doing the right thing, but won't discuss his reasoning with us. Is this just a phase? How can we stay connected to him, when he doesn't appear to want us in his life?

MGT: Oh, I wish I could read the future for you. I empathize with your anxiety about possibly "losing" your son, and I wish I could convincingly reassure you that it is "just a phase." It might be something temporary in his life, or it might be a path that leads to a lifelong commitment. No one can predict at this moment. I have known boys who have become followers of charismatic gurus or pseudo-religious movements like EST and Scientology and made extended commitments to them. I have known sons of Jewish families who became zealous followers of the "Jews for Jesus," to the chagrin of their families, and stayed with the movement—and distant from their parents—well into their thirties. Many of the Buddhist teachers in the United States are young Americans, originally Protestant, Catholic, or Jewish, who spent years in Asian monasteries and then returned to the States to teach meditation to American youths.

I also have known many young people who have become part of a meaningful, idealistic movement for a few years and then have gotten what they needed from it. At that point they have left it to start families, to be able to think more independently, to earn more money, to be closer to their parents. I sincerely believe that the "apple doesn't fall very far from the tree," but sometimes it takes years for that to be evident. Sometimes what a young person is doing is the mirror image of something his own parents did to their parents. If I had you sitting with me I would ask, "Did you ever do anything in your late teens or early twenties that made your parents worry that you had abandoned their values?"

In order to understand what your son is doing, you have to appreciate that young adulthood and the departure from home is perhaps the most stressful period in the life cycle. The great psychoanalyst Erik Erikson called the sudden changes of direction or commitment that many young adults go through an "identity crisis." He described this stage of life in a classic book entitled *Youth, Identity and Crisis*. I recommend it to you. A young person is suddenly asking himself, "Who am I, now that I am not just the obedient child of my family and the good student of my school?" And the answer that comes back to a young person is very often, "I don't know who I am." It can be a scary, even terrifying, time, because values and "what is true" become so uncertain. So young people seek out structure and answers.

Mental health professionals know young adulthood is a stressful time because it is the period of maximal psychological breakdown in life. Mental hospitals used to be full of young adults struggling with depression and identity issues. Erikson said that many young people need a "moratorium" in the predictable flow of their lives to think about their identities. Now, with managed care, we no longer use hospitals as holding places for late adolescents in identity crises, but they still need the structure. So they seek out the structures that society traditionally provides to give young people a "moratorium": the military, the Peace Corps, and missionary movements. Frankly, if it were up to me, we would require all late adolescents to serve two years somewhere and perform some service.

Your son, who has been very high achieving and dutiful, may suddenly wonder if he is his own person. He may be looking for a way to define himself as different than his parents and may also be seeking a comprehensive vision of the good that will reduce his sense of uncertainty in himself and the future. What better place to find out who he is than in a Third World country? What better place to test his idealism than a narrow and intolerant missionary movement? He undoubtedly finds it both comforting and, I suspect, a bit suffocating, which is why he cannot fully answer your questions about it. What better place to feel the value of a college education than an organization full of narrow-minded people or a country where people are desperate for education and will envy the opportunity he is discarding? Can you see him explaining to someone in Sri Lanka who yearns for education why he walked away from his place at a university?

I advise you to admire as much as you can about what he is doing. I suggest that you write letters to him and not get too bent out of shape when he doesn't answer them. I hope you will go and visit him in his first missionary placement. If you don't want to contribute money to his organization because you cannot respect its intolerance, then take two weeks and help build a house or a school for the village in which he is working. You will be modeling tolerance for him in the most powerful way.

Let him know that you love him, no matter what. The important thing for his life and for yours is that you stay connected. For a few years that connection may have to be on his terms. You may have to stretch yourselves and your life assumptions and your travel budget to meet him. Don't sit in your house and sulk about college. Psychology doesn't allow me to predict, but if I had to bet money, I would bet that your son will return to college and get his degree, and will become an educated person dedicated to work in the human services. He sounds like a wonderful person. Don't start grieving the loss of him. Love him and give him time.

Hate Prank No Joke

Q: An interracial family in my neighborhood recently found a KKK symbol spray-painted on their sidewalk, and police concluded it was just a teenage prank. A few days later the junior high boy who did it told my son about it, and my son told a

teacher, and eventually the police were contacted. The prank-
ster ended up doing some community service work for punishment, but his parents are furious and insist that he had
nothing to do with it. To be honest, I wish my son hadn't
snitched on this boy. I'm sure it was just a prank, and now we
have to deal with an uncomfortable situation because of it.
How can we talk to our son about minding his own business
in matters like this in the future?

MGT: Sometimes the young are both more sensitive to meaning and more idealistic than we are. There is so much hate in
the world, we become worn down and are ready to accept
things that we should not accept under any circumstances.
We conclude that things are just pranks because we do not
have the energy to do the right thing, which is find the culprit
and explain why the prank he has committed is too close to a
hate crime for anybody's comfort. He may be naïve; he may
not have much of a sense of history. He may have been, in an
important sense, "innocent." It is our job to help him understand the nature of racism and hate crimes so his lack of
knowledge does not hurt others.

For an interracial family, the letters KKK are a death
threat. The KKK lynched countless innocent black people
throughout the first half of this century. About a year ago
three men dragged to death a black man who had the misfor-
tune to ask them for a ride. No black person can ever feel
comfortable with the idea of the Ku Klux Klan, nor can he or

she feel protected by a police force that dismisses such things as pranks, or comfortable with neighbors who do not hold their sons morally accountable for such acts.

In this case, I believe your son is right. I think you should commend him on his sense of morality and his sensitivity to racism. There are some things we should not dismiss, and "hate pranks" are one of them. If we do not take them seriously, then the more troubled members of a community will feel licensed to engage in "real" hate crimes, and they will imagine that no one cares or that everyone supports them silently. A community must not be silent in these matters.

Vegetarian Moralist: Dinner Talk Hard to Stomach

Q: My son had to write a persuasive essay about vegetarianism for his sophomore high school English class. The next thing we know he's declared that he's a vegetarian and won't be eating dinner if it includes meat, chicken, or fish. I don't mind if he wants to pass up the main dish and just eat the vegetables and cheese, but he insists on lecturing us about cruelty to animals. My husband is especially offended by his attitude and he argues with my son, which only makes matters worse. The tension around family mealtimes is terrible now, and that's the only time we're really all together. What can I do?

MGT: This is not just a "boy" issue. I have heard this particular "vegetarian scenario" more from parents of girls than from parents of boys. However, cases of teenage boys sud-

denly adopting views contrary to their fathers' are common. I
know of Jewish boys—sons of Orthodox rabbis—rejecting Judaism. I know Catholic boys—former altar boys—who have
declared that they do not believe in God. I know athletic boys
with sports-minded, ambitious fathers who have suddenly
dropped out of football or ice hockey. And I have certainly
met children of psychiatrists and psychologists who reject
their parents' professions as pointless garbage, refusing ever
to see a mental health professional (I've sat through some
long appointments with some of them). I know a gifted, tolerant liberal educator who prided himself on how supportive
he was with his son, and never had any reason to doubt his
flexibility and tolerance until the day his son came home with
his tongue pierced.

Both girls and boys challenge their parents' values, but
boys often do it in a dramatic and confrontational way, just as
this vegetarian son is doing by attacking his father's dietary
habits at the dinner table. Why? Gertrude Stein had an answer at the beginning of one of her novels. She wrote: "One
day a young man was dragging his father by the feet through
the father's orchard. When they got to a certain tree, the father began to shout, 'Stop, stop, I didn't drag my father past
this tree.' "

Stein believed that every son had to test his father, every
boy had to drag his unwilling father past the point of the father's comfort. And so it is for every generation of fathers and
sons. That is the only way a boy can know he is different from
the man whom he has so loved and idealized. Suddenly that

childlike love for his father becomes a threat to his own sense of selfhood, and so he must challenge it. The more insecure he feels about his autonomy and his abilities, the more dramatic may be his philosophical rupture with his father.

So far I have emphasized a boy's need to challenge his father in order to "win" his adulthood. Yet, I also need to point out that this boy's vegetarianism emerges from his capacity for abstract thinking. The cognitive changes that adolescents go through in the years from twelve to fifteen give them an expanding worldview. They are able and motivated to think about moral issues and to call into question things that were absolute truths when they were children. When you are seven and going to McDonald's to get a Happy Meal, you are not thinking about the morality of butchering animals. A hamburger is a simple good because your parents feed it to you and they love you. You don't even think about meat as coming from animals, even though you know that it does (and if someone reminds you of it, you dismiss it with a "yuck," and refuse to think about it).

As you grow older you think more deeply about the ordinary assumptions of what is good and bad. It is precisely this development of an independent moral sense, a conscience, that we wish to encourage in boys. We don't want to be raising boys who are utterly conventional in their thinking, willing to go along with anything, nor do we want boys who are unwilling to take a moral stand. Such boys will be followers, "yes" men. They will lack moral courage.

Even though I am someone who eats meat, I admire your

son. I admire the fact that he researched a paper and took his own conclusions seriously. I respect that he is willing to forgo eating something that tasted good to him in the past because it is a matter of principle to him now. We call that "walking the walk." Good for him! Now, he doesn't have to be obnoxious about it by attacking his father, but his father shouldn't attack his son's eating habits, either. They don't have to needle each other at dinner. If they continue, you can always get up, pick up your plate, and go eat in front of the TV. Mom's leaving the table will give them both a message (and leave them with each other, which will be terrifying!).

My advice is this: buy a couple of vegetarian cookbooks and begin to serve meals where there are several "main dishes" at the table, because there are several "main adults" at your table now. Or, if he cooks his own meals, ask your son what he would like you to add to your shopping list so that you can meet his new dietary requirements. If you are so inclined, I would recommend that you read about vegetarianism yourself. (Did you read his paper thoroughly?) Without rejecting your husband, you can give your son some acknowledgment of his emerging adulthood and his unique, independent values. He is going to grow into a principled adult, and his vegetarianism is a sign of it.

Cancer Survivor Adopts Kosher Preference

Q: We are Jewish, and our son, now fifteen, has always been very comfortable and happy with our moderate style of religious observance, including the fact that we don't keep kosher. The problem is this: our son went through a very serious illness about six months ago and since then has pressured us to follow the more traditional dietary laws and keep kosher, which would require quite a change in the foods we eat and the way we prepare food. He now refuses to eat milk and meat at the same meal or any foods that combine them. This makes it much harder for him to eat what he needs to regain his health, and makes family meals much more complicated than ever before. We want to respect his desire to follow a more traditional path than we chose, but we're concerned about his health and about his singling himself out in this way in his community of non-Jewish friends. How can we understand what's brought about this change in him and respond in the best way?

MGT: Anyone who has ever had a life-threatening illness is changed by the experience. You do not take life for granted in the same way you did before the sickness. Your relationship to your God, your experience of faith, and your relationship to your body are likely to change. Can you imagine your son going through such an experience and having nothing in him changed? Can you picture him simply resuming the way he was before, with no acknowledgment of the seriousness of his encounter with mortality? If a boy didn't change at all, I would be puzzled by and worried about him. I would wonder if he had simply denied what had happened to him, or had in some way detached himself.

Your son's change in dietary habits is his way of announcing that he has been changed. He no longer takes his Jewishness and his God for granted. He is grateful for the gift of life and wants to honor it. He wants to be conscious and faithful and he does not want to forget. I respect him for that.

I have a friend who suffered from a serious malignant cancer. Despite bad odds, she beat the illness, but it affected everything she read. She didn't want to waste a moment of consciousness. Twenty years after having cancer she said that, at times, she regretted having returned to a state of taking life for granted again. She said she missed the "vividness" of life when she was closer to the threat of death.

I would suggest that you allow his experience to change you, too. I would see if you could find meaning in his new experience of Judaism. I would help him prepare food and I would do so for two reasons: first, to make sure he was getting good nutrition, and second, to acknowledge his new seriousness. If you cannot find meaning in his new expression of faith, I would show him that you are making the effort to understand by joining him. Don't make a huge production of it; do what you can do in a wholehearted way. I think he will appreciate it. Whether or not he continues to maintain his dietary restrictions I wouldn't venture to predict. At some point, he may decide to resume a more moderate attitude toward his meals, but I know many Jewish families who keep kosher in their homes and enjoy all the delights of friendship and community wherever they go. Your son may change his mind on this issue or he may have found a lasting, meaningful way of expressing himself through this particular piece of tradition.

Fifteen-Year-Old Doesn't Talk

Q: My fifteen-year-old doesn't talk to me. He doesn't initiate any conversations anymore and won't even answer my simplest questions. The only time he says anything is when he's looking for clean laundry or food. When I complain about this, it's bad enough that I feel like I'm begging for attention, but he just shrugs me off. He's so rude! My husband gets the same treatment and has stopped even trying to communicate with our son. I can tell that my husband's feelings are hurt. When I try to explain this to our son, he tells me that his father doesn't know anything about him and that there is no point in talking to him. They still share some interests—sports, for instance—but they do not really talk about anything important. Our son is a good kid and does his schoolwork and has friends, but we both miss the company of the boy we used to enjoy so much. How can we get our son to talk to us? Should I stop trying? Should I encourage his father to keep trying?

MGT: I have counseled boys and their families and boys and their schools for thirty years, and for the past two, since the publication *of Raising Cain: Protecting the Emotional Life of Boys*, I have been traveling across the United States speaking about boys and taking questions from parents about their sons. During that time, I have probably answered two or three thousand questions about the nature of boys, and that leaves me in a position to declare unequivocally that this is the number one question about boys!

Without a doubt, this is the boy behavior that most baffles, angers, and hurts mothers. It is the behavior that many fathers understand at an intuitive level but that can also hurt their feelings. It leaves fathers at a loss when they try to explain their sons to their wives. Groping for words, dads often end up saying, "Oh, leave him alone. He's okay." Many dads remember being this way when they were fifteen, but they cannot quite recall being so rude, and they had hoped that it might be different between themselves and their sons. They are discouraged to find the pattern repeating itself, and they can't remember the reasons they were so reluctant to speak to their parents.

The reason that boys fall silent has to do with the nature of boys' social training and the nature of adolescence. These two features in a boy's life come together to produce a boy who often does not want to tell his mother much about his life, or a boy who, even when he does want to talk to his mom or dad, feels he would be breaking the boy code to do so.

Here are the "rules" for fifteen-year-old boys:

1. You must act strong at all times.
2. Even when you don't feel strong, you should fake it.
3. Talking to your mother about how you feel is definitely not a masculine thing to do; it is something girls do with their mothers.

4. If you are going to become a cool, independent, sexual kind of guy, you have to avoid feeling the childlike feelings that you still have for your mother.
5. If you talk about your life with your mom, you are going to break rules 1 through 4.
6. Talking to your father might be cool, but not as long as he's such an asshole about grades and mowing the lawn.

Now, here are the rules for all fifteen-year-olds, both boys and girls:

1. Adults are so different from kids, they could not possibly understand what kids want.
2. Adults may appear friendly at times, but they are untrustworthy because of their need to control the behavior of kids.
3. If you are too close to adults, you cannot be in the cool group in school.

If you think I am overstating the case, I want you to know that yesterday I ran a one-hour assembly for the upper school at an excellent Catholic school in the Midwest. With their teachers present, these were all the things the students told me about the relationships between kids and adults. Individually they do not always behave this way, but these are the rules to which they hold one another.

Now that you have read all these rules, do you understand why boys don't talk much? They can't. They are afraid that they will be intruded upon or managed (the great teenage fear) or made to look weak (the great boy fear). They would prefer not to talk at all rather than to put themselves in this bad position.

What should you do? I have a number of suggestions.

First, don't get hurt and disappointed when your son doesn't talk to you or gives you short answers. Boys are allergic to mothers who are grieving for their lost little boys and who try to make them guilty about how they've changed: *"I don't know what's happened to you! You used to be such a sweet guy. We used to be able to talk about everything!"*

Second, have confidence that if you have had a good twelve years with your son, even though he makes himself distant in the years from age thirteen to sixteen, *he will come back to you!* The vast majority of boys (though sadly not all) are willing to open up to their moms again when they feel they have established their manhood, when they feel more secure as young adults. That's around age seventeen or eighteen.

Third, develop a sense of humor and don't be afraid or overly impressed by these big guys. When mothers get too bewildered or hurt by or actually frightened of their sons, their sons cannot respect them.

Please notice that in your question you say that your son is at least able to talk to you about how he cannot talk to his father. That suggests to me that he is prepared to speak to you about something meaningful and that he hopes you might be able to make a difference in that area of his life. It is probably

pretty painful for him to have you be so hurt and to have his
father give up on trying to converse with him.

There are a number of things your husband can do to
reestablish conversational contact with your son.

First—and this can be tough for fathers—he has to recover from his annoyance that he is not in control of his son
the way he used to be. Adolescent sons are acutely sensitive
to a father's need to control the conversation. If a boy senses
that his dad just wants to assert his seniority, the conversation
becomes a power contest that the son always wins with silence or an infuriatingly simple answer.

Second, if your husband is making the typical father's mistake of always focusing on the boy's achievements and future,
he needs to ask different kinds of questions. He has to ask
open-ended questions, questions to which he doesn't know
the answers. He cannot always be asking questions about doing homework, to which there is only one obvious answer—
"Yes, Dad, I know I need to work harder at my homework if I
am going to bring my grades up and get into a good college."
End of conversation!

Third, a father needs to share more about himself, about
his struggles, about his losses, about his heartbreaks as a
teenager. No, he shouldn't tell endless stories about his childhood. No adolescent has the patience for them. If he can
simply say, *"Yeah, when I was fifteen I hated my father because he was such a controlling guy. I'm trying to do better
than that, but I know that I tend to try to control our conversations."* Or if he can say, *"My father died when I was*

twelve. He had a heart attack when he was working in the garage, and I watched the emergency squad work on him. For years I acted as if it didn't hurt that much. I just tried to be the man of the house. It wasn't until I started going out with your mother that I ever cried about my father's death."

That's plenty. If a father can say something like that to a son, and the son doesn't ask a follow-up question right then or over the next couple of days, I would be astonished. If he does not retell that story to his closest friend in the next week, I would be amazed. If his friend hears that story and says, "Wow, that sounds pretty tough for your dad," your son is likely to see his dad in a new way. He is going to appreciate that his father did not spring from the head of Zeus as a fully formed annoying adult; he is going to remember that his dad too had a childhood and an adolescence and that he experienced losses. That is going to make your son want to learn more about the nature of life from his dad; sons always want to know, "Dad, what did you do in the war?"

You mention that your husband and your son still share an interest in sports. This would be a good time to use a bit more of the family budget on sports events for father and son, perhaps with another father-and-son combination. Adults often learn a lot from taking two teenage friends on an outing away from the house. Their boys will benefit from seeing the fathers enjoy each other's company. If your husband can spare the time, and this is an authentic interest for him, this might be the time for him to coach a Little League team or a youth soccer team. Most fathers coach when their own sons are young and on the team. At this time in life, your son might act—informally—as assistant coach. Certainly your son would be deeply touched by the fact that his dad is still interested in kids. That would send him a message. For the same reason, if a father donated his time to a charity, or performed some important community service, his son might be willing to work at his side.

Finally, if you want to get responses from a not-very-talkative fifteen-year-old, both you and your husband should ask specific and concrete questions that can be answered factually. Instead of saying "What did you do over at your friend's house?" ask a specific neutral question about the situation, about other people's motivations, about *facts*.

"I know Tony and Andy were over there with you; was anyone else there?" Follow your question with some indication that you are thinking about his life, not just requiring him to report to you. So you might ask, *"But weren't Tony and Andy fighting a couple of weeks ago?"* At the very least, he is likely to answer, "Yeah, but they got over it." That's six words. Congratulations!

Talk to your son in a way that honors his pride in his masculinity and does not shame him. Use him as an expert on his own life. Ask specific questions or make observations; talk about events external to him. Boys like to be experts and they like to "correct the record." So, for example, say to your son the soccer player, *"Mr. Jones shouts at the team much more than Mr. Smith did last year. Does that bother the players?"* (Notice that I am having you ask about what the other players feel, not him.) He may shrug and say, *"No, not really."* Then ask, *"Do you think it helps motivate the team, or do you just ignore it?"* If he says, *"I don't care about his yelling,"* and shrugs, don't give up. Count to ten silently and then say, *"I bet there are a few boys on the team who really hate it."* And then your son might let you in on a secret. He might say, *"He's a pretty good coach, but some kids think he's a jerk."* That's twelve words, an opinion, and some insight into the team. I congratulate you again. You are well on your way to having conversations with your fifteen-year-old. Who knows? If you're patient and don't press your luck, next week you might get twenty words out of him!

About the Authors

MICHAEL THOMPSON, Ph.D., is a school consultant, author, and child and family psychologist. He coauthored the best-selling *Raising Cain: Protecting the Emotional Life of Boys* with Dan Kindlon, Ph.D., and *Finding the Heart of the Child* with Edward M. Hallowell, M.D. Dr. Thompson has lectured widely on the development of boys and social cruelty in childhood. He has conducted workshops for more than two hundred public and private schools across the United States. For the past ten years he has been a faculty member of the Institute for New Heads of the National Association of Independent Schools and more recently of the Academy of Heads of International Schools. In those roles he has helped prepare many new heads of schools to take on the responsibilities of educational leadership. He is the psychologist for the Belmont Hill School, an all-boys school outside Boston. Dr. Thompson lives in Arlington, Massachusetts, with his wife, Theresa, and their children, Joanna and Will.

TERESA BARKER is a journalist and book writer whose recent collaborations include *Raising Cain: Protecting the Emotional Life of Boys* (Ballantine), *The Creative Age: Awakening Human Potential in the Second Half of Life* (Avon), and *The Mother-Daughter Book Club: How Ten Busy Mothers and Daughters Came Together to Talk, Laugh and Learn Through Their Love of Reading* (HarperCollins). She lives in Wilmette, Illinois, with her husband, Steve, and their three children, Aaron, Rachel, and Rebecca.